TAKING A BITE OF THE "BIG APPLE"

Some Thoughts on Visiting the United States

Du Jinqing

品味"大苹果"——访美漫谈

杜金卿　著

河北出版传媒集团

河北教育出版社

图书在版编目（CIP）数据

品味"大苹果"/ 杜金卿著 . -- 石家庄 ：河北教育出
版社 ，2015.6

ISBN 978-7-5545-1873-1

Ⅰ . ①品… Ⅱ . ①杜… Ⅲ . ①社会生活－美国－现代
②游记－作品集－中国－当代 Ⅳ . ① I267.4 ② D771.28

中国版本图书馆 CIP 数据核字 (2015) 第 138969 号

书名 / 品味"大苹果"—— 访美漫谈
作者 / 杜金卿 著

出版发行 / 河北出版传媒集团

河北教育出版社

石家庄市联盟路705号 邮编 050061
出 品 / 北京颂雅风文化传媒有限责任公司

www.songyafeng.com

北京市朝阳区望京利泽西园3区305号楼

邮编 100102 电话 010-84852503
编辑总监 / 刘 峥
责任编辑 / 刘 峥 闫 璐
英文翻译 / 李正栓 南 方 尹 晓 陈世杰
设计总监 / 郑子杰
装帧设计 / 杨 慧 周 帅
制 版 / 北京颂雅风制版中心
印 刷 / 北京永诚印刷有限公司
开 本 / 787mm×1092mm 1/16
印 张 / 17.5
字 数 / 150千字
出版日期 / 2015年6月第1版 第1次印刷
书 号 / ISBN 978-7-5545-1873-1
定 价 / 58.00元

CONTENTS

目　录

Preface

Currently, the power of the United States and its influence on the world are self-evident. For more than half a century, with its rise in the First World War and supremacy in the Second World War, especially after the collapse of the Soviet Union and the end of the cold war, America has become the top superpower in the world with unrivaled strength in economy, military, science and technology, and influence in culture, media, and etc. As a result, every word and deed of the American president, each action of the American government, any tendency in the field of American economy, science and technology and any kind of trend in American society and culture will attract the eyes of the whole world. It should be said that most countries in the world today admire, even imitate the strong power and creative vitality of America, and willingly or reluctantly accept the leading role of the American economy, science and technology and the impact of its culture.

However, the United States often boss itself and proclaim as the incarnation of democracy, freedom and justice precisely because of it power which no one has the strength to contend with. Its actions of value judgment, economic sanctions, military strikes and regime subversion of other countries together with its behavior of acting as the world police everywhere to frequently teach lessons to those so-called "disobedient" countries have aroused in many countries the dissatisfaction and anger, as well as the struggles against its hegemonic behavior. The attitudes of the international community towards the United States can be summarized as a love-hate relationship: admiring its powerfulness and dynamic, while disgusted with hegemony and unreasonable conducts.

The prosperity of the country should be ascribed to a combination of factors: the historical conditions, natural endowments, institutional culture and national quality. Or rather, the rise and strength of the United States originate from its realization of national independence, national unity, the establishment of market economy system, democratic political system and cultural value system in conform to the trend of the times and in line with its national conditions by seizing the opportunity in the specific historical circumstances. In more than 200 years of developing history, the United States has constantly adjusted and implemented these systems, making it constantly fresh with new vigor and vitality. We can see that, there must be many things for other countries and nations to learn from the rise and the economic and social construction of the United States. The economically and culturally backward countries must face their own shortcomings, and transform themselves by learning from others' strengths, in order to promote the progress of civilization and the prosperity of their country.

However, in this historical process of learn and self-innovation, all the countries should respect each other and not interfere with each other. Big and strong countries should not impose their own values and political systems on small, weak countries. No matter how closed and backward a country is in your eyes and makes you annoyed, it is internal matters of others. Some big and strong countries always appear to be self-righteous, overbearing and unreasonable, even oppressing the weak. Against this the weaker countries have to unite themselves and resolutely resist and protest. Otherwise, the spoiled "children" will make the world a mess.

The above is mainly the understanding and views of the international community towards the United States in recent years, from the perspective of the international status and state-to-state relations. However, what kind of country the United States actually is? What is the American society, the American people, the American territory and American culture actually like? The answers have been given by different kinds of media which provide people a rough idea of the United States even if they haven't understanding and judgment, not from one's own perception. As the saying goes, seeing is believing. In order to truly understand America, one has to personally have a look there, before drawing his own conclusions.

I have long desired to go to the United States to have a look. In May 2006, I had the honor to participate in the delegation to the U. S. which was organized by the China National Publications Import & Export (Group) Corporation (NPIEC). The major task of the delegation was to participate in the 2006 U. S. Book Fair which was held in Washington. I stayed in the United States for 12 days, from the east to the west, from the coast to the inland. In addition to participating in the Washington Book Fair, I also visited the cities, such as New York, Philadelphia, Los Angeles, Las Vegas and San Francisco. Though a quick glance it was, what I've seen and heard, felt and thought all gave me deep impressions and feelings.

When I came back from the United States, some of my colleagues and friends asked: how did you feel about America? It's hard to answer just in one sentence or two. Should I talk about the developed U. S. economy, the geographical landscape, the American social and cultural phenomenon, or what can we get when compare China with the United States? Since it is difficult to put them in only one answer, I prefer the travelogue, to describe the journey, to express my feelings, and try to make some rational thinking about the American phenomenon which I contacted with. At the same time, the book also touches some domestic issues and gives some exploration and discussion, to echo with those who have already been there and to offer some insights for those who haven't.

Du Jinqing
September 2006

前言

当今美国的强大、美国对世界的影响是不言而喻的。从一战崛起到二战称雄，半个多世纪以来，特别是前苏联解体、冷战结束以来，美国成为世界头号超级大国，它在经济、军事、科技等方面的实力和在文化、传媒等方面的影响力，是目前任何国家都不能匹敌的。因此，美国总统的一言一行，美国政府的一举一动，美国经济、科技领域的某种动向，美国社会、文化的某种潮流都会引起全世界的关注。应当说，当今世界大多数国家对美国的强大实力和创造活力是羡慕的，甚至是仿效的，情愿或不情愿地接受着美国经济、科技的引领和美国文化的影响。

但是，也正因为强大，因为没国家有相应的实力与之抗衡，美国往往就以老大自居，以民主自由等正义的化身自我标榜，经常对他国进行价值评判、经济制裁、军事打击、政权颠覆，到处充当世界警察，动辄教训那些"不听话"的国家，结果引起了很多国家的不满和愤怒，以及对其霸权行为的抗争。国际社会对美国的这种感受可以说是爱恨交加：既羡慕它的强大和活力，又反感它的霸道和无理。

一个国家的强盛是其历史条件、自然禀赋、体制文化、民族素质等综合因素作用的结果，或者说，美国的崛起和强大，是它在特定的历史条件下，抓住了机遇，实现了民族独立，维护了国家统一，建立起了顺应时代潮流并符合本国国情的市场经济制度、民主政治制度和文化价值体系，并在其200多年的历史进程中，不断调整和完善这些制度和体系，使其不断焕发新的生机与活力。可见，美国的大国崛起之路，美国的经济社会制度，必然有许多值得其他国家和民族学习的地方。经济文化落后的国家必须正视自己的缺陷，学习人家的长处，改造自己的社会，如此才能推动自己国家的文明与进步、繁荣与强盛。

但是，在这种学习借鉴和自我革新的历史进程中，各国之间应当是相互尊重、互不干涉。大国、强国不应将自己的价值观念和政治制度强加给小国、弱国，不管别的国家在你看来多么封闭落后、令你讨厌，那是人家内部的事。对于某些大国、强国自以为是、霸道无理、以强凌弱的坏毛病，弱小国家必须联合起来坚决予以抵制和抗争，否则，惯坏了的"孩子"会把世界搞得一团糟。

以上主要是从国际地位和国家关系的角度，谈谈近年来国际社会对美国的认识和看法。然而，美国究竟是一个什么样的国家？美国社会、美国人民、美国国土、美国文化究竟是一种什么样的情形？对此，各种媒介都有大量的报道和描述，这些信息使我们即使不亲身游历也会对美国有一个大概的了解。但是，媒体的报道，别人的讲述毕竟是他人的了解与判断，不是你所感知的美国。俗话说，百闻不如一见，了解真实的美国还是要亲自到那里走一走，看一看，然后得出自己的认识和判断。

去美国看看是我很久以来的愿望，2006年5月，我有幸参加由中国图书进出口（集团）总公司组织的代表团赴美访问，主要参访在华盛顿举办的"2006美国图书博览会"。在美国共逗留12天，从东部到西部，从沿海到内陆，除参加华盛顿书展外，还顺便造访了纽约、费城、洛杉矶、拉斯维加斯和旧金山等城市，虽说走马观花，浮光掠影，但所见所闻，所感所悟，应当说印象深刻，感触良多。

从美国回来后，有同事和朋友问我，到美国感觉怎么样？这很难用一两句话来回答。是说美国经济发达程度呢？还是说美国地理景观呢？是说美国社会和文化现象呢？还是说中国与美国比较怎样呢？既然难以用几句话来回答，那就用游记形式来记述此次访美行程和感受，并对所接触到的美国现象作些理性思考，同时联系国内有关问题作些粗浅探讨，以期对尚未去过美国的朋友有所裨益，使已经到过美国的朋友有所共鸣。

杜金卿

2006年9月

First Step on the United States

I thought we would fly directly across the Pacific Ocean to the United States. However, the international flights flew nearly halfway around the world. The immigration control made me feel that we were accepted as refugees rather than guests. But it was very nice to see our Chinese compatriots who came to the airport to meet us. Peter Cai, our driver and tour guide, a Hong Konger with a U.S. green card, spoke some kind of amusing Hong Kong-toned Chinese.

I remember it was in the early 1980s when at college I read Fei Xiaotong's *A Glimpse of the United States* and *American Kaleidoscope* soon after that. These two books left on me a deep impression of a very brilliant America. Then later I successively read Nixon's *Leaders*, and some American celebrities' biographies and literary works such as *A Biography of Lincoln*, *Iacocca Biography*, *The Winds of War*, etc. It can be said that when we were young we were very curious about America, a miraculous kaleidoscope. Even now in our forties and fifties, bombarded by media information every day, involved in a world situation agitated by U.S.A and tempted by Hollywood blockbusters and NBA games, who cannot be grabbed by it?

"U" Routes

It is my long-cherished wish to pay a visit to the United States. I had had many opportunities to visit it, but all of them were canceled for some reasons. So, I was a little excited this time. On May 17, 2006, eight of us from Beijing, Hebei and some publishers directly under central government met in Beijing airport, took flight CA981 to New York, and finally went to Washington D.C. to participate in the "2006 American Book Fair". At first, we were a bit puzzled: Why do we have to detour to New York first to take part in the Exhibition in Washington? Afterwards, we learnt that there wasn't any direct flight between Beijing and Washington at that time. Only by transiting from New York, Chicago, Los Angeles or San Francisco could we

Arriving New York

get to Washington.

When we boarded the Boeing 747, I thought we would fly directly across the Pacific Ocean to the United States. However, the plane departed from Beijing and went straight to the northeast of our country. After passing the cities of Chengde, Chifeng and Qiqihaer, it flew into Russian airspace. Then we passed over the Bering Strait, Alaska and Canada until we finally reached the United States. The plane flew halfway around the world for 13 hours before it arrived at Kennedy Airport in New York. The long flight was exhausting and tough with nothing to do except chat and take a little nap. The only interesting thing was that I watched the newly-released American blockbuster movie "King Kong".

The plane landed at 3 a.m. CST on the 18th. It was the 17th, 3 p.m. eastern time, a 12-hour time difference from Beijing. The temperature in Kennedy airport was 19 which was slightly cooler than Beijing.

Entry Setbacks

Anxiously, I left the cabin and entered the lounge, waiting in line for entry formalities. Just off the plane, a large group of travelers who looked dazed gathered in the hall. A young, dark-haired, white-skinned, slightly obese female police officer was loudly directing travelers to different windows for entry inspection. It made us feel like refugees instead of guests. When she waved and directed us to the check window, I was really happy and thought we could exit soon. However, we unexpectedly encountered trouble.

After the terrorist attack on September 11, the United States became like a frightened bird and took extreme measures to protect themselves against future attacks, implementing major precautions at airport security. After taking a photo and a thumbprint, security guards asked people to take off their shoes, unfasten their belts, have their bags checked and even frisked us. One could see how these extreme measures would be troublesome and embarrassing and could cause a civilized man to lose his manners and feel his dignity compromised.

Some of us didn't write our U.S. addresses clearly on the entry card. The immigration officer immediately returned the card and asked us to rewrite the information. I once studied a little English, but hadn't used it for years, and his accent was strange, so I didn't quite understand what to do. Fortunately, seeing us struggle, an American Chinese police officer who was next to us came over and helped us with the entry card. After we resubmitted them, all passed smoothly except me. The immigration officer who was responsible for the verification showed a special interest in my passport and visa. After the photographic and thumbprint procedure, a serious-looking white police officer with a pistol by his side repeatedly checked my passport, clicking the keyboard to check the system, or frowning at the passport seriously, as if there was something wrong. Although I was confident that my passport was official and valid until November, my heart still couldn't help beating fast when seeing this. I thought, because Americans are always overbearing, he might find some grounds to refuse my entry. The publishing staff of our province had gotten together for a delegation visit to the United States twice but been refused by the U.S. Embassy. I had also heard that someone was refused entry at the U.S. airport and had to go home.

Lingering for several minutes, the immigration officer finally affixed a seal to my passport reluctantly. "OK!" I felt relieved and picked up the passport, walking quickly out of the lounge. At the baggage claim area, seeing the Chinese compatriots who came to pick us up, I felt was relieved and in a better mood.

I was quite irritated by the whole experience. First there was the difficulty with my visa, then the indifference of the police officer and the immigration officer's reluctance to stamp my paperwork. It seemed that the Americans did not welcome us. I thought maybe the United States was too rich to care about our money. But what about the huge tourism market which is formed by more than 30 million Chinese passengers every year, didn't America really care? The most baffling thing was this: how could the United States, known for advocating freedom, democracy, openness and respect for human rights, treat Chinese tourists in such an unfriendly way? Is this caused by the ideology in their soul? Or because China is not strong enough to get America's due respect?

A Feeling of Deja Vu

I dragged my baggage out of the lounge and got in a large and bulky Ford station wagon. Lao Wu, the secretary-general, gave me favored treatment and asked me to sit upfront in the copilot position. This seat became mine during the whole tour in the United States. Each time we traveled by car I would sit in the front seat, where I would fasten my seatbelt and help the driver navigate. The driver and tour guide Peter Cai was a Hong Konger with a U.S. green card, very warm-hearted, talkative and humorous. He said that his father was from Ningbo, his mother from Shanghai, and he was "made" in Hong Kong and "used" in the States. He immigrated to the United States in the late 1980s, working as a tourist guide for more than 10 years and speaking some kind of humorous Hong Kong Chinese.

Soon the station wagon drove out of the airport and onto the expressway to downtown New York. When we saw the blue sky and the eyeful of green, we began to perk up, listening to the guide's explanation while constantly watching the scenery along the way. Within a short time, we arrived in Manhattan, the famous city we heard so much about. It's exciting to view the Empire State Building and many other high-rises in the distance. But at that moment, four helicopters were circling over New York for alert, which made us truly feel the sharply increased tension in the United States since the 9.11 terrorist attacks.

We drove over the Williamsburg Bridge on the East River of New York City, went through the Hudson River tunnel and then entered the urban area. I did not expect to be passing through Chinatown. The buildings were neat and orderly, but with little sign of bustling and downtown. On the contrary, everything looked obsolete. Suddenly I got a feeling of deja vu. Had I ever seen this place before? No, but it had appeared in the hot-broadcast TV series "A Native of Beijing in New York" in the 1990s. The tour guide explained that these old buildings were built 50 years ago when the fire safe passage was not a necessity. Later in order to comply with fire safety rules, an iron ladder was hung outside of the building which looked particularly conspicuous.

A Get-together of Chinese

Across New York City, we arrived at the neighboring city of Elizabeth in New Jersey and checked in at the Doubletree Hotel. After a short rest, we went to the nearby Linden city to visit the American branch of China National Publications Import & Export (Group) Corporation. The Vice President, Pang Lili, and some other compatriots welcomed us warmly and introduced the business of this branch company in the United States.

This overseas company is mainly to dispatch U.S. newspapers and a small amount of books (about 1500 types) to domestic subscribers. Its annual operating revenue is more than 14 million dollars. We discussed with great interest the prospect of Chinese publications' "going global". All agreed that books and periodicals about traditional Chinese medicine, children, literature and language would have a certain market in the United States at present. The problem was the lack of resource integration, channel unblocking and effective promotion. There was also a problem with money return. We enjoyed the talk very much and then visited the company's offices and warehouses. As a farewell, we took a group photo as a souvenir in front of the door. It was already nightfall, 8 p.m., and 18 hours passed since we left Beijing.

We were very hungry when we said goodbye to Vice President Pang. The guide took us to a nearby Chinese restaurant in Newark to have dinner. I didn't remember to call home and report I was safe until then. Before I left

China, I consulted the domestic mobile communication company about what type of mobile phone should be used in the United States. I was told to use the mobile phone with three frequencies of 1900 Hz. I also asked whether the common Motorola 760 would work. The answer was yes. However, when I got off the plane, no matter how I fiddled with it, the phone refused to work. It had no signal. Losing the call function, the cell phone turned out to be a watch and a notebook, where today's travel notes were originally written.

Setting foot on the United States for the first time, I finally relaxed and my mood improved Back at the hotel, the tour guide reminded everybody that in order to get rid of jetlag we needed to stay up until 12 o'clock midnight. So we played "tractor" (a kind of poker game) together till 1 a.m. 30 hours passed from the moment we set off for Beijing airport in our country at 7 a.m. on 17th; but none of us looked languid. It could be seen that man had great potential either mental or physical. Usually they would appear a little finicky, but as long as the real challenge came, hunger, fatigue, drowsiness and other physiological tests might all become a piece of cake.

Happy Hour with Compatriots

初踏美利坚

原以为会直接飞越太平洋进入美国，但国际航班却绕了半个地球。接受入境检查，感觉不像是迎接客人，似乎是在接受难民。见到前来接机的中国同胞，倍感亲切。司机兼导游蔡彼德是一位持美国绿卡的香港人，一口香港国语讲得颇为风趣。

记得上世纪 80 年代初，正在上大学时，读过费孝通先生的《访美掠影》，不久又看过《美国万花筒》，当时印象，这两本介绍美国的书写得精彩纷呈。后来又陆续读过尼克松的《领袖们》以及《林肯传记》、《艾柯卡传》、《战争风云》等美国名人传记和文学作品。可以说，年轻时代的我们对美国这个奇迹般的国家、万花筒式的社会充满了好奇。即便到了四五十岁，由于天天被媒体资讯轰炸着，被美国搅动的世界局势牵挂着，被好莱坞大片和 NBA 球赛诱惑着，又有谁会对美国不感兴趣呢？

曲形航线

去趟美国是我多年的夙愿，过去曾有多次访美机会都因故错过了，这次终于成行，不免有些兴奋。2006 年 5 月 17 日，来自北京、河北和中直出版单位的 8 位同行在北京机场会齐后，乘坐中国国际航空公司 CA981 航班飞往纽约，然后再辗转到华盛顿参加"2006 美国图书博览会"。开始有点纳闷，去华盛顿参展为何要绕道纽约？后来才知道，当时北京与华盛顿之间尚未开通直飞航班，去华盛顿只能从纽约、芝加哥、洛杉矶或旧金山等地转机。

登上波音 747 客机，原以为会直接飞越太平洋进入美国，但国际航班却是从北京起飞，然后直奔我国东北方向，在飞经承德、赤峰、齐齐哈尔后，进入俄罗斯领空，飞越白令海峡，掠过美国阿拉斯加州和加拿大，而后进入美国本土。飞机绕了半个地球，飞行 13 个小时才抵达纽约肯尼迪机场。漫长的飞行，令人困顿难熬，在机舱里只能是看书、交谈、打盹，途中唯一有趣的是观看了刚刚上市的美国大片《金刚》。

飞机降落已是北京时间 18 日凌晨 3 点，美国东部时间 17 日下午 3 点，比北京整整差了 12 个小时。肯尼迪机场地面气温摄氏 19 度，比北京稍凉。

入境周折

怀着期待的心情走出机舱，进入候机大厅，排队等候办理入境手续。刚下飞机、神情茫然的一大群旅客簇拥在大厅内，在一位黑头发、白皮肤、略显肥胖的年轻女警官喊叫指挥下，分别走向不同的窗口接受入境检查。感觉她不像是迎接客人，似乎是在接受难民。当女警官挥手指示我们走向检查窗口时，心里着实高兴，本以为很快就可出关，没想到却遇到了麻烦。

9·11 恐怖事件后，美国如惊弓之鸟，机场各种安全检查手段花样繁多，除了照相、按手印，还要脱鞋、解腰带、翻提包，甚至搜身，这些不胜其烦、令人难堪的安检手段可真让现代文明人斯文尽失、尊严扫地。

由于疏忽大意，我们几个同行没在入境卡上写清到美国后的具体住址，入境官员当即退回，让我们重新填写。我虽有点英语基础，但常年不用难以应急，尤其听不懂美国佬讲的美式英语。幸好旁边一位华人警官见此情景，主动过来询问情况，热情地帮助填写入境卡。再次提交后，其他人都顺利过关，可是负责验证的入境官却对我的护照和签证产生了兴趣。腰挎手枪、一脸严肃的白人警官在我履行照相和按手印程序后，拿着我的护照反复掂量，一会儿点击电脑键盘进行核对，一会儿皱着眉头翻看护照，神情凝重、煞有其事。虽然我心中有数，自己拿的是大公务护照，签证有效期到 11 月份，理应没有任何问题。但见此情景，心里也不免敲起鼓来，心想老美霸道，说不定会找出点什么理由拒绝入境。因为此前我省出版系统自己组团访美，已经被美国大使馆拒签过两次，还听说有人在美国机场被拒绝入境、打道回府的事也曾发生过。

磨蹭了好几分钟，入境官总算不情愿地在我的护照上盖了章。"OK!"我如释重负，拿起护照快步走出候机厅。来到行李领取处，见到前来接机的中国同胞，倍感亲切，稍微冲淡了刚才的一丝不快。

这件事让我颇受刺激，先是签证困难，再是入境冷淡近乎刁难，看来，美国人不欢迎我们。我想，也许美国富得流油，不太在意我们这点银子，但是，对于中国每年 3000 多万人次出国（境）旅游的巨大市场，难道美国人也不在意吗？尤其令人感到困惑的是，在美国这个以自由、民主、开放和尊重人权著称的国度里，竟以如此不友好的态度对待中国客人，究竟是心灵深处的意识形态作怪，还是中国不够强大，得不到美国人应有的尊重？

似曾相识

拖着行李走出候机厅大门，登上一辆宽大笨重的美国福特牌旅行车。秘书长老伍优待我，让我坐在副驾驶位置上，不承想初次的座位竟成了我的专利，在整个访美期间，每次乘车我都坐在前座，代表大家系好安全带并帮司机看路。司机兼导游蔡彼德是一位持美国绿卡的香港人，热心健谈，讲话幽默，说他的父亲是宁波人，母亲是上海人，自己是香港制造，美国使用，上世纪 80 年代末移居美国，做了 10 多年的旅游接待，一口香港国语讲得颇为风趣。

中巴车驶出机场，开上通往纽约市区的快速公路，当看到湛蓝的天空和满眼的绿色，大家开始活跃起来，一边听着导游讲解，一边目不暇接地观察沿途景致。汽车快速行进，眨眼到了市郊，慕名已久的纽约曼哈顿进入视野，从远处眺望帝国大厦等高楼群煞是兴奋。此刻，纽约上空正有四架直升飞机在盘旋警戒，使人真实地感受到美国自遭受 9·11 恐怖袭击后陡增的紧张气氛。

汽车通过纽约市东河上的威廉斯堡大桥，穿过哈得逊河隧道，开始进入市区，没想到第一处景观竟是路过唐人街看街景。街道建筑虽整齐但看不到繁华景象，反而显得陈旧。此地似曾相识？对了，上世纪 90 年代曾在热播电视剧《北京人在纽约》里出现过。导游介绍，这些旧楼都是 50 年前建的，当时楼内未建消防安全通道，后来便在楼体外侧加挂一个铁梯，看上去格外显眼。

同胞欢聚

穿过纽约市区，进入邻近的新泽西州伊丽莎白市，入住双树饭店 (Doubletree Hotel)。稍事整理，就去附近的林登 (Linden) 市拜访中图美国公司。公司副总裁庞莉莉等同胞非常热情地接待了国内同行，向大家介绍了该公司在美开展业务情况。

这家驻外公司主要是向国内订户发送美国报刊和少量图书，约有 1500 多种，年经营收入 1400 多万美元。大家饶有兴趣地讨论起我国出版物"走出去"的前景，认为目前我国中医、少儿、文学、语言类书刊在美国应有一定市场，问题是缺乏资源整合、渠道疏通和有效推介，回款也有问题。大家交谈甚欢，随后参观了公司的各间办公室和库房，告别时在门前合影留念。此时已是夜幕降临，晚上 8 点，离开北京已经有 18 个小时了。

告别庞副总等，已是饥肠辘辘，导游拉着我们赶到附近的纽瓦克 (Newwark) 市中餐馆用餐。这时才想起给家里打电话，报平安。行前曾咨询国内移动通讯公司，到美国该用何种型号的手机，告知必须使用三频 1900 赫兹的。我问平时常用的摩托罗拉 760 型如何？答复可以。结果下了飞机，我的手机怎么摆弄也没有信号。打电话派不上用场，手机倒成了看钟点和记事的工具，今天的游记文章最初恰恰是手机的功劳。

初次踏上美利坚国土，第一天总算顺利，略感不安、疲劳怠倦的心境逐渐踏实下来。回到饭店时，导游提醒大家，倒时差最好熬到 12 点以后入睡。于是大家便凑在一起打"拖拉机"（一种扑克玩法），直到深夜 1 点钟才上床。算起来，从国内 17 日早 7 点动身赶赴北京机场，到此时已整整过去了 30 个小时，全团没有人撑不住。看来，人的精神和体力弹性很大，平时显得娇气，但只要遇到较劲的事情，就能经得住饥饿、疲劳、困倦等生理考验。

Taking a Bite of the "Big Apple"

New York is the symbol of the United States. In the world, I'm afraid there are not many cities as globally attractive as New York. Wall Street, Broadway, the site of the World Trade Center, the Empire State Building, the headquarters of the United Nations, Rockefeller Center, Times Square, the Statue of Liberty ... New York is indeed a world metropolis: not only bustling and dignified, but also elegant and comfortable, aptly nicknamed the "Big Apple".

Although I had never been to New York before, it was already in my mind for a long time: a world-class metropolis of skyscrapers, bustling style, tremendous wealth which everyone is longing for. So many dazzling sights not only attract the attention of the world, but also become the target of terrorist attacks. The earthshaking explosions of "9.11" was still vivid; as was the noisy and intense scene of the New York Stock Exchange; "To be heaven or hell," the suspense about New York left by the TV series "A Native of Beijing in New York" had haunted our minds all the time... so we couldn't wait to tour New York and enjoyed ourselves to the fullest degree.

Call at the "9.11" Ruins

New York's most prosperous places of interests are mostly all on the Manhattan Island. So on May 18, we spent the whole day in Manhattan.

At 9 a.m., the station wagon took us into the hustling and crowded flow of traffic, through the river-bottom tunnel, and then arrived in the downtown Manhattan. With mixed feelings of curiosity, we first went to visit the ruins of the Twin Towers of the World Trade Center. The World Trade Center was built in 1973 as the "Window of the World". It used to be the tallest building in the world, and was also the landmark of Americans' miraculous creation. On September 11, 2001, two huge passenger aircrafts which were hijacked by terrorists roared to hit the two buildings one after another. The buildings immediately burst into flames, and then collapsed suddenly which led to death of 3201 people and tens of billions of dollars' economic loss.

The "September 11" event shocked the United States and the world. It changed the global strategy of the United States and also the world pattern. The United States quickly responded to this event by taking pre-emptive military actions. First, it sent troops to Afghanistan to destroy the Taliban regime and severely hit Bin Laden's al-Qaeda; then, it attacked Iraq and arrested Saddam Hussein, which opened the prelude of the global anti-terrorism.

The "September 11" attack was nearly five years ago, but the Americans were still haunted by the shadow of pain. The construction plan of the new World Trade Center had been worked out for a long time, but until now nothing had happened. The building foundation had been cleaned up, and a small number of workers were working at the site. The ruins were surrounded by tall mesh wire. Though it was a large area of land, it was in the middle of high-rises, and looked very cramped and narrow.

The Explosion Moment of World Trade Center

We stepped onto the building corridor in the north of the ruins to have an overview of it through the glass windows and to take pictures. But after looking for a while, we did not feel comfortable, so we went to the south to look out. There we found that a mourning platform was put up temporarily near the inside of the mesh wire in the southwest corner of the ruins. A plastic board with a piece of white curtain was erected on the steps. The curtain was adorned with a variety of police badges, epaulettes. A few hats of police officer and firefighter, as well as photos, flowers, fire engine models, and other items were placed on the steps. A few lines of English words were written on the curtain, roughly the idea was "Thank you America for your prayers and support for all those lost and their families"and was signed by "From the port authority NY & NJ Police." The scene was very touching. How much unspeakable pain and grief was behind this piece of writing and all those mourning items! I mused carefully, and a lot of feelings rose in heart. Then I quickly put the camera lens through the mesh wire hole to snap a few pictures and left in a hurry.

Encountering the Bull

Leaving the World Trade Center site, we went to visit the famous Wall Street, the world's financial center. The car was running through the narrow streets in downtown Manhattan, when we caught sight of the U.S. Federal Reserve Bank Building, where the renowned Alan Greenspan was once in power. Greenspan was once the pivotal person in the global financial world and was called "one of the world's most powerful people" by the Western media. He served as the chairman of the Federal Reserve from 1987 to 2006, with great power that no one could rival.

When we arrived on Wall Street, we suddenly noticed the Wall Street Bull at the intersection of two streets in the plaza at Bowling Green. This world-famous bronze Bull sculpture, which was the source image of many souvenirs sold by merchants, was designed by the Italian artist Dimo Decca and was erected here in 1989. The power and grandeur of this charging bull is considered to be the symbol of "American strength and courage". As an exquisite work of art, the significance of the bronze bull is already far

The Memorial Platform of World Trade Center

The Wall Street Bull

beyond that of an urban sculpture. It is not only the epitome of Wall Street, but also the symbol of the soaring optimism and arrogance of the New York Stock. Seeing the Charging Bull, a familiar figure to us, we hurried to get out of the car, grabbing our cameras to take pictures. Measuring nearly five meters long, this huge 6,300-kilogram bronze bull is carved lifelike and imposing. Gazing at the statue and feeling its body, head and horns, one could not help but be lost in imagination and we were reluctant to leave.

After driving around for a long time the driver finally found a parking space at the southern end of Wall Street. We never thought that Wall Street, which holds the world's financial lifeline, was only a ten-meter-wide and less than one-kilometer-long small street of slings and arrows. Only rows of famous buildings like the Tower Bank and the Stock Exchanges, which stand on both sides of the street, serve as a testament to the world financial center. It was said that a mountain is not famous for height but for immortality, so a street is not well-known for width but for wealth.

The Goddess: Safe and Sound

At about 11 o'clock, we gathered at the pier on one side of the Brooklyn Bridge and then toured the Hudson River by boat to appreciate the Statue of Liberty.

Speaking of the Statue of Liberty, one must remember the famous short poem named "The New Colossus", composed by a Jewish poet Emma Lazarus for the Statue of Liberty. It goes like this:

Give me your tired your poor,
Your huddled masses yearning to breathe free,
The wretched refuse of your teeming shore.
Send these, the homeless, tempest-tossed to me;
I lift my lamp beside the golden door!

The Statue of Liberty is located on "Liberty Island" at the entrance to New York Harbor in the Hudson estuary. The height of the copper statue is 46 meters, while it is 93 meters high from the foundation of the pedestal to the tip of torch, and it weighs 225 tons, which makes it the most unique huge bronze statue in the world. The imposing appearance and demeanor of fortitude is considered to be the symbol of American national spirit. In 1885, the French people sent the statue to the United States as a gift to celebrate the 100th anniversary of American Independence. Since the ceremony of dedication was held in 1886, the statue has served as a spiritual icon to encourage people to pursue a free and happy life, and is an inspiration for people all over the world to immigrate to the United States. In recent years, especially after the end of the Cold War, the U.S. government often sent troops overseas to interfere with other countries' internal affairs in the name of democracy and freedom, which has been strongly criticized by the international community. As a result of this, the moral power and the symbolic meaning represented by the Statue of Liberty are questioned. The statue is mainly appreciated by the visitors all over the world for its distinctive image.

After the tourists boarded, the yacht cruised quickly to the center of the Hudson River, leaving lines of waves. When the yacht slowed down, we could see the clusters of skyscrapers in Manhattan Island, which turned out to be like a splendid and colorful oil painting, a contrasting silhouette against the blue sky and white clouds in the center of the sparkling river.

Standing on the bow of the boat, I looked into the distance. Under the bright sun, clouds and birds were playfully chasing each other in the blue sky, while the boats were busy shuttling across the rippling river. The suspension bridge across the sky, the rows upon rows of skyscrapers, the circling and roaring helicopters, and the flying white seagulls over the river ... All of this, at the moment, reminded me of Fan Zhongyan's famous lines, though I was in a foreign country. "What an unbounded joy! In such a case, ascent to the pavilion gives one a broadened mind and eased heart, with credit and discredit both forgotten. Holding a wine cup in the wind, one is overflowing with happiness."

When the yacht approached the Statue of Liberty, it slowed down, allowing

Statue of Liberty

Hudson River

A Corner of Rockefeller Center

tourists to get a good look and take pictures. Immediately, tourists on board all cheered, with some speaking highly of it, some running back and forth taking snapshots and some just gazing at the statue. At that moment, the tourists seemed to hope that time could stop to let the goddess be with them forever.

Staying there and feeling the beauty in person, I was also lost in thoughts:

Across the Atlantic the Goddess came,
Standing gracefully in New York Harbor;
And holding high the light of freedom,
How could she take New York for her home?

The yacht docked at 12 o'clock. We left the ship reluctantly and went ashore. After lunch, we visited Rockefeller Center on Fifth Avenue. We had thought that Manhattan was full of skyscrapers and bustle with crowds and cars. But quite contrary, Rockefeller Center, the icon of wealth and luxury, looked quite different. Along one side of the center street lay rows of benches, where tourists wandered leisurely, while on the other side

Twisted Pistol

Hall of the UN Security Council

was a large beautiful fountain and flower beds decorated with greenery. What a unique example of moving with silence! New York is indeed a world metropolis: not only bustling and dignified, but also elegant and comfortable. No wonder it has the gracious nickname "Big Apple".

Feelings about the United Nations

In the afternoon, we went to visit the United Nations Headquarters. At the entrance of the building stand two unique sculptures a broken earth and a twisted pistol, which intend to warn us of the ruin of human beings and the earth caused by nuclear war, and to demonstrate the hope to destroy weapons and the wish for peace.

In the hall, waiting for the interpretation of the guide, we first took pictures with the portraits of the former seven United Nations Secretary-Generals. Then, led by the docent, we visited the three conference halls of the Security Council, the Economic and Social Council and the UN General Assembly. Then we went to the UN exhibition, which aimed to promoting world peace and eliminate poverty and hunger. It should be said that we had admired the United Nations for a long time, so we felt a great honor to have the opportunity to visit it. However, when we really came into this "state within a state," perceiving its existence and imagining its function, we could not help feeling strange. This international organization by the name of the United Nations is mainly a global political stage for every member country to consult and debate. Or it can be recognized as an international coordination mechanism, with much stronger moral influence than its real strength. But in a modern world full of power politics, military hegemony and oligarchs economy, the United Nations as an international institution supported by every member country has no managerial function of a super-government, so it is difficult for it to intervene and exert impact on major international affairs. It is especially beyond its capability to coordinate and solve the conflicts that occurred throughout the world. The history professor Paul Kennedy of Yale University pointed this out in an article published entitled *The United Nations: the World's Scapegoat*, stating: In terms of world affairs, the United Nations actually does not play a centralized big role, so it has no corresponding power and ability. On issues like the Lebanese-Israeli conflict and the Palestinian-Israeli peace process, some big countries shift the blame to the United Nations in order to disguise their failures in diplomatic policy.

"The Empire Gloom"

After visiting the United Nations building, we went to the Empire State Building which is known as the symbol of U.S.A and the landmark of New York. It was exciting to feel the mighty presence of the Empire State Building. On the 86th floor, visitors could heartily enjoy the panoramic view of Manhattan on the observation deck. However, after we took the elevator to the 80th floor, all visitors were asked to line up and pose for pictures before going on to the 86th floor to sightsee. After the sightseeing, we had to get our photos with the list from the photo claim. Some tourists who couldn't understand English would take the list directly and then spent 20 dollars on an unnecessary fake photo which they might not actually want. Though it was voluntary and looked insignificant, we could not help feeling disrespected.

Because of the "photo event" and a sudden rainfall, the visit to the Empire State Building did not bring any pleasure. After dinner, night fell. We hurriedly rushed to Times Square which was named after *the New York Times* and turned out to actually be an area of long triangular avenue. The skyscrapers in the center and both sides of the streets were ablaze with lights, bright and charming. The various electronic advertisements on the large screens were especially shining and eye-catching. In addition to the bustling streetscape and noisy crowd, there was nothing special about Times Square. But a kind of bicycle being ridden by 6 people at the same time aroused our interest. It was another reflection of the creative spirit of the Americans and their unrestrained attitude toward life.

Times Square

品味 "大苹果"

　　纽约是美国的象征，世界上恐怕没有几座城市能像纽约那样经常吸引全球关注的目光。华尔街、百老汇、世贸中心、帝国大厦、联合国总部、洛克菲勒中心、时代广场、自由女神……纽约不愧是世界大都会，不但繁华凝重，而且舒适娴雅，品位独特，难怪有"大苹果"的雅号。

　　纽约是美国的象征，世界上恐怕没有几座城市能像纽约那样经常吸引全球关注的目光。以前虽然没有到过纽约，但心中早就对纽约形成了一种印象：那是一个高楼林立、繁华气派、财富横流、令人向往的世界大都会，那里有闻名于世的华尔街、百老汇、世贸中心、帝国大厦、联合国总部、洛克菲勒中心、时代广场、自由女神……一幅幅令人炫目的景象，既吸引了全球的目光，也成为恐怖袭击的对象。9·11那一幕惊天动地的爆炸场面至今仍历历在目；纽约证券交易所那喧闹激烈的场景想来便令人心动；电视剧《北京人在纽约》给了纽约那个到底是"天堂"还是"地狱"的悬念，一直萦绕心头……这一切都驱使我们在踏上美国国土后，第一站就想把纽约看个究竟、游个尽兴。

探访 "9·11"

　　纽约有"大苹果"的别称，纽约的繁华名胜都汇聚在曼哈顿岛上，5月18日，我们一天的行程全都在曼哈顿度过。

　　上午9点，旅行车载着我们汇入喧嚣拥挤的车流，穿过河底隧道，进入曼哈顿市区。怀着好奇复杂的心情，我们首先来到世贸中心双子座大厦遗址参观。有着"世界之窗"之称的世贸中心建成于1973年，曾是世界上最高的建筑，也是美国人创造奇迹的地标。2001年9月11日，两架遭恐怖分子劫持的大型客机先后呼啸着朝两座大厦撞去，大厦立即爆炸起火，接着轰然坍塌，造成3201人死亡和上千亿美元的经济损失。

9·11 事件震撼了美国，震惊了世界，改变了美国的全球战略，也改变了世界格局。9·11 事件后，美国迅速作出反应，采取先发制人的军事行动，先是出兵阿富汗，摧毁塔利班政权，重创拉登基地组织；接着攻打伊拉克，捉拿萨达姆，拉开了全球反恐怖主义的序幕。

9·11 事件已经过去将近 5 年了，但其伤痛和阴影在美国人的心目中挥之不去。世贸大厦的新建方案早就拟定，但至今未见动静。大厦地基已经清理干净，有少量的工人在现场作业。遗址被一人多高的铁丝网围了起来，夹在周围高楼中间，偌大一片地方显得局促狭小。

我们登上遗址北侧的大楼走廊，隔着玻璃可以居高临下朝里观察和拍照。看了一会儿，觉得不解渴，又急步走到南面观望，发现遗址西南角靠近铁丝网里侧的一处空地上，临时搭起了一个悼念台，台阶上竖立着塑料板，板墙上挂着一块白色幕布，幕布上面挂着各种各样的警察胸章、肩章，台阶上摆放着几顶警察和消防队员的帽子，还有照片、鲜花和消防车模型等物品。幕布上面写着几行英文字，大意是："感谢所有为这些失去生命的人和他们的家庭而进行祈祷和给予支持的美国人。"落款为纽约和新泽西州警察局。眼前的情景令人感动，短短的一篇文字，各式各样的悼念物品，其中饱含着多少难以言表的伤痛和哀思啊！仔细端详，心中感慨，赶紧把相机镜头伸进铁丝网孔，抓拍了照片，然后匆匆离去。

遭遇公牛

离开世贸中心，前去参观著名的世界金融中心华尔街 (Wall Street)。汽车在曼哈顿市区狭窄的街道上穿行，刚好路过美国联邦储备银行大楼，这里曾是大名鼎鼎的格林斯潘主政的地方。格老曾是世界金融界呼风唤雨的人物，被西方媒体誉为"世界上最有权势的人士之一"，他从 1987 年担任美联储主席到 2006 年卸任，其影响力无人能及。

快到华尔街时，忽然发现竖立在两条街道交叉路口上的华尔街公牛。这头名扬世界、被许多商家仿制成纪念品的铜牛雕像，是由意大利艺术家狄摩迪卡设计，1989 年竖立在此的。这头威武雄壮的铜牛以其奔腾向前的气势，被认为是"美国人力量与勇气"的象征。作为一件精美的艺术作品，铜牛的形象早就超出了一座城市雕塑的意义，它既是华尔街的缩影，也寓意着纽约股市的冲天牛气。见到早就熟悉喜爱的华尔街公牛，大家赶紧下车，抢上前去拍照留影。这头身长近 5 米、重达 6300 公斤的巨大铜牛，雕铸得栩栩如生，威风八面。仔细端详着公牛雕像，触摸着牛身牛头和牛角，令人产生许多联想，不愿即刻离去。

开车后绕了一大圈儿，司机好不容易在华尔街南端找到了泊位。出乎意料的是，这条掌握着全世界金融命脉的华尔街，只不过是一条十来米宽、不足千米长的矢石小街，只有街道两侧耸立着的一座座著名银行大厦和证券交易所大楼，方能显示出其世界金融中心的雄风。可谓山不在高有仙则名，街不在宽有钱则灵。

女神无恙

大约 11 点，在布鲁克林大桥一侧码头集合，乘船游览哈得逊河，前去观瞻自由女神像。

说起自由女神像，不能不提及那首题为《新巨人》的著名短诗，它是犹太诗人爱玛·拉扎露丝为自由女神而创作的。诗中写道：

> 送给我
> 你那疲乏的和贫困的挤在一起渴望自由呼吸的大众
> 你那熙熙攘攘的岸上被遗弃的可怜的人群
> 你那无家可归饱经风波的人们
> 一齐送给我
> 我站在金门口
> 高举自由的灯火

自由女神像位于哈得逊河口纽约港入口处的"自由岛"上，女神像高46米，连同基座高93米，重达225吨，是世界上独一无二的巨大铜像。铜像气宇轩昂，神态刚毅，被认为是美利坚民族精神的象征。整座女神像是1885年法国人民作为庆祝美国独立100周年的礼物赠送给美国的。自1886年揭幕以来，她曾作为追求自由和幸福生活的精神力量，激励着欧洲及世界各国移民投奔美国。近年来，特别是冷战结束后，由于美国政府经常打着民主自由的旗号到处出兵和干涉别国的内政，遭到国际社会的强烈批评，美国人引以为豪的自由女神所代表的道德力量和象征意义也受到了质疑。现在，女神雕像更多的是作为一处独特景观而受到各国游人的青睐。

　　来自中国、韩国等国的游客登船后，游船快速向哈得逊河中心驶去。游船划过河面，泛起道道波澜，随着白色浪花的远去消失，耸立在曼哈顿岛上的摩天大楼群像一幅浓墨重彩的油画映衬在蓝天白云下，浮动于波光粼粼的河中央。

　　站在船头，举目眺望，但见天空蔚蓝，阳光灿烂；白云飘动，鸟儿飞翔；游船穿梭，河水荡漾。横空飞架的悬索大桥，鳞次栉比的摩天大楼，盘旋轰鸣的直升飞机，掠过河面的白色海鸥……此刻，身在异国他乡，耳边却回响起范仲淹的名句："登斯楼也，则有心旷神怡，宠辱皆忘，把酒临风，其喜

Brooklyn Bridge

洋洋者矣。"

当游船驶近女神雕像时，开始低速盘桓，让游客观望和拍照。一时间，船上游客欢呼雀跃，嘴上啧啧称奇，脚下前后跑动，手中相机频闪，目光久久凝望。此时，游人骚客恨不得让时光停住，让女神永伴。

身临其境，感受美景，作者也不免心神熠动，浮想联翩：

女神横渡大西洋，亭亭玉立纽约港；
痴情高举自由火，怎把他乡做故乡？

游船靠岸已是中午 12 点，大家依依不舍地离船上岸。午餐后又去参观第五大道上的洛克菲勒中心 (Rockefeller Center)。原以为曼哈顿到处是高楼林立、人车熙攘，没想到代表财富与奢华的洛克菲勒中心却是另一番情景。只见中心街头一面是座椅成排、游人悠闲，另一面是喷泉如瀑、花坛绿茵，可谓闹中有静，景物别致。我想，纽约不愧是世界大都会，不但繁华凝重，而且舒适娴雅，品位独特，难怪有"大苹果"的雅号。

感受联合国

下午去参观联合国总部大厦。大厦入口处有两座独特的雕塑：破碎的地球和扭曲的手枪。意在警示世人核战争将对地球和人类造成的毁灭以及销毁武器、祈盼和平的愿望。

进入大厅后等待讲解，先在联合国原七位秘书长画像前拍照留影，然后在讲解员带领下进入安理会、经社理事会和联合国代表大会三个会议大厅参观，同时参观联合国在促进世界和平、消除贫困饥饿方面的展览。应当说，我等国人对联合国仰慕已久，对有机会参观联合国大厦深感荣幸。可是，当你真正走进这个"国中之国"，体会它的存在，联想它的作用时，你就会产生异样的感觉：眼前这个以联合国命名的国际组织，主要是一个供各成员国协商辩论的国际政治舞台，或者说是一个国际协调机构，其道义影响大于实质力量。在当今这个依然是强权政治、霸主军事、寡头经济的世界上，联合国作为一个由各成员国供养的国际机构，并没有超级政府的管理职能，很难干预影响重大国际事务，尤其在协调解决世界各地发生的冲突中，联合国往往是心有余而力不足。对此，美国耶鲁大学历史学教授保罗·肯尼迪在他去年发表的《联合国：世界的替罪羊》一文中指出，在世界事务中，联合国本不是一个中央集权的大角色，因而也就没有相应的权力和能力。在诸如黎以冲突和巴以和平进程问题上，某些大国为掩饰其失败的外交政策，把联合国当作了替罪羊。

"帝国" 不悦

从联合国大厦出来，就去登临号称美国象征、纽约标志的帝国大厦（The Empire State Building)。登临霸气十足的帝国大厦是件令人兴奋刺激的事，在大厦 86 层，游客可以在观光台上尽情欣赏曼哈顿市区全景。可是，当我们乘坐电梯抵达 80 层后，所有游客都必须排队经过一道照相程序，与帝国大厦照片合影留念，然后再转升至 86 层观光。从观光台下来，又得经过照片领取处拿上单子领取照片。虽说照片要不要自愿，但有些听不懂老美英语的游客，拿了单子就得花 20 美元，买一张本人并不一定想要的假合影。尽管是件小事，但让人感觉有点强拍强卖、不尊重游客的味道。

因为"照片事件"，加上突然降雨，参观帝国大厦没有带来心情的愉悦。晚餐后已是夜幕降临，抓紧时间赶往时代广场 (Times Square) 。以《纽约时报》命名的时代广场，实则是一块长长的三角大街。街道中央和两侧的大厦灯火辉煌、流光溢彩，特别是各种大屏幕电子广告闪亮夺目，耀眼迷人。除街道繁华、人群喧闹外，时代广场并无特别之处，倒是一种 6 人同骑的圆形自行车引起了大家的兴趣，它从一个侧面反映了美国人的创造精神和无拘无束的生活态度。

Glory of Philadelphia

During the American War of Independence, Philadelphia was the birthplace of the American Revolution and is known as the cradle of the U.S.A. On every National Independence Day of the United States, the bell symbolizing the independence of the United States will toll. Mr. Gu Yuxiu once asked the former Chinese Premier Zhu Rongji to take good care of himself for the country, and shared with him the motto: "The wise will not feel puzzled. The brave will not feel fear. The honest has integrity. The benevolent has no enemy."

On the morning of the 19th, we left Elizabeth New Jersey for Washington D.C. We stopped at the Cherry-Hill Mall for a while to experience the consumer life of American middle-class people. After lunch, we entered Philadelphia to have a short visit before passing through New Jersey, Pennsylvania, Delaware, Maryland and Virginia, and traveling a total of 450 kilometers.

Cradle of Republicans

We had little knowledge about Philadelphia before we came. We only

On the Street of Philadelphia
(The one is Zhao Hengfeng, in the same delegation with the writer)

knew that it was a city with a glorious history and beautiful scenery. The full name is Philadelphia. "Feicheng" is its shortened name in Chinese. It is located along the Delaware River in Pennsylvania and has an area of 336 square kilometers and a population of about 2 million. On the way there, our tour guide Peter Cai described it with a vivid comparison: Philadelphia is America's "Yan'an."

To be exact, Philadelphia is the birthplace for American Revolution. During the Revolutionary War, many important historic events took place here. In 1774 and 1775, two continental congresses were held in this city; On July 4, 1776, the "Declaration of Independence" declaring liberty, equality and fraternity was signed here; in 1787, the first constitution of the United States was born here; from 1790 to 1800, it was also the temporary capital of the United States. Philadelphia became known as the cradle of the United States. George Washington, Benjamin Franklin, Thomas Jefferson, Thomas Paine and other great historical figures had adorned it with their wisdom and left glorious achievements. Today, Philadelphia still preserves the monuments with this period of glory, such as the Independence Hall,

Philadelphia Street Scene

the Liberty Bell, Franklin Museum and so on. At the entrance of downtown Philadelphia, we passed the Franklin cemetery.

Many Chinese people have heard of the name of Franklin and know that he was a great scientist and inventor of the lightning rod. In order to prove the existence of electricity from thunder and lightning, Franklin made an experiment by flying a kite in a thunder and lightning storm at the risk of his life, which took the whole world by storm. Franklin is also one of the early famous political activists and educators of the United States. He started out as a printer's typesetter, but studied hard to become proficient in all walks of life, whether natural science or social science.

Franklin, the self-taught elite, exerted far-reaching influence on U.S.A. The United States always advocated "self-study." As early as in the colonial period, a variety of reading materials were published. But the daily wages of the ordinary workers were only two shillings, so they could not afford to buy books to read. In order to meet the reading needs of the autodidacts, especially the ordinary workers, in 1731, Franklin mobilized people to donate money and jointly founded the first public library in the United States. In 1743, he created the first cultural society, the North American Philosophical Society. In 1751, he helped Jefferson to establish the University of Pennsylvania. Philadelphia had many firsts in the history of the United States. For example, it is also the birthplace of the first bank, the first stock exchange, the first coin foundry and so on. So, it is indeed the city of history and culture.

Motto Gift from the Master

The communication between China and Philadelphia has lasted for more than 100 years. According to the records, in 1876, when the United States commemorated the 100th anniversary of the "Declaration of Independence," China sent a group of delegation to attend the International Exposition which was held in Philadelphia. After the founding of New China, the famous Philadelphia orchestra came to visit China many times. In 1980, Tianjin and Philadelphia became friendly cities. Jiang Zemin, who was the

Chinese President at that time, visited the United States in October 1997 and especially went to Philadelphia to see his teacher Gu Yuxiu.

If not for President Jiang's visit, many Chinese people would not have known Gu Yuxiu. Gu Yuxiu is a famous academic master who has a thorough knowledge of the East and the West, and is proficient in both literature and science. He is not only a famous scientist and educator of many achievements, but also is a quite good writer. Mr. Gu was born in Wuxi, Jiangsu Province in 1902. In 1923, he went to study at Massachusetts Institute of Technology (MIT) in the United States, where he earned a Bachelor and Master degree in Electrical Engineering and obtained his Doctorate degree in Science. After he came back to China in 1929, he served as the headmaster of the National Government Central University, the vice Minister of Education and so on. In 1950s, he went back to MIT to serve as a professor, and settled down in the United States. Because of his outstanding contributions in dynamo theory, in 1972, he won the Lamb Medal which is known as "the Nobel Prize in the motor area."

In April 1999, the former Premier Zhu Rongji visited the United States. Mr. Gu Yuxiu was 98 years old then, but he specially went to Washington D.C. from his home in Philadelphia. Zhu Rongji presented the famous Huangshan Tea to Mr. Gu as a gift. In return, Mr. Gu asked the Premier to take good care of himself for the sake of the country, and presented him with such words: "The wise will not feel puzzled. The brave will not feel fear. The honest has integrity. The benevolent has no enemy." These words are very instructive for doing great things in life and being a great person.

The "Bell" as a Favorite

Today, Philadelphia is the fifth largest city in the United States. Factories clustered round the outskirts; a large number of boats shuttled back and forth on the river; the city was covered with green, Philadelphia is famous for its lasting appeal of an ancient city and has attracted a large number of tourists from other parts of the United States and all over the world.

Liberty Bell

We stayed in Philadelphia for just more than 2 hours, and mainly visited the Liberty Bell and Independence Hall, which were both crowded with tourists. Because of the delay of the security check, people could not move forward smoothly, and they consciously lined up at the entrance of the Liberty Bell Memorial. At this moment, a few old-fashioned carriages came down the street, carrying tourists viewing the city. An empty carriage came near us. A tall and thin black coachman was joking with the American tourists, aiming to persuade them to ride his carriage. A disabled girl in a wheelchair, accompanied by a middle-aged woman (presumably her mother), was also on line.

Looking at the American tourists who were lining up and especially the mother and daughter, I could not help thinking: Do these ordinary Americans interested in and cherish their own country's history? Throughout our visit, we really got that impression. The Chinese tour guide once described to us with great emotion: No matter on what kind of occasion, formal or recreational, as long as they hear their national anthem "The Star-Spangled Banner" or see the rising of the American flag, the Americans would immediately take off their hats, put their right hand on the chest, and all stand still facing the flag, which shows a kind of conscious and devout patriotism.

Before we entered the exhibition hall, we had to take off our shoes, untie our belts, and have our bags checked. After going through all these and some other security procedures, we finally went into the hall. The memorial was not physically big but simple, with displays of pictures, words and some historical objects. What people mainly wanted to see was the iron bell of special commemorative significance. Approaching the Liberty Bell, tourists all stepped forward to take pictures. Some American children snuck under and stuck their hands in to explore the inside of the bell curiously. The Bell is nearly one meter high and weighs 943 kg. It was cast in London and was shipped to the United States in 1752, symbolizing the independence and free spirit of America. On July 4, 1776, the bell was rung to mark the reading of "Declaration of Independence;" On April 16, 1783, the ringing of the "liberty bell" declared the victory of the American War of Independence. Since then, on every July 4, the National Independence Day, the bell which symbolizes this independence is rung. Now, the 250-year-old bell has cracked, but the Americans still have a unique preference towards it, and place some kind of spirit and ideal on it.

Opposite the Liberty Bell, on the other side of the street, is Independence Hall, a two-story old red brick building with milky windows, wooden doors and a steeple. A big clock is inlaid between the house and steeple. In this plain building, the Declaration of Independence and the Constitution of the United States were born. Here also was the headquarters of the American War of Independence. So, it became one of the American historic sites and is called "Independence Hall." What a pity that we did not have time enter the Hall! We just took a few pictures outside of the red building, and then drove on.

光荣的费城

美国独立战争期间，费城是美国革命的发祥地，被称为美利坚合众国的摇篮。每逢美国国庆日，都要敲响象征美国独立的钟声。顾毓琇先生嘱咐朱镕基总理为国珍重，并赠其 16 字箴言："智者不惑，勇者不惧，诚者有信，仁者无敌。"

19 日上午，我们从伊丽莎白市出发赶往华盛顿，途经新泽西、宾夕法尼亚、特拉华、马里兰和弗吉尼亚五个州，全程 450 公里。途中在新泽西州的超级大商场 (Cherry-Hill Mall) 停留，参观了解美国中产阶层的消费生活，午餐后进入费城作短暂参观。

共和摇篮

对于费城，我们事先了解得不多，只知道它是一座历史光荣、风景秀丽的城市。它的全称叫菲拉德尔菲亚 (Philadelphia)，"费城"是其中文简称。这座位于宾夕法尼亚州特拉华河畔的城市，面积 336 平方公里，人口约 200 万。在赶往费城的途中，导游蔡彼得形象地比喻说，费城就是美国的"延安"。

准确地说，费城是美国革命的发祥地，在美国独立战争期间，许多具有重要历史意义的事件都发生在这里：1774 年和 1775 年两次大陆会议在这里召开；1776 年 7 月 4 日，昭示着自由、平等、博爱思想的《独立宣言》在这里通过；1787 年美国第一部宪法在这里诞生。1790 至 1800 年间，费城还曾是美国的临时首都。因此，费城被称为美利坚合众国的摇篮。乔治·华盛顿、本杰明·富兰克林、托马斯·杰斐逊、托马斯·潘恩等历史名人都曾在费城挥洒下他们的智慧，留下了光辉的业绩。如今费城完好地保存着记载这段光荣历史的名胜古迹，如独立宫、自由钟、富兰克林博物馆等。当我们进入费城市区时，恰好路过富兰克林墓地。

富兰克林像

很多中国人都听说过富兰克林的名字，知道他是一名伟大的科学家、避雷针的发明者。为了证明雷电的存在，富兰克林甘冒生命危险，在电闪雷鸣的暴风雨中放风筝，做了一个轰动世界的实验。富兰克林还是美国早期著名的政治活动家和教育家，他从小当过印刷厂的排字工人，边工作边勤奋学习，从自然科学到社会科学，无不通晓。

富兰克林通过自学而成为杰出人物，这对美国社会影响深远。美国是个崇尚"自学"的国家，早在殖民地时期，美国出版的各种读物就非常多，但普通工人每天的工资只有两个先令，买不起书看，为了满足广大自学者特别是普通工人的读书需求，1731年，富兰克林发动人们捐款，共同创办了美国第一个公共图书馆；1743年，他又组织创办了第一个文化学会——北美哲学学会；1751年，他协助杰斐逊创办了宾夕法尼亚大学。费城拥有美国历史上很多个第一，比如还诞生过美国第一家银行、第一个证券交易所、第一家硬币铸造厂等等，因而是名副其实的历史文化名城。

名师箴言

中国和费城的交往已有100多年的历史。据记载，1876年，美国纪念《独立宣言》100周年时，中国曾派团参加在费城举行的万国博览会。新中国成立后，赫赫有名的费城交响乐团曾多次访华，1980年中国天津市和费城结成友好城市。1997年10月，时任中国国家主席的江泽民访美，特意到费城看望了他的老师顾毓琇先生。

如果不是江主席看望，或许很多中国人并不了解顾毓琇先生。顾毓琇是一位学贯中

顾毓琇

西、文理兼通的学术大师，是建树卓越的著名科学家、教育家，还是一位颇有造诣的文学家。顾先生 1902 年出生于江苏无锡，1923 年赴美国麻省理工学院留学，获该校电机系学士、硕士和科学博士学位。他 1929 年回国后，曾担任国民政府中央大学校长、教育部次长等职。50 年代到美国麻省理工学院任教授，后在美国定居。由于顾先生对电机理论的突出贡献，他于 1972 年荣获被誉为"电机领域诺贝尔奖"的兰姆奖章。

1999 年 4 月，朱镕基总理访美，98 岁的顾毓琇先生特意从费城家中赶到华盛顿。朱镕基向顾毓琇先生赠送黄山名茶，顾先生则嘱咐朱镕基为国珍重，并赠其 16 字箴言："智者不惑，勇者不惧，诚者有信，仁者无敌。"对人生做大事、成大器很有教益。

情有独"钟"

如今的费城是美国第五大城市，郊外工厂林立，河上轮船如梭；市内则是绿荫如盖，名胜繁多，浸透出浓厚的古城韵味，吸引着来自全世界及美国国内的大量游客。

我们一行进入费城只停留了两个多小时，主要参观自由钟和独立宫。前来参观的人很多，由于安全检查耽搁，人流不畅，人们自觉地在自由钟纪念馆入口处排起长队。这时大街上驶过来几辆老式马车，正拉着游客浏览市容，一辆没拉上客人的马车靠近我们，又高又瘦的黑人马车夫走过来与美国游客逗嘴说笑，游说客人乘坐他的马车。有位中年妇女推着轮椅陪着一位残疾小姑娘也在等待参观。

看着前后排队的美国游客和这对母女，不禁令人思忖：这些普通的美国人也喜欢了解和珍视自己国家的历史吗？一路访美下来，给我们的印象的确如此。华人导游曾颇为感慨地给我们讲述了如下场景：不论是在正式场合或在娱乐场所，只要听到国歌《星条旗》，看到美国国旗升起，现场的美国人都会立刻脱帽，右手抚胸，齐刷刷地面向国旗，肃然而立，表现出一种自觉而虔诚的爱国情怀。

经过脱鞋、解腰带、搜提包等安检手续才得以进入展览馆。场馆不大、陈设简单，除图片和文字外，还有一些实物。人们想要看的，主要是那口具有特别纪念意义的铁钟。走近自由钟，游客纷纷上前拍照，有的美国少年儿童还好奇地趴到地上朝铁钟里面观看。这口象征着美国独立、自由精神的铁钟铸于英国伦敦，高约一米，重 943 公斤，1752 年运到美国。1776 年 7 月 4 日，当《独立宣言》宣读之际，钟声响彻长空；1783 年 4 月 16 日，"自由钟"的钟声又宣告了美国独立战争的胜利。此后，每逢 7 月 4 日美国国庆日，都要敲响象征美国独立的钟声。现在这口 250 多年的铁钟已经裂缝，但美国人对它仍情有独钟，寄托着某种精神和理想。

从自由钟纪念馆出来，就看到街道对面的独立宫。这是一座两层旧式红砖楼房，乳白色的门窗和尖塔，正屋和尖塔之间镶嵌着一座大时钟。就是在这座朴实无华的楼房里，诞生了《独立宣言》和美国宪法。这里还曾是美国独立战争的指挥部，故而成为美国历史文物建筑，被命名为"独立宫"。遗憾的是，因时间仓促，我们未能进入独立宫内参观，只在红楼外面拍了两张照片就登车前行了。

Getting to Know Washington D. C.

The capital is the heart and soul of a country. People begin to know a country usually by its capital. The design of Washington is centered on its capital administrative function. The layout of the city is logical and scientific with wide development space. In contrast, Beijing carries too many functions in politics, economy, culture, education, sports, scientific research, medical treatment, military affairs and transportation. The complexity of its roles plus the big city disease has made Beijing hard to breathe and unbearable, which make people feel haunted by a strong anxiety about the current situation and the future of Beijing.

The full name of Washington, the capital of U.S.A, is Washington District of Columbia. The total area of the district is 6094 square kilometers and its population is about 4 million while the urban area covers only 177 square kilometers with an urban population of 550, 000. As the capital of U.S.A, the superpower, Washington D.C. is both the political center and the focus of global attention. Every important message sent out from here will affect the world situation more or less. Due to the high media exposure of the city, even the people who have not been to Washington will be familiar with the

Downtown of Washington City

famous buildings such as the White House, the Capitol and the Washington Monument.

New Look of the Capital

On May 19, with a long journey of sightseeing, we arrived at Washington D.C. at dusk. We stayed in a suburban hotel and did not enter the urban area until the next day when we were to participate in the book fair and tour the city.

On the way to the downtown area, the roads were wide with dense forests on both sides. The famous Potomac River, clear and charming, flowed across Washington D.C. The downtown area of Washington D.C. is located on the north bank of the Potomac River, which was originally a bushy virgin land with only a few cottages scattered over 200 years ago. It was coincidence of history that enabled it to become the capital of the United States.

In 1789, the federal government of the United States was formally established and George Washington was elected the first president. In the first conference of the Congress in New York, the location of the capital caused a heated debate. The north and south both hoped to have the

Graduation Ceremony of Georgetown University

The U.S. Capitol

capital located in their own territory. After repeated consultations, they finally agreed on a compromise: Philadelphia served as the temporary capital. The congress authorized the government to select the natural boundary of the south and the north — Potomac River became the new site of the capital, and the French engineer Pierre L'Enfant, who had participated in the American War of Independence, was appointed to preside over the overall planning and design of the new capital.

The designer had a blank slate, allowing him to heartily imagine a new city without any burden of history. Based on plans of European cities and in reflection of the governing ideals of democratic countries, Pierre L'Enfant designed the new capital to be not only dignified but also fresh and beautiful, in an air of the emerging metropolitan powers. He put the top legislative body — the Capitol, at the top of Jenkins Hill which is the highest point downtown, to make it the center and focus of the city. The White House, the Capitol and the Supreme Court building were located in the form of a triangle. The famous "independence" and "constitution" boulevards lie on both sides of the Capitol which is located with the White House by Pennsylvania Avenue. On the same axis, broad avenues named

White House

after different states radiate out from these two buildings and lead to many monuments, memorial halls, town plazas and other important buildings.

Therefore, Washington D.C. is designed for the capital administration functions. The overall arrangement is quite scientific and reasonable, with broad space for further development. In addition to a dozen federal departments and other government agencies, there are also hundreds of libraries, museums, galleries, art centers, universities, research institutions, many memorials, monuments of famous people, etc. These places are most elegant and luxuriant with green grasses and trees. More than 300 big or small parks dot the city, where the per capita green space is 40 square meters. The highlight is the central administrative region. It is only less than 10 square kilometers but just like a big park. All buildings in it are exquisite and the scenery is beautiful everywhere.

Exploring Washington

In the District of Columbia, the Washington Monument is located in the center, west of the Capitol Hill and east of the Lincoln Memorial. They line up side by side on a horizontal axis. On the south is the Jefferson Memorial and on the north is the White House, which forms the vertical axis. This kind of layout not only shows the majesty of the capital, but also avoids the noises and crowdedness brought by the high buildings and large number of commercial ports. Tourists who first arrive in Washington mainly visit the District and the surrounding attractions.

In the past, visitors could freely enter the White House, the Capitol Hill and other places to have a visit. But since the "September 11" terrorist attack, the United States has taken strict vigilance measures on all the important buildings and places, not to mention the key places such as the White House and the Capitol Hill. On the afternoon of May 21, when we parked the car and came across the meadows and woods, near the White House, we found that the channel outside of the White House South Lawn and the main entrance of it north on the Pennsylvania Avenue were both blocked by isolation zone and concrete barriers. The police were all heavily armed and keeping watch. Absolutely no tourists dared to come closer. We could only stand outside the barricades, watching at a distance and taking pictures carefully.

The White House is a three-story white marble building. Viewed from afar, against the background of the blue sky, white clouds and lush greens, the White House seems extremely elegant and beautiful. In the modern viewpoint, the White House as the presidential palace of the world's most powerful country is not large; however, the denizen of it is the most powerful figure in the world. It is said that there are a total of 132 rooms in the White House. Besides the President and his family, 431 White House working staff also live there.

It is slightly less inhabited to visit the Capitol Hill than the White House. Tourists were allowed to come close to the foot of the building to see and take pictures, but they were not allowed to walk up the steps and go inside. The Capitol was built at the highest point in the center of the city, so it was called "Capitol Hill". Like the White House, the Capitol Hill is also the symbol of Washington as well as the United States, and often appears in the TV media. This milky white building is composed of a main domed building and the interconnected east and west wings. One hundred senators and 435

Group Photo of Our Delegation

representatives of the U.S. Congress all work in this building. Whether seen from a distance, or observed closely, Capitol Hill looks like it is exquisitely carved in white ivory, is elegant and dignified, and can be called a classic of the world's architecture.

In addition to the White House and Capitol Hill, the Department of Defense is also a major attraction for tourists. The Pentagon which is located on the other side of the Potomac River is the U.S. Department of Defense, the headquarters of army, navy and air force and also Joint Chiefs of Staff. It is a huge pentagon shaped building with a total construction area of 608,000 square meters, formed by five connected 22-meter-high buildings, which may accommodate 23,000 people at the same time.

As a military institution which holds the world's most powerful army, the U.S. Department of Defense has not only the largest building in Washington, but also huge overseas military bases. According to media reports, the Pentagon has nearly 1,000 military bases around the world, covering a land area of more than 2.2 million hectares, and it is one of the largest landowners in the world. In the "September 11" event, one side of the Pentagon was destroyed by a plane and even after the repair, traces of the crash can still be seen. During the American Book Fair, each time we drove from our quarters in the suburb to downtown Washington we would see the Pentagon, but we never had the chance to see it closely.

Moreover, there are so many other places of interest in Washington, which I will not describe. The one thing that is worth mentioning is the Chinese "Friendship Archway," or Paifang in Washington's Chinatown, which is 23 meters wide and 14.33 meters high, with two huge pillars onto stone bases, and seven eaves bound together. It is known as the highest, the best and the largest single span Chinese archway in all Chinatowns of the major cities of the United States. For the sake of traffic, its original 4-pillar base was reduced to 2, and seven roofs were designed in three stories. This Chinese Paifang is decorated with more than 7,000 pieces of yellow glazed tiles and wooden stones with the total weight of 128 tons, and fully in the style of the Ming and the Qing dynasties. Some people say that it is born out of the "Hanxu, Jingyuan" archway which is located in front of the door of the Orient House in the Summer Palace in Beijing. The archway in Washington is painted in the style of "Jinlonghexi," with 270 golden dragons on it, which used 50 kilograms of gold. In the center of the archway beam it reads "Zhong Guo Cheng" (China Town) in Chinese characters, which was written by the famous Chinese painter Wu Zuoren. These archway were jointly built in 1984 when Washington and Beijing became sister cities after the mayor of Washington visited Beijing. It was completed in 1986 and there was a ceremony. Behind the archway, we can see both the connotation and charm of Chinese culture and the tolerance and tension of Washington.

As a city Washington is beautiful and as a capital it is atmospheric. It mirrors the unique national spirit of the United States and the air of a big country. Just as Professor Shi Peijun at Beijing Normal University said in an article, "The capital is the heart and soul of a country. People begin to know a country usually with its capital. The capital is also the political and cultural center. Whether old or young, the civilization of a great country first accumulates in the land of the capital. So, the capital city is the microcosm of a country, and also the recorder of the history and culture of a state and nation."

Indeed, Washington is the microcosm of the United States. It has been more than 220 years since the United States chose its capital. From the founding fathers to today's celebrities, all of them have left distinct traces

Archway of China Town

in Washington. As the capital of a big country, Washington attracts the attention of the whole world by its powerful international influence. At the same time, the city's urban beauty, classic architecture, grand culture and its clear rivers, lush forests and picturesque countryside all attract about 20 million tourists from all over the world every year.

Hopes and Fears of Beijing

Washington and Beijing are both capitals of big countries in the center of the world's attention, and also the cities which deserve the title of the capital. With the differences in history and national conditions, it is rash to draw a simple analogy between the two. In terms of location and status, they have many things in common. The latitudes of the two cities on the earth are close to each other: both are located on the continent's eastern coast, near the ocean, beautiful and magnificent. But as for the design planning, the architectural style and the urban scale, especially the capital function of the city, there are many differences between the two. The famous Chinese historical geographer Hou Renzhi, a professor in Peking University, had once made a comment on this. He thought that Washington's spatial layout is more conformed to the architectural design style of landscape aesthetics, while the city layout of Beijing can better reflect the features of the oriental culture. From the perspective of sustainable development, the spatial layout of Washington, with its beautiful environment, convenient transportation, good services and other aspects, can really provide today's city planners with a lot of enlightenment.

Urban planning and design, construction and layout mainly depend on the orientation of the urban functions. The United States is a young country whose economy develops at a high speed. Its industrial, financial, cultural and educational functions are respectively shared by New York, Los Angeles and many other big cities and regional central cities, while Washington only plays the role of the political center. However, Beijing, as the capital of a big country, with a history of 800 years and a population of nearly 16 million people, carries too many functions in politics, economy, culture, education, sports, scientific research, medical treatment, military affairs and transportation. The complexity of its roles plus the big city disease has made Beijing hard to breathe and at times, unbearable.

The college entrance examination of 2006 in Beijing chose "The Symbol of Beijing" as the topic of the composition to test the Chinese. This topic sparked heated social repercussions, and all of a sudden, all kinds of unsatisfactory phenomenon in Beijing became the hot topics of netizens. Some people playfully said that "In Beijing, the house price is always rising, the road is always in jam and buses and subways are always crowded," "The capital city is becoming the 'jam city'". Though these words are a bit harsh, they indeed reflect some prominent problems in Beijing.

It should be said, whether in comparison with other domestic cities, or to be measured as the world's capital city, Beijing, with its grandeur and majesty, grace and elegance, is unparelleled. But the constant superimposing of functions, the rapid growth of population and the over-expansion of the city have put Beijing in an increasingly severe test of housing, transportation, environment, especially in terms of the water usage. Facing this, together with the natural disasters such as sandstorms and acid rain, people cannot help feeling haunted by a strong anxiety about the current situation and the future of Beijing.

认识华盛顿

首都是一个国家的心脏和灵魂，人们认识一个国家，通常从它的首都开始。华盛顿主要是围绕首都行政功能而设计的，城市布局科学合理，发展空间游刃有余，而北京却承载了太多的政治、经济、文化、教育、军事等功能，首都重担加上大城市病把北京压得气喘吁吁，不堪重负，不由得使人对北京的城市现状深感焦虑，对它的未来充满担忧。

美国首都华盛顿，全称叫"华盛顿哥伦比亚特区"(Washington District of Columbia)。特区总面积 6094 平方公里，人口约 400 万，市区面积仅 177 平方公里，城市人口 55 万。作为超级大国的首都，华盛顿既是美国的政治中心，也是全球关注的焦点，这里发出的每一条重要信息，都会对世界局势产生或大或小的影响。由于被媒体高度关注，即使没有到过华盛顿的人，也能经常在电视上看到白宫、国会大厦、华盛顿纪念碑等标志性建筑。

新都新貌

5 月 19 日，我们经过长途跋涉，一路观光，到傍晚时分赶到了华盛顿特区，先是在郊区宾馆住下，第二天才得以进入市区，参加书展，游览市容。

从郊区赶往市区，沿途道路宽阔，森林茂密，著名的波托马克河从华盛顿特区蜿蜒流过，河水清澈，风光旖旎。华盛顿市区就位于波托马克河北岸，200 多年前，这里原本是一片灌木丛生的处女地，只有一些村舍散落其间，是历史机缘让它成为美利坚合众国的首都。

1789 年美国联邦政府正式成立，乔治·华盛顿当选为首任总统。当国会在纽约召开第一次会议时，因首都选址问题引起激烈争吵，南北两方的议员都想把首都设在本方境内。经过反复协商，达成折衷协议：以费城为临时首都，由国会授权政府选定南北方的天然分界线——波托马克河畔作为首都新址，并交由参加过美国独立战争的法国工程师皮埃尔·朗方主持新首都的总体规划和设计。

一张白纸可以描绘最新最美的蓝图，一座没有历史包袱的新城可以让设计者尽情发挥他的想象力：吸收欧洲城市的建筑特色，体现民主国家的治国理念，展示新兴大国的都市风采，皮埃尔·朗方把美国新首都设计得既庄重大方又清新美丽。他把立法机关——国会选在市区最高的詹金斯山山顶，使它成为全城的中心和焦点；白宫、国会和最高法院形成三角形状；在国会大厦两侧，建有著名的"独立"和"宪法"两条林荫大道；国会大厦和白宫以宾西法尼亚大街相连接，在同一轴线上，以美国各州州名命名的一条条宽阔的大道从这两处建筑放射出去，通向众多的纪念碑、纪念堂、城市广场和重要建筑物。

可见，华盛顿主要是围绕首都行政功能而设计的，城市布局科学合理，发展空间游刃有余。除十几个联邦政府部门和其他政府机构外，华盛顿还拥有数以千百计的图书馆、博物馆、美术馆、艺术中心、大学、科研机构以及众多的名人纪念堂和纪念碑等，这些地方环境幽雅，草木葱郁，遍布市区的大小公园、绿地达 300 多处，人均绿地 40 平方米。特别是不到 10 平方公里的中央行政区就像一座大公园，园内座座建筑精美，处处景色秀丽。

华府探秘

在华盛顿中央行政区内，以华盛顿纪念碑为中心，东面是国会大厦，西面是林肯纪念堂，一字排开成横向中轴线；南面是杰斐逊纪念堂，北面是白宫，成纵向中轴线。这种布局，既体现了美国首都的雄伟壮丽，也避免了高楼林立、商埠云集的嘈杂拥挤。初到华盛顿的游客，主要是在中央行政区和周边景点参观游览。

从前，游客可以自由地进入白宫和国会大厦等处参观，自 9·11 恐怖事件后，美国对所有重要建筑和场所都采取了严格的警戒措施，何况白宫、国会这样的首脑重地。5 月 21 日下午，当我们把车子停好，穿过草地和树林，来到白宫 (The White House) 附近参观时，只见白宫南草坪外面的通道和北面的宾州大街白宫正门都已被隔离带和水泥墩堵死，而且警察荷枪实弹，戒备森严，游客哪个还敢靠近，只能站在路障外面远远地观望，小心地拍照。

白宫是一座三层楼高的白色大理石建筑，远远望去，在蓝天白云和绿树草丛的映衬下显得极为典雅，非常漂亮。以今天的眼光看，白宫作为世界头号大国的总统府，建筑的体量并不大，但它的主人却是当今世界上最有权势的人物。据说白宫共有 132 间房屋，除美国总统和他的家人外，还有为总统服务的 431 名白宫工作人员。

参观国会大厦 (Capitol Hill) 比白宫略好一些，游客可以到大厦下面近距离游览拍照，但不能走上台阶和到大厦里面参观。国会大厦建在市中心最高处，因此被称为"国会山"。和白宫一样，国会大厦是华盛顿也是美国国家的象征，经常在电视媒体上露面。这座乳白色的建筑有一个圆顶主楼和相互联结的东、西两翼大楼，美国国会 100 名参议员和 435 名众议员都在这座大楼里办公。无论是从远处眺望，还是近处观察，国会大厦犹如一座白色象牙雕刻，玲珑剔透，精美凝重，堪称世界建筑的经典之作。

除了白宫和国会山，对游客最有吸引力的地方还有五角大楼 (Dept.of Defence)。位于波托马克河彼岸的五角大楼，是美国国防部和陆、海、空三军军部以及参谋长联席会议的所在地，这是一座巨大的五边形建筑物，总建筑

波托马克河

面积 60.8 万平方米，由 5 幢 22 米高的楼房连接而成，可供 2.3 万人办公。

作为一个掌握着世界最强大军队的军事机构，美国国防部不但在华盛顿拥有最大的建筑，而且在海外还拥有庞大的军事基地。据媒体报道，五角大楼在全世界有近千个军事基地，所占土地面积达 220 多万公顷，是世界最大的地主之一。在 9·11 事件中，五角大楼一侧遭到飞机撞毁，修复后的痕迹依稀可见。美国书展期间，我们乘车从郊区住处来往华盛顿市区，每次路过都能看到五角大楼，却无缘走近参观。

华盛顿还有很多名胜古迹，这里不再赘述。值得一提的是位于华盛顿唐人街的中国城牌楼。这是一座两柱七楼檐一字形的牌楼，宽 23 米，高 14.33 米，被誉为美国各大城市唐人街中等级最好、跨度最大、也是最高的中式牌楼。为了不影响交通，改四柱为两柱，三层排列七楼檐式样，用 7000 多块黄色琉璃瓦和木石建造，重达 128 吨，完全是明清建筑风格，有人说它是脱胎于北京颐和园东宫门前那座"涵虚、静远"牌楼。该牌楼采用"金龙和玺"彩绘，画有金龙 270 条，耗金 1000 两，牌楼正中是中国大书画家吴作人手书的"中国城"三个金光闪闪的大字。这座牌楼是 1984 年华盛顿市长访华与北京市缔结为姊妹城时决定共同兴建的，1986 年完工并举行落成仪式。透过这座牌楼，让人看到的既有中华文明的内涵和魅力，也有华盛顿的包容和张力。

华盛顿作为城市是美丽的，作为首都是大气的，它就像一面镜子，折射出美利坚独特的民族精神和大国风采。正如北京师范大学史培军教授在一篇文章中所说的："首都是一个国家的心脏和灵魂，人们认识一个国家，通常从它的首都开始。首都是一个国家的政治和文化中心，无论古老还是年轻，伟大国家的文明首先积淀在首都的土地上，因此，首都是一个国家的缩影，是一个国家和民族历史文化的记录者。"

华盛顿的确是美国的一个缩影，美国定都 220 多年来，从开国元勋到当今风云人物，都在华盛顿留下了鲜明的痕迹。作为大国首都，华盛顿不仅以其强大的国际影响力吸引着全世界关注的目光，而且还以它漂亮的城市、经典的建筑、气派的文化以及清澈的河流、茂密的森林、如画的郊野……每年吸引着约 2000 万来自全世界的人前去访问。

北京喜忧

华盛顿与北京，两者都是世界瞩目的大国首都，都是无愧于首都称号的城市。由于历史和国情不同，二者不能简单地类比，但从地理位置和首都地位上看，华盛顿与北京有许多相似之处。这两座城市在地球上的纬度相近，都处于大陆东岸，靠近海洋，美丽恢宏。若从城市规划、建筑风格、城市规模特别是首都功能来看，两座城市又有许多不同之处。我国著名历史地理学家、北京大学教授侯仁之先生对此曾有过一番评论，他说，华盛顿的空间布局更符合景观美学的建筑设计风格，北京的城市布局更能体现东方文化的特色。而从可持续发展的角度来看，华盛顿的空间布局，即环境优美、交通便利、服务性强等方面，确实能给今天的城市规划者以许多启示。

城市规划和设计，城市建设和布局主要取决于城市功能定位。美国是一个经济社会高度发达的年轻国家，它的工业、金融和文化、教育等功能分别由纽约、洛杉矶等多个大都市和区域中心城市分担，华盛顿只担当美国政治中心的角色。而北京作为拥有800多年历史、近1600万人口的大国首都，承载了太多的政治、经济、文化、教育、体育、科研、医疗、军事、交通等功能，如此庞杂的首都功能加上大城市病把北京压得气喘吁吁、不堪重负。

2006年，北京市高考出了一篇名为《北京的符号》的作文题目，没想到此事竟引起了社会反响，一时间关于北京种种不尽如人意的现象，成为网民热议的话题，有人戏谑北京"房价永远都是涨的，马路永远都是堵的，公交地铁永远都是挤的"，"首都正在变成'首堵'"。话虽然有些牢骚，但也的确从一个侧面反映了北京市面临的突出问题。

应当说，不论是以国内城市来比较，还是拿世界首都城市来衡量，北京都是天骄雄风、雍容气派、不可替代的，但由于北京功能不断叠加，人口急剧增长，城市过度膨胀，导致住房、交通、环境、特别是水源问题日趋严峻，加上沙尘暴袭击、酸雨降临等自然灾害，不由得使人对北京的城市现状深感焦虑，对它的未来充满担忧。

The American Book Fair and National Reading

So far, books are still the main bearer of the wisdom of human civilization. Reading is the most effective way for people to obtain true knowledge, to cultivate abilities of independent thinking, imagination and creativity. Reading is actually a matter of the nation's spiritual pursuit and value orientation. In a social atmosphere full of temptation and utilitarianism, everybody is pursuing quick success. How many people can calm down to read and study?

The main activity of this visit to the United States was to attend "the 2006 American Book Fair" which was held in Washington. Fortunately, I got the chance to attend this global book exhibition and copyright trade event personally. What I saw and heard was beautiful and enjoyable. and inspired me.

Enduring Appeal of English Books

An Authoress Signing Her Book

The yearly American Book Fair is a great event in English publishing industry. A main part of this fair is the gathering of the professionals who come from four fields: booksellers and retailers, librarians and educators, copyright agents and professionals, publishers and other insiders. Attending this fair personally, I found that Americans have many novel ideas and successful practices in holding book fairs. What we have drawn from its organizers, the organization of the event, the construction of the platform and the service of this fair would be useful and enlightening for similar events for domestic, publishing and national readings in China.

First, the American book fair was large-scale and high-grade. It is normally held in May or June every year and lasts three to four days. It was jointly organized by the American Booksellers Association and the American Publishers Association. During this book fair, about 25,000 publishers, distributors and agents who came from more than 90 countries and regions gathered in Washington. All of the most famous publishers were there, including Oxford University Press, and the five major U.S. publishing groups, Random House, Penguin Group, Harper Collins, Simon & Schuster and Time Warner. Copyright trade was a popular topic of the book fair. It is said that the financial turnover of the American Book Fair is more than $25 billion every year.

Second, the fair is designed in novelty forms with good effect. It consists of not only exhibitions of all kinds of books, but also a rich variety of activities including lectures, awards, autograph sessions of the writers etc. In this book fair, 80 keynote lectures were held, and. 400 bestseller authors were invited to come to book signing and to solicit donations. It also organized the so-called "world's largest book autograph session." Most of the signed books were free, and a few books cost only one dollar. On May 20, when we came to the crowded signature hall of autograph session in the book fair, I lined up and got a copy of the bestseller *Time Soldiers* with the signature of its author Kathleen Duey, an American woman writer.

Third, the American network publishing has shown its great power and potential. Out of the traditional press group, the network publishing was an eye-catcher at this fair. Almost every press had set up its own website. Companies like AOL and Google had multi-page advertisements in the Book Fair Manual to publicize their online book sales. The Amazon and other famous online professional bookselling websites also did their part by setting up big booths. Books on-demand printing companies like Booksinprint.com also took part in it. From this, we can see that the growth of the network publishing is rapid and strong, and its impact on the traditional publishing industry is self-evident.

Fourth, books in English were in large varieties and were most influential. Every year, many large international book fairs are held all around the world,

This Book's Writer in front of the Exhibition Hall

for example, the Frankfurt Book Fair, London Book Fair, the Paris Book Fair, etc. However, the American Book Fair is considered to be the world's largest Book Fair of English books. In a world where English language and American culture take the upper hand, even if one doesn't read Jack London or is not interested in *Harry Potter*, the impact of English information is still huge. The visit to the American Book Fair made us feel deeply the sustained prosperity and enduring charm of English books.

Fifth, Chinese reading materials were desirable and needed to be developed. Among various fascinating booths of the English-speaking countries' booksellers, the Chinese booth organized by the China International Publishing Group and other domestic presses also stood out. For this fair, the China International Publishing Group brought nearly 500 kinds of books, among which the teaching materials and reference books for Chinese language learning, the large albums for introducing Chinese scenery and the ancient Chinese academic and literary classics occupied a prominent position. The vibrant colors and classic content of these Chinese books attracted the attention of the professionals and visitors all over the world. But, it was really a pity that, in the ocean of English books, Chinese books appeared only in a small number and with minor influences due to the lack of English translation and English introduction of the materials, which was incongruous with the status of China as a growing great power and the newly rising boom of Chinese language learning all over the world.

Worries about China's National Reading

Participating in the American Book Fair, we were prompted to think of the Chinese Book Fair, domestic publishing and Chinese people's reading habits. Book fairs aim to display books and promote sales, to inspire publishers to publish good books, prompt distributors to sell good books and attract readers to read good books. It promotes not only the prosperity of the publication, but also the development of cultural industry. The Book Fair in China or National Book Fair is held every year and becomes more and more popular and prosperous. The annual Beijing International Book Fair keeps gaining its reputation rapidly and has turned out to be Asia's largest internationally renowned book fair. The popularity of book fairs brings up the prosperity of publishing. Consequently, in recent years the number of book categories and their printing has been rising steadily. In 2005, more than 570 Chinese publishing houses published 222,473 kinds of books with a total printing number of 6.466 billion copies, compared with 140,000 kinds in the year of 1995. So, in only one decade, there was an increase of about 60%. In terms of quantity, China has become one of the world's few publishing powers. However, as for the market scale of publications, the publishing profits and especially the influential original works, China is still left behind.

Although the number of book categories and printing copies have been rising, and the total amount of book pricing and book sales has also increased slightly, the volume of book sales and publishing profits have been in the trend of overall decline. In 2005, the Xinhua Bookstore System and the Self-issuing of the publishing houses sold only 6.336 billion copies. It had decreased 8.5% from the number of 6.925 billion in 2001. Corresponding to the downturn situation of the publications market, the conditions of our nationals' book acquisition and reading also fill people with dread. According to the statistics, in 2003, the Chinese book acquisition

A Book Fair in China

cost spent per capita was 35.79 Yuan, the U.S. was $107.42 (equivalent to RMB 882,4 Yuan), the UK was £ 58.8 (equivalent to RMB 836.7 Yuan), France was 84 Euros (equivalent to RMB 756 Yuan), and Japan was ¥ 7,567.4 (equivalent to RMB 553.96 Yuan). It was reported that, in 2005, China's book acquisition was 2.54 copies per capita, while the developed countries' in Europe and America were generally about 10 to 20 copies, which was several times more than China's. Except for students' textbooks and a large amount of public funds acquisition, which accounted for more than 50% of the total number of publishing books, in fact, the average number of books bought personally is just about 1 copy.

The poor bookselling results directly stem from inactive book reading. According to an authoritative survey of the Chinese Institute of Publishing Science, in recent years, the national reading rate (that is, the ratio between the number of people who read at least one book per year and the total number of literates) keeps decreasing: In 1999, the number was 60.4% but declined to 54.2%. in 2001, 51.7% in 2003, and even 48.7% in 2005, which was the first time it was below 50%; Currently, the Chinese who have developed reading habits cover only 5% of the total population. This ratio is not only lower than the developed countries, but even lower than India. According to the report, in 2005, the average number of books read by Chinese readers was 4.5 copies, while it was 14 in France; In 2004, the reading rate of adult Koreans was 76.3%, and 11 books per capita; It is the Jewish nation that has the largest group of readers and its annual amount of reading was 64 books per capita. The Indians spent the most time reading, which is 10.7 hours per week. The drop of the national reading rate is a worldwide problem. However, the situation is particularly serious in China. It is not convincing to ascribe this kind of cultural phenomenon to the underdeveloped economy and the big differences between urban and rural areas. Looking back to the beginning of the reform and opening up, we still feel encouraged by the enthusiasm of the the Chinese quest for knowledge. How upsetting to see the flippancy of Chinese readers today!

In the past 30 years since China's reform and opening up, our economic strength has been greatly enhanced. The living standards of most Chinese have been much improved. However, the number of book buyers has not yet grown as expected. Instead, the proportion of book reader has declined. On the one hand, it is the rapid development of economy and society; on the other hand it is the declining reading rate of the citizens. If not for the data, this dichotomy is really hard to believe.

We may explain that times are different and people's ways of obtaining knowledge and information have changed. Social media and the Internet have stunted many young readers. It makes sense. But, can online reading take the place of turning paper pages? Can answers like "having no time," or "not used to it" be excuses for not liking books? So far, the books are still the main bearer of the wisdom of human civilization. Reading is the most effective way for people to obtain true knowledge, to cultivate abilities of independent thinking, imagination and creativity. Assume that, if more than 50% of the literate people do not like reading, how can we improve the overall quality of our nation and cultivate the spiritual temperament? If China wants to become one of the first-class powers in the world, where can it get the necessary innovation ability and development vigor?

Rekindling the Passion for Reading

Only when reading becomes a habit can the country become prosperous and hopeful. Challenged by the current declining national reading rate and reduced numbers of reading groups, the decision makers at all levels of Party committees and governments should take note. As the supervisors of the economic and social management, they indeed should attach importance to the construction of highways and skyscrapers and the accumulation of GDP and fiscal revenue, but for the prosperity of a nation is there anything more important and more meaningful than the national study and education? In competing for strength among countries and regions, soft power such as cultural education and innovative spirit has played a more and more important role. Soft power is crucial for the long-term development of a country or region. Therefore, the implementation of a harmonious society, a scientific development and a modern country all depend on the promotion of education and reading, the cultivation of the national spirit, the improvement of the national quality and the building of the culture foundation.

Chinese leaders at all levels should become introspection. As a social public model, have you set a good example of diligent reading? "If we still have energy after we become officials, we should do some study." Only by reducing consciously the engagement in social activities, releasing interpersonal fetters and developing a good habit of reading and learning can leading cadres improve constantly their own knowledge and superior insight and be better qualified to take the responsibilities of leadership.

The publishing industry and writers should also self-examine. As a cultural body gathered to create culture and inherit civilization, how many good books have we written which are welcomed by readers, and how many masterpieces have we published which exert a profound impact on enlightening people's wisdom and uniting the national spirit? Within our reach are a large number of junk books, which are grandstanding, hyped, with a lack of penetrating ideas, facing the inventory burden and the ignorance of the readers, should we not feel ashamed and guilty? Just as famous writer Ji Xianlin said, "The professionals a nation needs the most are those who create and spread culture." For us publishers and writers, we should be quite aware of our own social roles and historical responsibilities. We should stay away from flippancy and fame, and turn toward reading, thinking, creating and producing bestsellers with profound ideas and wonderful language, catering to both refined and popular tastes.

The educators should be self-reflexive. The intellects, the so-called "social conscience," had assumed the responsibility of the world from the ancient times. But now, in an environment of market economy, are they still practicing the old saying "Never be contented with your study, never be impatient with your teaching" and still teaching earnestly or studying steadily? Suppose the educators are busy all day chasing fame and fortune, and doing falsehood in study, how can they see to it that the learners will patiently read and be men of integrity? "Peaches and plums do not have to talk, yet the world beats a path to them". Only the teacher who has good ethics and professionalism, who likes reading, is willing to teach and is good at teaching can be a model for others, and let knowledge, character, moral and ideals be passed on to students, generation after generation.

Others from all walks of life also need to think it over. In modern China, is reading really unimportant? Taught by the painful lessons of the knowledge desert which resulted from the Cultural Revolution, will the faith be once again shaken in the importance of reading and learning? Today there is nothing wrong with people's pursuit of material wealth. What is more, a considerable number of people in our country are still rushing for living every day. But as a human being, in addition to material comforts, one should also have a rich spiritual life or spiritual pursuit. Books are the shared spiritual wealth of mankind, acting as the ladder of human progress. Reading can enrich and expand people's limited life.

The first issue about reading is about publishing. If there are not many good books or the book prices are too high, then who will buy and read? Reading is also related to education. The passion, gains and habits of reading all come from education. At present, how can the teenagers' interest in reading be cultivated under this grade-targeted and Gaokao-oriented (with an orientation of taking exams for entrance into universities) education system? Reading is actually a matter of the nation's spiritual pursuit and value orientation. In a social atmosphere full of temptation and utilitarianism, everybody is pursuing quick success, how many people can calm down to read and study?

Therefore, we need leaders at all levels to attach virtual importance to advocating nationwide reading and encouraging people to study diligently and to making progress. There also needs to be a concerted effort from publishers, educators and all sectors of the community to create the system, environment and atmosphere for the nationals, especially the youth, to "love reading and read good books".

Reading makes a man noble, fulfilled, rich and wise. Reading is not a burden but fun and enjoyable. These words are proven by not only the inculcation of the ancient sages and masters, but also the personal experiences of the contemporary Chinese scholars.

A few days ago, I learnt a lot from a cell phone message sent by one of my friends who said, "More reading cultivates literary talent. More caution in words and manners develops noble sentiment. More value on friendship brings popularity. More temperance fosters harmony. More responsibility improves morality. More care about people builds up confidence. Less care about fame and fortune breeds justice. Lack of vulgarity promotes strength of character. Boldness in action incubates courage." In my opinion, to obtain the above "Ten Virtues," one must concentrate on constant reading and constant practice.

美国书展与国民阅读

到目前为止，书籍仍是人类文明智慧最主要的承载者，阅读乃是人们获取真知灼见、培养独立思考能力和想象力、创造力以及修身养性的最有效途径。读书，说到底是一个民族的精神追求、价值取向问题，在一个充满诱惑、急功近利的世态风气下，又有多少人能够静下心来读书学习呢？

这次访美的主要活动，是参加在华盛顿举办的"2006美国图书博览会"，有幸亲历这次全球图书展览和版权贸易盛会，耳目所及，赏心悦目；思考所至，颇多启示。

英文图书经久不衰

一年一度的美国图书博览会是英语出版界的盛事，这届博览会的主要活动为四个方面行业人士的聚首：书商和零售商、图书馆与教育界人士、版权代理人和专业人士、出版商和其他业内人士。亲历博览会，感到美国人举办书展有许多新颖的思路和成功的做法，从主办单位、活动组织到平台搭建、展会服务等各方面，对国内举办同类活动均有借鉴意义，对国内出版和国民阅读具有启发作用。

一是书展规模大、档次高。美国图书博览会由美国书商联合会和美国出版商联合会共同组织，每年约于五六月间举办，为期3~4天。这次书展期间，约25000名来自90多个国家和地区的出版商、发行商和代理人云集华盛顿，世界各国的著名出版社如牛津大学出版社、美国五大出版集团、兰登书屋、企鹅集团、哈珀·柯林斯、西蒙·舒斯特、时代华纳等无一缺席。版权贸易成为此次书展的一大亮点，据了解，美国书展交易额每年都在250亿美元以上。

二是各种活动形式新、效果好。此次展会不仅限于各类图书的展示，还组织了丰富多彩的活动，包括讲座、颁奖、作家签名等。这次书展期间举办

哈利波特与阿兹卡班囚徒　　哈利波特与混血王子　　哈利波特与火焰杯

的各种主题讲座达 80 多场次，还邀请了 400 多位畅销书作家前来签名赠书，组织了号称"全球最大的图书签名活动"。签名的大部分图书是免费赠送，有少量图书仅需付 1 美元即可得到。5 月 20 日，我们在书展现场参观时，来到人头攒动的签名大厅，排队后也得到了一本由美国女作家凯瑟琳创作并签名的畅销书《时间战士 (Time Soldiers)》。

　　三是网络出版势头强、后劲足。在传统出版社群体之外，网络出版在此次展会上十分抢眼，几乎每家出版社都建立了自己的网站。美国在线、GOOGLE 公司等都在书展手册上做了多版广告，宣传其在线图书销售。亚马逊等著名在线专业图书销售网站也当仁不让，设立了大型展台。 Booksinprint.com 等图书按需印刷公司也参与其中。由此可见一斑，网络出版增长势头迅猛，对传统出版业的冲击不言而喻。

　　四是英语图书种类多、影响大。每年全世界都要举办许多大型国际书展，如法兰克福书展、伦敦书展、巴黎书展等等。但美国图书博览会被认为是全球最大的英文书书展。在英语强势和美国文化称霸的今天，即使你不阅读杰克·伦敦，不屑看《哈里·波特》，但英语图书、英文信息对我们的影响还是巨大的。参观美国书展，我们深刻地感受到英文图书的持续繁荣和经久不衰。

　　五是汉语读物有市场、待开发。在英语国家书商琳琅满目的展台中间，由中国国际出版集团和其他国内出版社组织的中国展台也颇为引人注目。这次中国国际出版集团带来了将近 500 种图书，其中学习汉语的教材和工具书、介绍中国风光的大型画册、中国古代学术与文学名著等占据了显著位置，鲜明的色彩和经典的内容引起了各国同行的注意和参观者的兴趣。但是，在英文图书的海洋里，中国参展的图书数量少、影响小，尤其缺乏英译本图书和英文资料介绍，令人感到遗憾。这种状况，与中国日益增强的大国地位和正在全球兴起的汉语学习热潮很不相称。

国民阅读令人堪忧

参加美国书展，自然联想到中国书展、国内出版和国人读书情况。书展是图书展示促销活动，目的是激发出版商出好书，促使发行商卖好书，吸引读者读好书，既为促进出版繁荣，也为推动文化产业发展。中国国内图书博览会即全国书市年年搞，而且越办越抢手、越办越热闹；一年一度的北京国际图书博览会声誉日隆，已经成为亚洲最大、国际知名的大型国际书展。书市火爆，出版繁荣，近些年，我国图书出版种类和印刷数量不断攀升。2005年全国570多家出版社总共出版图书222473种，总印数64.66亿册（张），与1995年的14万种相比，10年间增长了约60%。仅从数量上看，我国已成为世界上屈指可数的出版大国，但是，如果从出版物市场规模、出版效益特别是有影响力的原创作品来看，中国还不能说是出版强国。

近年来，虽然我国图书出版种类和印刷数量不断攀升，图书定价总金额和销售总额略有增长，但图书销售数量和出版效益却成整体下滑的趋势，2005年全国新华书店系统和出版社自办发行单位纯销售63.36亿册，比2001年的69.25亿册下降了8.5%。与出版物市场不景气状况相对应的是，我国国民购书、读书情况令人堪忧。据有关资料统计，2003年，中国人均购书为35.79元，美国人均购书为107.42美元（折合人民币882.4元），英国为58.8英镑（折合人民币836.7元），法国为84欧元（折合人民币756元），日本为7567.4日元（折合人民币553.96元）。有媒体报道，2005年中国人均购书为2.54册，欧美发达国家人均购书一般在10~20册，是中国的几倍。如果扣除占图书出版发行总量50%左右的学生课本和大量的公款购书，实际上真正由个人自费购买的一般图书平均每人也就是一本左右。

售书不畅是读书不旺的直接表现，据中国出版科学研究所权威调查，近几年国民阅读率（即每年至少有读一本书行为的读者数量与识字者总体之比）

持续走低：1999 年为 60.4%，2001 年为 54.2%，2003 年为 51.7%，2005 年降到 48.7%，首次低于 50%；而且，目前我国国民有阅读习惯的人仅占总人口的 5%，这个比率不仅比发达国家就是比印度也低得多。据报道，在我国图书阅读者中，2005 年人均读书 4.5 本，而法国人均读书 14 本；2004 年韩国成年人阅读率为 76.3%，人均阅读一般图书 11 本；读书数量最多的是犹太民族，每年人均读书 64 本；读书时间最多的是印度人，平均一周 10.7 个小时。国民阅读率下降是一个世界性的问题，然而中国的情况尤为严重，这种文化现象不是经济欠发达、城乡差别大的解释就能令人信服的。回想上世纪 80 年代改革开放初期，那种人人渴望知识、全民读书学习的情形多么令人鼓舞，看看眼下国人的浮躁又多么令人不安。

我国改革开放近 30 年，经济实力大大增强了，大多数国民的生活富裕了，但是，买书的人未见增长，读书的人比例下降，一方面是经济社会的快速发展，一方面是国民阅读率的逐年下降，如果不是一连串真实的数据摆在那里，这种状况令人难以置信。

对此，我们可以说，时代不同了，传媒发达了，人们获取知识和信息的方式改变了，尤其是互联网分流了许多年轻的读者，这话有一定道理。但是，网络阅读能代替图书阅读吗？"没时间"、"不习惯"能成为多数国民不爱书香的理由吗？应当说，到目前为止，书籍仍是人类文明智慧最主要的承载者，阅读乃是人们获取真知灼见、培养独立思考能力和想象力、创造力以及修身养性的最有效途径。试想，我国 50% 以上有阅读能力的国民群体不喜欢读书，那我们民族整体素质的提高、精神气质的涵养靠什么呢？中国要成为世界一流强国所必需的创新能力和发展活力又从哪里来呢？

重新唤起读书热情

读书盛，才能国运兴。面对国民阅读率持续走低、读书人群逐渐减少的现状，各级党、政府的决策者应当反思：作为经济社会的管理者，修建高速公路、高楼大厦，积累生产总值和财政收入固然重要，但对于一个国家民族的强盛而言，还有比国民学习教育更重要、更具有根本意义的事情吗？在当今国家和地区综合实力竞争中，文化教育、创新能力等软实力的作用日益凸显，软实力对于一个国家或地区长远发展的影响愈显重要。因此，构建和谐社会，实现科学发展，建设现代国家，必须重视抓学习、抓教育、抓读书，涵养民族精神，提高国民素质，铸就文化基石。

各级领导干部应当自省：作为社会公众的表率，我们是否做到了以身作则、勤奋读书？"仕而优则学"，领导干部只有自觉地减少应酬，松解人际关系的羁绊，养成读书学习的好习惯，才能不断提高自身的知识涵养和卓越识见，更好地胜任所肩负的领导责任。

出版界和作家群体应当反省：作为创造文化、传承文明的文化群体，这些年我们究竟创作了多少受读者欢迎的好书，出版了多少对启迪民众智慧、凝聚民族精神产生深刻影响的上乘佳作？面对大量思想贫乏、哗众取宠、跟风炒作的各种垃圾图书，面对库存码洋的增长和广大读者的冷漠，我们是否应当感到汗颜和愧对国民大众。正如季羡林先生所说："一个民族最需要的是创造和传播文化的人。"我们广大的出版人、作家群应当清醒自己的社会角色和历史责任，应该离浮躁和名利远一点，真正静下心来，读书、思考、创作，不断推出思想深刻、语言精彩、雅俗共赏、既叫好又畅销的精品力作。

教育界应当内省：自古以来就以兴天下为己任、被称为社会良心的知识分子，在市场经济环境下，我们是否还在践行"读书不厌，诲人不倦"的古训，认认真真地教书育人、踏踏实实地钻研学问？试想，倘若教育者成天忙于追名逐利，甚至虚假为学，怎能让受教育者耐心读书、诚实做人呢？桃李不言，下自成蹊，只有具备良好的职业道德和职业素养，爱读书、肯教书、善育人的教师才能为人师表，才能让知识、品格、道德、理想在莘莘学子中薪火相传。

其他各界人士也应当思考：当今中国，读书真的不重要了吗？经过"文化大革命"那场知识荒漠的惨痛教训，我们对于读书学习重要性的认知还会再次发生动摇吗？当今社会，人们追求物质财富无可非议，何况，目前我国仍有相当一部分民众每天还在为生计而奔波。但人生在世，除了物质享受之外，还应该有丰富的文化生活和精神追求。书籍是人类共同的精神财富，是人类进步的阶梯，读书可以丰富一个人的有限人生。

读书首先是一个出版问题，没有好书，书价过高，又有谁来买，谁来读呢？读书，更是一个教育问题，读书的激情、收获和习惯都来自教育，目前以考分为指标、以高考为导向的应试教育体制怎么能培养青少年读书的乐趣呢？读书，说到底是一个民族的精神追求、价值取向问题，在一个充满诱惑、急功近利的世态风气下，又有多少人能够静下心来读书学习呢？

因此，倡导全民阅读，鼓励勤学上进，需要各级领导干部真正重视并率先垂范，需要出版界、教育界人士以及社会各界齐心协力，共同创造使国民大众特别是青少年"爱读书、读好书"的体制、环境和氛围。

读书使人高尚，读书使人充实，读书使人丰富，读书使人聪慧，读书不是负担而是一种乐趣和享受，这些话不仅是先哲大师们的谆谆教诲，更是当代中国读书人的切身体会。

日前，收到朋友一则手机短信，读来颇为受益："多读书以养才气，慎言行以养清气，重情义以养人气，能忍辱以养大气，温处事以养和气，讲责任以养贤气，系苍生以养底气，淡名利以养正气，不媚俗以养骨气，敢作为以养浩气。"我想，要养成这"十气"，均离不开长期的潜心阅读和人生的不断修炼。

Approaching the Great Men

It is said that the United States was founded by Washington, expanded by Jefferson, saved by Lincoln and rescued by Franklin Roosevelt, who salvaged the market economy of the United States and even the West. These four great presidents have accomplished immortal feats for their country. The contemporary China is now at a historically crucial juncture of millennium changes. The development of economy and military strength, the rebuilding of culture and the cohesion of beliefs all rely on great and strong leaders. Without such first-rate figures, it is very difficult for China to become the world's leading power.

The most impressive historical sites in Washington D.C. are the Monument, Memorial Hall and Memorial Park in commemoration of these four great presidents. The specific location is as follows: directly south the center of the Washington Monument is the Jefferson Memorial, east is the Capitol, west is the Lincoln Memorial and north is the White House, while the Roosevelt Park is located in the southwest. This design has considerable ingenuity and profound meaning.

The Washington Monument: A Wordless Milestone

In the center of the capital stands the Washington Monument, which was built to commemorate the first president George Washington. It is 169.3 meters high and is the highest stone building in the world. Washington D.C. has declared that the height of any other building in this region shall not exceed the monument. The construction of this monument started in 1848, with its necessary building materials and funding donated by other states and countries. It's erection was suspended in 1855 because of the chaos and capital shortage brought by the disputes between the south and the north. Its construction did not resume until after the Civil War in 1880. As a result, the color of the stones used before and after the suspension appear different. Two-thirds of the stones built after 1880 are

Washington Monument

Thomas Jefferson Memorial

slightly darker. In the United States, the Washington Monument is the first building to commemorate the founder of the nation. In addition to the majestic and straight body, the monument should also have been engraved with a beautiful epitaph to eulogize George Washington's feats and convey people's admiration for him. However, what you can see is only a tablet with no word on it.

Talents in Literature and Military Affairs

Across the Potomac Park and a lake, directly south of the Washington Monument is the Jefferson Memorial, which was built in 1943 to commemorate the third President of the United States, Thomas Jefferson, on his 200th birthday. In the center of the dome-shaped marble hall stands the 5.8 meter-high bronze statue of Jefferson. Part of the *Declaration of Independence* drafted by him and some of his famous political speeches are engraved on the wall. Washington and Jefferson are regarded by Americans as "Two Great Men Adept with Pen and Sword". Foreigners often know much about Washington's feats but little about Jefferson's contribution and literary talent. The visit to the Jefferson Memorial enabled us to know more about Jefferson accomplishments. It is Jefferson who drafted the *Declaration of Independence* and, as a result, he became one of the founding fathers of the United States. It is said that so far nobody in the U.S. has transcended Jefferson's literary talent. In 1803, during his presidency, Jefferson bought large areas of land between the Mississippi River and the Rocky Mountains from the French Emperor Napoleon at the price of only 15 million dollars, which, as a result, doubled the territory of the United States.

A Memorial Temple

Facing the Washington Monument across a distance is the Lincoln Memorial, a classical building built in the style of the ancient Greek Parthenon. It is slightly larger than the Jefferson Memorial in appearance and looks solemn and elegant. Abraham Lincoln was the 16th president of the United States and there were 36 states in the United States at that time, so the main hall of the Memorial was designed to be supported by

36 marble columns. In 1921, at the time of the Memorial's completion, the number of the states increased to 48 and on the attic frieze are inscribed the names of the 48 states. Later the names of Alaska and Hawaii were added and engraved beneath the balcony. The words from "I have a dream" by the famous leader of the blacks, Martin Luther King, were also carved on the granitic ground close to the entrance of the memorial. In 1965, in the same place, facing 250 thousand people, King delivered this famous speech. Opposite the entrance in the memorial hall is a prominently large sculpture of Lincoln seated, with a peaceful and profound look. The sculpture, made of white marble, is 5.8 meters tall. Above its head, a few lines are engraved on the wall:

IN THIS TEMPLE
AS IN THE HEARTS OF THE PEOPLE
FOR WHOM HE SAVED THE UNION
THE MEMORY OF ABRAHAM LINCOLN
IS ENSHRINED FOREVER

To the left and right sides of the sculpture are inscriptions of two well-known speeches by Lincoln, his Second Inaugural Address and fragments of The Gettysburg Address, with its most quoted line, "The government of the

Lincoln Memorial

IN THIS TEMPLE
AS IN THE HEARTS OF THE PEOPLE
FOR WHOM HE SAVED THE UNION
THE MEMORY OF ABRAHAM LINCOLN
IS ENSHRINED FOREVER

Lincoln Statue

people, by the people, for the people".

Roosevelt Park

West of the Jefferson Memorial and south of the cherry trees by the Potomac River is the Roosevelt Park, named after Franklin Roosevelt, the 32nd President of the United States. Different from President Washington, Jefferson and Lincoln, Roosevelt was commemorated by way of a park, which also reflected the significance of the times. In the open-style Roosevelt Park, soft waterfalls and streams run through grass and flowers, full of twists and turns and magnificent scenery. The highlights are two full-length copper statues of Roosevelt with different expressions to indicate different times, One is Roosevelt in time of peace, wearing a hat, looking slightly younger with an air of ease and confidence; the other is Roosevelt in the Second World War, dressed in a military uniform, old but with a commanding and proud look. His dog crouches beside him staring forward. When we were there, we met an American dressed as a veteran soldier who was delivering a speech about Roosevelt's New Deal and his contributions. A lot of people were watching and listening to him.

We finished visiting the Memorials of the four American Presidents with a lot of sighs of emotion. As an ancient Chinese once said, a person should have high moral character, make his words recorded and contribute greatly to his country. Washington and Jefferson are the founding fathers of the U.S. One commanded the war of independence and established the federal state. The other drafted the *Declaration of Independence* and expanded the territory of the country. Lincoln, who was born in a common family, won the Civil War, freed the slaves and avoided the division of the nation. Roosevelt helped the United States overcome the economic crisis, carried out the New Deal, led the American people and the world anti-fascist alliance to have won the Second World War, and together with Churchill and Stalin helped build the foundation for the post-war world. Therefore, in a sense, it is Washington who founded the United States, Jefferson who expanded it, Lincoln who saved it from division and Roosevelt who rescued the American and Western market economy. The four great presidents

THEY WHO SEEK TO ESTABLISH
SYSTEMS OF GOVERNMENT BASED ON
THE REGIMENTATION OF ALL HUMAN
BEINGS BY A HANDFUL OF INDIVIDUAL
RULERS... CALL THIS A NEW ORDER.
IT IS NOT NEW AND IT IS NOT ORDER.

Roosevelt Statue

have performed immortal feats for the independence and liberation, the unity and prosperity of the United States which won them the recognition and admiration of Americans and the people all over the world. In order to commemorate their great contributions, immortal words and noble virtues, the monument, memorial and park were set up to remember them and inspire future generations.

A Bit of Expectation

The former President of the United States Richard Nixon said in his book *Leaders*: "Great country and great event create great men." In my eyes, it's vice versa: Great men also create great country with great events. The historical roles played by the great men are decisive and in a certain period the wheel of history is also to be pushed forward by the great men, just as Mao Zedong who led people to win the independence and liberation of the Chinese nation and Deng Xiaoping who promoted China's reform and opening up. Of course, the historic functions of great figures work only when they are conforming to their people and the trend of their times.

In China's history of over 5000 years, heroes and saints keep appearing like the stars shining in the sky. Standing on the forefront, they inspired our ancestors to depict historical scenes in the art world and promoted the continued prosperity of our nation and the progress of our civilization.

Contemporary China is now at a historically crucial juncture of millennium changes. The development of the economy and military strength, the rebuilding of culture and the cohesion of beliefs, the accomplishment of national prosperity and rejuvenation all rely on great and strong leading figures, not only the epochal political leaders but also a large number of world-class business leaders, and master thinkers, philosophers, scientists, educators, literary and artistic giants, etc. Without such first-rate figures, it is very difficult for China to become the world's leading power.

走近伟人

华盛顿创立了美国，杰斐逊拓展了美国，林肯拯救了美国，罗斯福挽救了美国和西方的市场经济，这四位伟大总统为美国建立了不朽功勋。当代中国正处在一个千年巨变的历史关头，经济发展、军事强大、文化重塑、信仰凝聚都需要伟大而坚定的领袖人物来担当历史的重任，没有一批这样的一流人物，中国很难成为世界一流强国。

在华盛顿特区参观名胜古迹，给人留下深刻印象的是纪念四位伟大总统的纪念碑、纪念堂和纪念园。具体坐标是：以华盛顿纪念碑为中心，东面是国会大厦，西面是林肯纪念堂，北面是白宫，南面是杰斐逊纪念堂，西南面是罗斯福公园，如此安排设计颇具匠心和深意。

功高无言

为纪念第一任总统乔治·华盛顿而修建的华盛顿纪念碑耸立在首都中心区域，碑高169.3米，是世界最高的石质建筑。华盛顿特区规定，特区内所有建筑高度不得超过此碑。这座纪念碑自1848年开始兴建，资金、原料来源于各州和各国捐赠的石材和基金。1855年因南北分裂混乱、资金不足而停工。此后又经历南北战争，直到1880年才恢复建设。由于分两次施工，中断前后的石料颜色有差异，后建的三分之二颜色显得稍深一些。华盛顿纪念碑是美国第一座纪念开国总统的建筑物，除碑身的雄伟挺拔外，似乎还应当刻上一篇赞颂乔治·华盛顿丰功伟业的优美文字，以表达人民对他的敬仰之情，但它却是一座无字碑。

文圣才略

　　隔着波托马克公园和一湾湖水，华盛顿纪念碑南面是杰斐逊纪念堂，它是 1943 年为了纪念美国第 3 任总统托马斯·杰斐逊诞辰 200 周年而兴建的。杰斐逊纪念堂建筑成圆顶型，由大理石砌成的纪念堂大厅中央竖立着 5.8 米高的杰斐逊铜像，墙壁上刻着由他起草的《独立宣言》的部分文字和他发表的一些著名政治言论。华盛顿和杰斐逊被美国人称作"文武二圣"。外国人对于华盛顿的丰功比较了解，而对杰斐逊的业绩和文采所知不多，这次参观杰斐逊纪念堂才略长见识，知道杰斐逊也是一位了不得的伟大人物，是他起草了美国《独立宣言》，和华盛顿等开国元勋一道，缔造了美利坚合众国，据称至今美国无人能超越杰斐逊的文采。1803 年，在杰斐逊任总统期间，仅以 1500 万美元的代价就从法国皇帝拿破仑手中买下了从密西西比河到洛基山之间的大片土地，把美国的疆域扩大了一倍。

纪念圣殿

　　与华盛顿纪念碑遥遥相对的是林肯纪念堂，这是一座仿古希腊巴特农神庙式的古典建筑，比杰斐逊纪念堂规模略大，外形庄重典雅。美国第 16 任总统亚伯拉罕·林肯在任时美国有 36 个州，故纪念堂大殿用 36 根大理石圆柱支撑。1921 年纪念堂落成时美国增加到 48 个州，48 个州的名字刻在纪念堂的裙楣上，后加入的阿拉斯加和夏威夷两个州的名字则刻在阳台下面。在接近纪念堂门口处的花岗岩地面上刻有著名黑人领袖马丁·路德金的名言：我有一个梦想 (I have a dream)。1965 年他正是站在此处面对 25 万人发表了这篇著名的演说。进入纪念堂大厅，正面端坐着用白色大理石雕塑的林肯雕像。林肯雕像神情自若、目光深邃。像高 5.8 米，头顶上方石壁上镌刻着几行大字："在这座殿堂内，永远供奉和纪念的是，因为拯救了联邦而活在人民心中的亚伯拉罕·林肯。"塑像的左首墙壁上刻着林肯在第二次就任总统时的演说辞，右侧墙壁上刻有林肯著名的葛底斯堡演说片断，最著名的一段话是"人民的政府，来自人民，为了人民"（"The government of the people, by the people, for the people"）。即"民有、民治、民享"之意。

罗斯福公园

1972 年毛泽东会见尼克松

与杰斐逊纪念堂相邻的西侧，樱花树林的南面，波托马克河河畔，是以美国第32任总统富兰克林·罗斯福名字命名的公园。与纪念华盛顿、杰斐逊和林肯三位总统的方式不同，对罗斯福的纪念是通过兴建一座公园来表达，反映出时代意义。开放式的罗斯福公园不但花草如茵、瀑流潺潺，而且迂回曲折，别有洞天。特别是两尊罗斯福全身铜雕像因反映的时代不同，神采各异。一尊是和平时期的、头戴礼帽、略显年轻的罗斯福，看上去轻松自信；另一尊是二战时期的、身着戎装、显得苍老的罗斯福，一副运筹帷幄、雄视全球的神态，他的爱犬俯卧身边，虎视前方。我们参观时，碰上一位老战士打扮的美国人正在那里绘声绘色地演讲罗斯福新政的功绩，引来不少人围观和倾听。

游历四位美国总统的纪念场馆，令人产生许多感慨。中国古人讲，人生当立德、立言、立功。华盛顿和杰斐逊为开国元勋，一个统帅指挥独立战争、建立联邦国家，一个起草《独立宣言》、开疆扩土；平民出身的林肯统帅打赢了南北战争，亲自解放了黑奴，避免了国家分裂；罗斯福则从美国经济大危机中力挽狂澜，推行新政，又领导美国人民和世界反法西斯同盟打赢二战，同丘吉尔、斯大林等一道缔定战后世界新格局。因此，从某种意义上说，是华盛顿创立了美国，杰斐逊拓展了美国，林肯拯救了美国，罗斯福挽救了美国和西方的市场经济。这四位伟大总统为美国的独立解放、国家统一、繁荣强盛建立了不朽功勋，赢得美国乃至世界人民的认同和景仰，故为纪念他们的盖世之功、不朽之言、高尚之德，而为他们立碑、建堂、开园，以缅怀先圣，激励后人。

一点期盼

美国前总统尼克松在他的《领袖们》一书中讲道：伟大的国家、伟大的事件造就了伟大的人物。我想反之亦然：伟大的人物因领导伟大的事件，同样造就了伟大的国家。伟人所起的历史作用是有决定意义的，某个时代的历史车轮是要靠伟人来推动的，正如毛泽东领导中华民族的独立解放，邓小平推动中国的改革开放一样。当然，伟大人物的历史作用是建立在合乎民心、顺应时代潮流基础上的。

中华民族在长达 5000 多年的历史长河中，英雄豪杰、圣人贤哲如同星汉灿烂、辈出不穷，正是他们站在历史潮头，率领先民大众，绘就了一幕幕波澜壮阔的历史画卷，推动着中华民族的不断强盛与文明进步。

当代中国正处在一个千年巨变的历史关头，经济发展、军事强大、社会转型、制度改造、文化重塑、信仰凝聚……都需要伟大而坚定的领袖人物来担当历史的重任，完成国家强盛、民族复兴的大业，使中国成为不再衰落的世界强国。为此，当代中国既需要划时代的政治领袖，也需要一批世界级的企业领袖，同时更需要一批大师级的思想家、哲学家、科学家、教育家和文学艺术巨匠等等，没有一批这样的一流人物，中国很难成为世界一流强国。

Talks on Wars before the Monuments

It is hard to count the wars that America participated in after its Independence, but three monuments with records of different war elegies can reveal something. War is a contest of military strength, leaders' willpower and national mobilization capacity between different countries or political groups. When the footsteps of war are coming closer and there is nowhere to dodge, one must stand up to battle and dare to show courage. Even if it sets back the economy of a country 20 years after the war, it is far better than letting a nation be humiliated for 100 years.

During the 200 years since the outbreak of the War of Independence in 1775, Americans have participated in many wars. These wars are commemorated in many monuments, such as the War of Independence Monument, the Monument of the Civil War, the World War II Memorial, the Vietnam Memorial and so on, to remember those soldiers who died. We visited three war memorials in Washington and got quite different feelings after each due to the different American participations. But the one thing they have in common is, all of them are elegies of wars.

Heroism in World War II

On the morning of the 20th, on our way to attend the American Book Fair, we passed the Navy Soldier Monument and stayed there for a short while. The monument was built in the suburb of Washington, to the north of the Arlington National Cemetery. It displays the scene of the Pacific War during the Second World War, when the American army captured Iwo Jima, and the marines courageously rushed ashore to plant the Stars and Stripes (the American flag) in the ground. The brave images of the five naval soldiers, unafraid of death, fighting together, are carved vividly on the base of the monument.

This group of sculptures is based on a photo of the battlefield at the wartime. The publishing of the photo in the United States was a sensation and greatly inspired the lofty aspiration and patriotism of the Americans. Althought the army photographer, Joe Rosenthal, didn't know it at the time, the snap photo he took after which sculpture are based became the symbol of national victory and the eternal legend of American heroism. Last year, based on this story Hollywood shot a movie called *The Flags of our Fathers* in which the war scenes are extremely heroic and tragic while the plot is real and touching.

Pain from the Vietnam War

On a lawn to the northeast of the Lincoln Memorial, an area of slope gradually sinks into the ground, and with a sudden turn the apex stretches to two sides and highlights on it two black gabbro walls as smooth as mirrors. One points toward Washington Monument, the other is in direction of the Lincoln Memorial. On the walls are carved the names of more than 57,000 American soldiers, who were confirmed as KIA (Killed in Action) or remained classified as MIA (Missing in Action) in the Vietnam War. These walls represent the famous Vietnam War Memorial Monument, which is also called "A Scar in the History of the United States".

From May 14, 1961 when the United States "Special Operations Forces" invaded Vietnam to the liberation of Sai Kung by the Vietnamese soldiers on April 30, 1975, the entire Vietnam War lasted 14 years, which is considered as the longest and the most intense large-scale local war since World War II.

Marine Corps War Memorial

During the Vietnam War, the United States dropped 8 million tons of dynamite onto Vietnam, far beyond the total amount dropped on all the battlefields of the Second World War. This caused the death of more than 1.6 million people in Vietnam, and more than 10 million refugees in Vietnam, Laos, Cambodia and other surrounding areas became destitute and homeless. The United States itself also suffered heavy losses. The casualty number was up to 360,000, of which more than 58,000 people were dead or missing, and the war took a total of more than 400 billion dollars.

During the War, the U.S. economy remarkably declined and the once-supreme dollar took a heavy blow, causing a huge deficit. Meanwhile, the Vietnam War completely changed the pattern of the hegemony of the U.S. and the U.S.S.R: Throughout the 1970s, the global strategic position of the United States turned to the defensive, while the Soviet Union started to be offensive.

The former Secretary of State, Henry Kissinger said, "Perhaps the Vietnam War is a tragedy, and the United States shouldn't have been involved."

After the Vietnam War, the former U.S. Secretary of Defense, Robert McNamara, who had been retired for nearly 30 years, was encouraged to published a memoir called *In Retrospect: The Tragedy and Lessons in Vietnam* in 1995. In it, McNamara says that the U.S. decision makers had little understanding of the facts: "Whether it is our people or our leader,

Vietnam Veterans Memorial

Maya Ying Lin

The Statue of Vietnam War Soldiers

they are all not omnipotent. When the affairs do not involve our own
survival, if we want to judge what the best interest of another country or
people is, we should let the international community to conduct a public
debate and decide. We do not have the inborn power to use our own ideals
or choices to shape any other country. But until today, in many parts of the
world, we are still repeating the similar mistakes."

The Vietnam War brought immeasurable trauma to the American people.
In order for people to remember this period of "painful history" forever, on
July 1, 1980, the U.S. Congress approved the construction of the "Vietnam
War Memorial Monument," and elicited design ideas all over the country.
Surprisingly, among the total 1,421 ideas received, the one made by a
21-year-old American-Chinese female university student became the first
choice. Her name is Maya Ying Lin. Her uncle is the renowned architect
Liang Sicheng and her aunt is the remarkably talented woman of the
ages, Lin Huiyin. Maya Ying Lin was then a student of the department of
architecture at Yale University. She happened to see the solicitation for

design ideas on the school bulletin board and decided to have a try. Within only two weeks, she completed a design model, and later won over the jury, which was comprised of 8 internationally renowned artists and master architects, with her concise but profound idea.

In Maya Ying Lin's design, the monument stands like an opened book below the lawn. The visitors walk on the pathway along the 151-meter-long black marble walls, and look upon the names of the dead and missing soldiers with the same shock, sorrow and pain felt in reading a long death notice.

May 21, the day we went to the Memorial was a Sunday and there were a lot of visitors. Some mourning flowers as well as a photo of a handsome young soldier who was killed in the battle were placed in front of the monument. There were three bronze statues of servicemen looking sad and tired carved on the south side of the wall, silhouetted against the long black monument.

Reflection on the Korean War

South of the Vietnam War Memorial is the Korean War Memorial. It was built and unveiled in 1995. Whether the war was forgotten by the Americans or for some other reasons, it was not until more than 40 years after the Korean War that the United States started to build the Memorial, even 15 years later than the construction of the Vietnam War Memorial.

When we visited the Korean War Memorial — actually a Memorial Park, the first thing that we saw was a group of 19 stainless steel statues of soldiers in different positions on a slope-shaped grassland, larger than life-size, representing a squad on patrol. In a triangle, in front and on the right and left side of the statues lie three groups of black granite monuments. The 15 participant countries that fought for the United Nations are carved on the stone tablet on the left front, namely: the United Kingdom, Australia, the Netherlands, New Zealand, Canada, France, the Philippines, Turkey, Thailand, South Africa, Greece, Belgium, Luxembourg, Colombia and Ethiopia.

Group Statues of Korean War Soldiers

Engraved on the front granite block are the casualty statistics for the United Nations soldiers who were killed, missing, captured and wounded in the war. The total number is 242,9370, among which 36,574 people of the U.S. forces were killed, 8,176 were missing, 7,245 were captured and 103,284 were wounded. The total number of the U.S. casualties is 139,858. On the right front side is a black granite monument wall on which four prominent English words are carved: Freedom is not free! This is a conclusion the Americans came to 42 years after the Korean War.

Yes, for this war the two sides finally invested 3 million soldiers. (The United Nations forces was reported to have invested 1.2 million while the Korean and Chinese army 1.88 million.) They fought fiercely in the bitter cold and scorching heat for three years, started from the "demarcation line." fought a few back and forth, south to north and finally stopped again at the "demarcation line," which resulted in millions of casualties and a huge cost of heavily damaging the beautiful Korean Peninsula.

After the war, the supreme commanders of the two sides both made thought-provoking speeches. The chief commander of the United Nations Forces and the U.S. Army General Mark Clark said in his memoirs, "In the execution of the instructions of my Government, I got an unenviable reputation: In history, the first American commander who signed on the Armistice Agreement in which the United States lost the war. "

Peng Dehuai, the commander of the Chinese People's Volunteers said, the Korean War "proved eloquently that, the era has ended which lasted for hundreds of years, when the Western invaders could occupy a country only by setting up a few cannons on an East Coast."

Fifty years have passed, and this war has already become an indelible memory, but there is no permanent peace. Looking back upon the local wars and armed conflicts happening all over the world since the end of the Korean War, and considering again the war-threatening and battle-ready situations of the Korean Peninsula and its surrounding areas in recent years, how can we easily believe the promise of peace?

Daring to Show the Sword

War is cruel. No country wants war to break out. However, in this world, which is seemingly civilized but actually power-dominated by nature, in the irreconcilable conflicts between nations, war as the final means to solve political disputes is often inevitable. The one-sided wishes, compromises or concessions are just like holding a snake in the bosom and looking for insults. The living lessons of this can be found in the British and French policy of appeasement to Nazi Germany before World War II, and Chiang Kai-shek (Jiang Jieshi)'s compromise and concessions to Japan as it occupied the three northeastern provinces of China. When a country's territory and sovereignty are violated and a nation's dignity is insulted, when your opponent comes to corner and bully you, would you still talk with him about peace and friendship? When this happens, any nation of courage and uprightness will fight to survive at the cost of life.

Of course, war needs power and strength, enough material and spiritual preparation, and appropriate political and military strategies. To fight rashly is nothing but an emotional impulse and a reckless behavior. However, when meeting on a narrow road, the brave man always wins. When fighting is inevitable, one needs to show his sword. Any excessive balance between the two sides or any lack of confidence and courage to fight would put oneself into adverse circumstances. War is a contest of military strength, leaders' willpower and national mobilization capacity between different countries or political groups. Once a military and economic strength is established, the key to winning lies in the willpower of the ruling group, especially the leaders, the morale of the army and the cohesion of people bound by a common hatred for the enemy, all of which would have a decisive impact on the outcome of the war. The proof of this can be seen in the both the War of Resistance against Japan and the Korean War. When it comes to a moment of life and death for a nation, there should be no weakness, cowardice or fear of death. To die heroically is far better than to live for the sake of remaining alive. Even if joining war would drag its economy backward for 20 years, a nation would never permit itself to accept a century's humiliation for refusing to face the war. Otherwise, it would result in irreparable trauma on the national psyche and spirit, and would damage and shame the country for a long time. As the saying goes, "Good at fighting first, then you can talk about peace". For a nation at a certain historical stage, war is the necessary means to obtain peace and it is also the price a generation has to pay to win peace for their offspring.

No country wants war, but war is not determined by man's will. When you are faced with war and have nowhere to hide, you must stand up to battle and dare to show your sword.

纪念碑前话战争

自独立战争以来，不知美国参与了多少次战争，三座纪念碑记录了不同的战争悲歌。战争是不同国家或政治集团之间军事实力、领袖意志力和国民动员能力的较量，当战争的脚步向你走来、使你无法回避时，你必须挺身应战，敢于亮剑。战争即便使一个国家倒退 20 年，也不能让一个民族屈辱 100 年。

自 1775 年爆发独立战争以来的 200 多年间，不知美国参与了多少次战争。为此，美国兴建了不少纪念历次战争阵亡将士的纪念碑，如独立战争纪念碑、国内战争纪念碑、二战纪念碑等。这次在华盛顿参观了三座战争纪念碑，因每次美国参战的情况不同，参观后的感受也就大不一样。可以说，三座纪念碑记录了不同的战争悲歌。

二战豪情

20 日上午，在去参加美国图书博览会的途中，路过海军战士纪念碑，在那里停留片刻，驻足参观。纪念碑建在华盛顿郊外阿灵顿国家公墓北侧，表现的是二战太平洋战争期间，美军攻占硫磺岛时，海军陆战队员奋勇争先地将星条旗插上阵地的情景。纪念碑底座上雕铸的 5 名海军战士前赴后继、视死如归的形象栩栩如生，英气逼人。

这组雕塑取材于一幅当年的战地照片。当年，这幅照片发表后在美国引起了轰动，极大地激发了美国人的豪情壮志和爱国情怀。令随军摄影师乔·罗森塔尔没有想到的是，他抓拍下的这张照片和根据照片制成的雕塑，已经成为一个国家胜利的象征符号，成为代表美国英雄主义精神的不朽传奇。去年，以这个故事为题材，好莱坞拍摄了一部电影，名叫《父辈们的旗帜》，战争场面异常惨烈，故事情节真实感人。

越战伤痛

　　在林肯纪念堂东北侧的一片草坪内，有一块坡地缓缓下陷，然后突然转弯向两边伸开，托起两面黑色大理石磨成的、像镜子般光滑的碑墙，那上面雕刻着57000多名因参加越南战争而阵亡和失踪的美国军人的名字，它就是被称为"美国历史上的一道伤痕"的越南战争阵亡将士纪念碑。

　　从1961年5月14日美国"特种作战部队"入侵越南，到1975年4月30日越南军民解放西贡，整个越南战争历时14年，是第二次世界大战以后持续时间最长、程度最激烈的大规模局部战争。

　　越战期间，美国向越南投下了800万吨炸药，远远超过第二次世界大战各个战场投弹量的总合，造成越南160多万人死亡和越南、老挝、柬埔寨等周边地区1000多万难民流离失所。美国自身也损失惨重，美军共伤亡36万多人，其中死亡和失踪5.8万人，战争共耗费了4000多亿美元。

　　越战期间，美国经济出现大幅度滑坡，美元的世界霸主地位遭到沉重打击，美国财政出现了巨额赤字。同时，越战彻底改变了美苏两国争霸的格局：整个20世纪70年代，美国在全球的战略地位转为守势，而苏联则处于战略攻势。

　　美国前国务卿亨利·基辛格说："越南战争也许是一场悲剧，美国本来是根本不应该闯进去的。"

　　越战之后，卸任近30年的美国前国防部长麦克纳马拉，在众多越战反省者的鼓励下，于1995年发表了《回顾：越南的悲剧与教训》一书。麦克纳马拉认为，美国政府决策人没有意识到，"无论是我们的人民，还是我们的领袖，都不是万能的，在不涉及我们自身存亡的事务中，要判断什么是另一个国家和人民的最大利益，应由国际社会进行公开辩论来决定。我们并不拥有天赋的权力，来用我们自己的理想或选择去塑造任何其他国家。可是直到今天，在世界上许多地方，我们仍然在重复着类似的错误"。

　　越南战争给美国人民造成了无法估量的心灵创伤，为了让人们永远记住这段"伤痛史"，1980年7月1日，美国国会批准建造"越南战争阵亡将士纪念碑"，并向全国征集设计方案。出人意料的是，在总共收到的1421个方案中，一位年仅21岁的华裔女大学生的设计方案成了首选。她叫林璎，其姑父是中国著名建筑大师梁思成，姑姑是旷世才女林徽因。林璎是耶鲁大学建筑系的学生，她偶然在学校的告示牌上看到了征集告示，决定尝试一下，仅用了两个星期就做出了设计模型，并最终以简洁而又蕴含无限深意的构思，获得了由 8 位国际知名艺术家和建筑大师组成的评委会的认可。

林璎把纪念碑设计成一本打开的书本形状横卧在草坪下面，前去参观的人沿着长达 151 米的黑色大理石走过去，一路观看着阵亡和失踪军人的名字，就像是在默读一本长长的死亡通知书，其心灵的震撼、悲哀和隐痛可想而知。

5 月 21 日，我们前去参观的这天正值星期日，参观的人络绎不绝，纪念碑前摆放着几束悼念的鲜花，还有一张年轻英俊的阵亡士兵的照片。在碑墙南侧雕立着 3 位神情悲哀、面色疲惫的士兵铜像，与黑色长碑相互映衬。

朝战反思

越战纪念碑南面是朝鲜战争纪念碑。朝鲜战争纪念碑于 1995 年建成揭幕，不知是朝鲜战争被美国人遗忘了还是其他原因，美国修建朝鲜战争纪念碑是在朝鲜战争停战 40 多年以后，而且也比越南战争纪念碑晚了 15 年。

走到朝鲜战争纪念碑——实际是一座纪念园前，首先映入眼帘的是，在一片坡形草地上站立着 19 尊形态各异的士兵群组雕像，成三角队形搜索前进。与真人一样大小的雕像是用不锈钢雕制成的。群雕正前方和前方左右两侧横卧着三组黑色花岗岩碑，左前方石碑上刻有以联合国名义参战的 15 个国家的名字，他们是英国、澳大利亚、荷兰、新西兰、加拿大、法国、菲律宾、土耳其、泰国、南非、希腊、比利时、卢森堡、哥伦比亚、埃塞俄比亚。

正面石碑上刻着联合国军阵亡、失踪、被俘和受伤的人数，共计 2429370 人，其中美军阵亡 36574 人，失踪 8176 人，被俘 7245 人，受伤 103284 人，美军总共伤亡 139858 人。右前方是一面黑色花岗岩碑墙，墙面上镌刻着四个醒目的英文单词：Freedom is not free（自由不是无代价的！）这是美国人在朝鲜战争停战 42 年后得出的结论。

是啊，为一场战争双方最后投入了 300 万兵力（据有关资料介绍，联合国军投 120 万，中朝军队投 188 万），在严寒和酷暑中浴血拼杀了三年，从"三八线"打起，从南到北打了几个来回，最后又打停在"三八线"，造成几百万人伤亡。把一个美丽的朝鲜半岛摧残得千疮百孔，代价也实在太大了。

战后，中美双方的最高指挥官分别讲了一段耐人寻味的话。联合国军总司令、美国陆军上将马克·克拉克在他的回忆录中说："在执行我的政府的指示中，我获得了一个不值得羡慕的名声：历史上第一个在没有胜利的停战协定上签字的美国司令官。"

中国人民志愿军司令员彭德怀说，朝鲜战争"雄辩地证明，西方侵略者几百年来只要在东方一个海岸上架起几尊大炮就可以霸占一个国家的时代，一去不复返了"。

50 多年过去了，这场战争虽已成为永久的回忆，但和平并没有真正到来。回顾一下朝鲜战争停战 50 多年来世界各地所发生的局部战争和武装冲突，再看看近年来朝鲜半岛及其周边地区战云密布、厉兵秣马的局势，怎能让人轻易相信和平的诺言呢？

敢于亮剑

战争是残酷的，任何国家都不希望发生战争。但是，在这个貌似文明、实则强权的世界上，在国家和民族利益不可调和的情势下，战争作为解决政治冲突的最后手段往往是不可避免的，仅靠一厢情愿、妥协退让无异于养虎遗患、自寻欺辱。二战前英法等国对纳粹德国的绥靖政策，蒋介石对日本占领我东三省的妥协退让，都是活生生的教训。当一个国家的领土和主权遭到侵犯，一个民族的尊严受到侮辱，当你的对手欺负你到家门口、把你逼到墙角使你无法躲避时，你还能再跟人家讲和平友好吗？这时，任何一个有血性的民族都要不惜一战，以死求生。

当然，打仗是需要有实力的，是需要讲究政治和军事策略的，没有充分的物质和精神准备，妄言动手只是书生意气和鲁莽行为。但是，狭路相逢勇者胜，该亮剑时要亮剑。如果总是考量敌我双方实力的对比，缺乏奋起一搏的信心和勇气，那就使自己先处下风了。战争是不同国家或政治集团之间军事实力、领袖意志力和国民动员能力的较量，在军事和经济实力既定的前提下，统治集团特别是领袖的意志力、军队的士气和全体国民同仇敌忾的凝聚力是非常关键的，对于战争的结局往往有着决定性的影响。抗日战争的最终胜利、朝鲜战争的平手结局都充分证明了这一点。所以，当一个民族到了安危存亡的重大关头，任何人都不应该软弱怯懦，贪生怕死。苟且偷生不如壮烈赴死，战争即便使一个国家倒退 20 年，也不能让一个民族屈辱 100 年，那样对民族心理和民族精神造成的创伤是无法挽回的，会让你的国家和人民长期在世界上挺不起腰来。古人言"善战方能言和"，对于一个民族的某个历史阶段而言，战争也是和平的必要手段，是一代人为几代人赢得和平环境所必须付出的代价。

还是那句话，任何国家和民族都不希望战争，但是，战争不是以人的意志为转移的，当战争的脚步向你走来，使你无法回避时，你必须挺身应战，敢于亮剑。

Museums of Boundless Beneficence

Today, the United States has the world's most developed museum cluster. Almost every city possesses at least one museum or more than one. The museums play a huge and subtle role in the edification of cultural and artistic qualities and the cultivation of scientific spirit of the American nation, especially for the youth. China, a big oriental country with 5,000 years' history of civilization, has the endowment to develop museums.

Like visiting churches in Europe, going to museums in the United States is a must. After attending the American Book Fair in Washington, we took a quick trip to the National Gallery of Art , the National Museum of Natural History and the National Air and Space Museum.

Visit to Three Museums

The National Gallery of Art is the most famous American institution for the collection and exhibition of the Western European and American works of

National Gallery of Art

Specimen of African Elephant

Airplane Models

art. The museum contains a large number of works ranging from the 13th century to the contemporary, including more than 40,000 oil paintings, prints, sculptures and other decorative works of art. The collection contains the paintings of great artists such as Leonardo Da Vinci, Raphael, Rembrandt, Monet, Van Gogh, Picasso. The museum and its contents were endowed or donated by more than 400 people. In 1937, the Croesus Andrew Mellon, who was the Minister of Finance at that time, donated 15 million dollars to start the construction of the Gallery. It was opened to the world after the completion in 1941. The main axis of this neoclassical building is 240 meters long and it covers a bottom construction area of 47,000 square meters. It is centered on a domed rotunda. A pair of high sculpture halls are located on the east and west sides of the rotunda leading to the garden court, which is decorated with fountains and lush flowers and trees. The sculpture hall is surrounded by 125 exhibition galleries full of exquisite artwork, which can be overwhelming and enchanting.

The National Museum of Natural History is located to the west of the National Gallery. It mainly exhibits the history of all kinds of animals and their various habitats, and also gives a retrospect of the past and present living conditions of the American Indians. The first floor of the museum is a special exhibition hall of mammals. The world's largest specimen of the African giant elephant is in the center of the domed rotunda. It is said that the elephant weighs 12 tons when it is alive. On the second floor are the skeletal remains of the mammoths and dinosaurs. The third floor is the Hall of Gems and Minerals, which includes a large 44.5-karat diamond named the "Hope Diamond," which was discovered in India in 1640. It is the world's largest known blue diamond and once was owned by Louis XIV of France. This hall of geology also contains a large number of various meteorites in different sizes.

The National Air and Space Museum is the world's largest museum of flight at present and is also the most visited museum in Washington, with more than 100,000 visitors per month. In its first year, it set the record of the highest number of visitors with a total of 10 million, more than any other museum in the United States. It is a modern-style building made of marble, glass and steel, displaying a variety of aircrafts, engines, rockets, lunar landing vehicles and other mock-ups. Some implements that were used by famous pilots and astronauts are also on display. There are many historical aircrafts exhibited here. From the first air vehicle invented by the Wright brothers to the Boeing airliners used in World War II, there are more than 300 different types of airplanes. The most famous exhibit in the museum is the moon rock which was brought back by the Apollo moon-landing spacecraft. It is a small piece of black smooth rock, inlaid in the showcase in the front of the hall of the museum, attracting the visitors to view it. Full of curiosity, we also carefully observed and touched the rock to feel the moon.

The above three museums all belong to the famous Smithsonian Institution, which was set up through posthumous donations of the British scientist James Smithson. Now as the only semi-official institution funded by the U.S. government, it consists of fourteen museums belonging to this institution, and thirteen others located in Washington and free of charge for people to visit.

Six Points of Revelation

A museum aims to convey and display the heritage and environmental outlook of mankind. It is also the microcosm of history and culture for a country or a nation. By visiting the American Museums, and coming to know their development history and current status, we can get a lot of enlightenment and revelation.

There are lots of museums in the America.Nowadays,it has the most developed museum systems.Almost every city has more than one museum. According to statistics, there are more than 6, 600 museums in the United States, among which the most famous ones are The National Gallery of Art in Washington, D.C. , the New York Metropolitan Museum of Art and the Boston Museum of Art. Unlike the European museums that were founded by royal family and the nobility on the basis of their long-term collection and accumulation, museums and collections in the United States were funded and donated generously by a large number of wealthy tycoons, such as the

National Gallery of Art,Ginevra de' Benci,42×37cm
Leonardo da Vinci 1474

Auto magnate Ford, the steel king Andrew Carnegie, the petroleum magnate Rockefeller, and the financial giant JP Morgan, etc. These industrial magnates donate large sums of money to found museums, or donate a large number of collections. They have become the important driving forces for the development of the American Museums.

Second, the architecture of American museums is generally high quality and unique in character. Many famous American museums and art galleries are either majestic and impressive or beautiful and elegant in appearance; while bright, spacious and well-equipped indoors, such as the East Building of the National Gallery designed by the famous American-Chinese architect Ieoh Ming Pei. It was extended in 1976 to commemorate the 200th anniversary of the founding of the United States with a total investment of 905 million dollars donated by the relatives and children of Andrew Mellon and the Mellon Foundation. It is designed in modern style, with outstanding character of neat geometrical lines. In order to be consistent with the West Building, the external walls of the entire East Building are all made of rose bengal and milky white marbles. The exquisite art collection and the elegant style of the architecture attract more than 2.5 million people every year.

Third, a visit to American museums is generally free or low cost. Although some museums sell tickets, the ticket price is usually very low or not mandatory. Free admission or cheap tickets are in accordanc with the nature of museums as a kind of nonprofit cultural institution. According to the latest definition revised by the International Council of Museums in 1989, "The museum is a non-profiting-making permanent institution in the service of the society and its development and open to the public." It can be seen that, being "non-profit-making" is very important for a museum. Those "museums" aiming at profits are never real museums but only enterprises in the name of museum.

Fourth, museums are mainly donated and found by private persons. American museums whether national or local, are mainly supported by private donations and trusts. According to the classification of the American Association of Museums, among over 6,600 museums in the United States, 65% are private non-profit-making museums; 23.6% are the state-owned museums, 10.4% are university museums and 0.7% profit-making ones. An important feature of the American Museums is that they are based on private donations and are created by private institutions. Once the museum is established, whether they were founded by nation or by private people, they will become a nonprofit public cultural institutions.

Fifth, there are a large number of first-class collections in the United States. In our visit this time, we did not go to famous museums like the New York Metropolitan Museum of Art, but the collections we browsed in the three museums in Washington were indicative of the variety and value. It is said that the New York Metropolitan Museum of Art has over two million pieces in its permanent collection, and can be referred to as "the encyclopedia of all the galleries". The museum contains about 365,000 works of art spanning 5,000 years, from prehistoric times to modern times. The collection is divided into four major categories: Ancient art, Oriental art, European art and American art. These works are all-inclusive and priceless, and are presented in various styles including: architecture, sculpture, painting, sketching, print, ceramics, glassware, metal products, textiles, ancient rooms, furniture, weapons, armor and musical instruments, etc.

Sixth, American museums have many social functions and strong impact on the community. They are not only for people to visit, but also the places for men and women, old and young, interact, study and relax. For example, concerts, recitations and all kinds of lectures are often held in museums. There are also amateur schools and training courses held for primary and secondary students, counseling students to engage in a variety of extracurricular literary, artistic, scientific and technological activities. Therefore, the contemporary American Museum is not only the center of collections, but also the center of culture, education, academics and entertainment. Just as advocated by the International Council of Museums: "Museum is the projector of the old heritage, but it is also to become a generator of new culture."

"Museum," another word for elegant taste and noble class, has become a very attractive symbol in the United States. It represents elegant taste and noble level. The U.S. government and all sectors of the community pay great attention to the construction, collection and utilization of the museum. The museum plays a huge and subtle role in the edification of cultural and artistic quality and the cultivation of scientific spirit of the nation, especially the youth. In recent years not only do Americans like to visit the museum, but there are many visitors from Asia, especially China, who also haunt here and have become one of the ethnic groups growing the fastest.

A Little Hope

China started developing museums late and slowly. Influenced by the European countries, at the end of the 19th century and the beginning of the 20th century, China set up some museums, and the modern western mode of museum was introduced.

However, during the more than 100 years from 1840 to the founding of PRC, China had been in wars and unrest: the Opium War, the Taiping Rebellion, the Sino-Japanese War, and the Power Allied Forces aggression, etc. The corrupt and incompetent Qing dynasty signed a series of humiliating treaties, which not only let the Western powers fragment our territory, but also allowed them to take by force countless cultural relics and treasures of the Chinese nation. According to incomplete statistics, over one million Chinese treasures are in the collections of more than 200 museums in nearly 50 countries. When the Chinese people go to visit the European countries, they feel very sad at seeing the treasures of their own country

The Dunhuang Mural in the Metropolitan Art Museum

being part of the collections of foreigners.

"In the golden age, relics are the most valuable, while in troubled times, gold is the most useful thing." The poor and weak old China did not have time to care about the development of museums until the founding of New China ushered in a good period. But the catastrophic "Cultural Revolution" later not only destroyed a large number of cultural relics and classics, but also controlled the development of museums. It was not until the time of reform and opening up that China's museums quickly developed. From central to local, from governmental to nongovernmental, all financed for the establishment of various types of museums, collected cultural heritage and promoted the display of national culture. In recent years, I had the opportunity when traveling on business to visit many domestic museums, both magnificent and rich in collections or small but distinctive, such as Museum of Shaanxi Province, Henan Provincial Museum, Tianjin Museum, the Tibet Autonomous Region Museum, the Xinjiang Autonomous Region Museum, Xixia Imperial Tombs Museum, Museum of Chifeng City, Handan Museum, Huanghua Museum, Inner Mongolia Museum of Ewenki, etc. Each visit was like enjoying a sumptuous historical and cultural feast.

So far, there are more than 2300 museums of various kinds in China, of which 80% were built during the past 20 years, and the construction of museums around our country is still growing. Within this short period, the progress of our museum development should be recognized as historic. However, compared with western countries, especially the United States, whether in collections and exhibition or operation and management,

ShanXi History Museum

we are still left much behind. The biggest problem lies in the shortage of professionals and managerial talents, and the backwardness of management system. Many museums were completed but few came to visit and, as a result, the museums' cultural and educational functions are limited. Therefore, museums in China are in urgent need to learn from the advanced experiences of the United States and other countries, such as encouraging private donations and creations of museums, establishing Museum Development Fund, implementing the Board of directors system, expanding the scope of the exhibition, and strengthening the collection awareness and the museum's educational, cultural, tourist and recreational functions.

As a great oriental nation of 5,000 years history, China has very rich conditions to develop museum systems. With the nearly 30 years of development after the reform and opening up, the state and the local economic strength has been improved a lot, and people's cultural needs become more obvious. Therefore, an important issue has to be seriously considered by all levels of government and sectors of the community, that is, how to further accelerate the development of China's museums, especially to improve the operation and management, to promote collection and exhibition level, and to fully play the its role in cultivating national scientific and cultural qualities and national spirits.

功德无量博物馆

当今美国拥有世界上最发达的博物馆群，几乎每座城市都有一家以上的博物馆。博物馆对美利坚民族特别是青少年文化艺术素质的熏陶，科学精神的培养产生了巨大的、潜移默化的作用。中国作为有着 5000 年文明史的东方大国，发展博物馆事业具备得天独厚的条件。

在美国参观博物馆如同到欧洲参观教堂一样，是必看的节目。在华盛顿参加美国图书博览会之后，我们用半天时间匆匆参观了美国国家美术馆、国家自然史博物馆和国家航空航天博物馆。

三馆浏览

国家美术馆是美国最著名的收藏和展览西欧和美国艺术品的机构，馆内收藏了大批从 13 世纪至当代的欧美艺术家的作品，有油画、版画、雕塑和其他装饰艺术品 4 万余件，其中有达·芬奇、拉斐尔、伦勃朗、莫奈、梵高和毕加索等艺术大师的作品。美术馆及其收藏品都是由 400 多人赠送和捐款修建起来的。1937 年，时任财政部长的大富豪安德鲁·梅隆捐资 1500 万美元开始兴建艺术馆，1941 年建成对外开放。这是一座新古典式建筑，长 240 米，底层建筑面积为 47000 平方米。美术馆中央是圆型大厅，两侧是雕塑厅，可以通向建有喷泉和栽植着繁茂花木的庭院。雕塑厅四周设有 125 个展览厅，陈列品极为丰富，令参观者目不暇接，流连忘返。

国家自然史博物馆位于国家美术馆西面，主要展出各类动物生长史及其不同的栖息地，并介绍美国印第安人过去和现在的生活实况。该馆一层是特别展厅，圆形大厅中央有世界最大的非洲巨象的标本，据说生前体重达 12 吨；二层是长毛象、恐龙的骨骼标本；三层是宝石厅，有一颗 44.5 克拉大钻石，名"希望钻石"，产自印度，发现于 1640 年，是已知世界上最大的蓝色钻石，加工后曾为法国路易十四王冠上的宝石之一。馆内还收藏了数量众多、大小不一的各种陨石。

国家航空航天博物馆是目前世界上最大的飞行博物馆，也是华盛顿吸引观众人数最多的博物馆，每月接待观众达 10 万之多，开馆第一年参观人数超过 1000 万人次，创美国各博物馆最高纪录。它是一座由大理石、玻璃和钢材构成的现代化建筑。馆内陈列着各种飞机、发动机、火箭、登月车等实物模型，还有著名飞行员和宇航员用过的器物。飞机展品非常丰富，从莱特兄弟发明的第一架飞机到二战时期的波音客机，各种类型的飞机样品达 300 余架。该馆最为出名的展品应是阿波罗登月飞船带回的月球岩石，这是一小块黑色光滑的岩石，镶嵌在博物馆大厅前的玻璃框内，引得游人纷纷观看。我们也怀着好奇心，仔细观察并用手触摸岩石，体会了一下接触月球的感觉。

上述三家博物馆均隶属于著名的史密森学会。这个学会是根据英国科学家詹姆斯·史密森的捐赠遗言设立的，它是唯一由美国政府资助的半官方性质的博物馆机构，学会下辖 14 家博物馆，其中 13 家设在华盛顿，供人免费参观。

六点启示

博物馆是展示人类遗产及其环境面貌的窗口，是一个国家和民族历史文化的缩影。通过参观美国博物馆，了解美国博物馆的发展历史和现状，我们可以得到很多启发。

一是美国博物馆数量众多。当今美国拥有世界上最发达的博物馆群，几乎每座城市都有一家以上的博物馆，据统计，全美博物馆数量达到 6600 多家，最著名的有华盛顿国家美术馆、纽约大都会艺术博物馆、波士顿艺术博物馆等。虽然美国没有像欧洲王室、贵族那样长期的收藏积累作为后来博物馆的基础，但是美国造就了一大批财富大亨，如汽车大王福特、钢铁大王卡内基、石油大王洛克菲勒、金融巨头摩根等，这些产业巨头或慷慨出资建馆，或捐赠大量藏品，成为美国博物馆发展的重要推动力量。

二是建筑档次高、有特色。美国许多著名的博物馆、美术馆建筑或巍峨壮观，或精美典雅；馆内宽敞明亮，设施齐全。如由著名美籍华裔建筑师贝聿铭设计的国家美术馆东楼，是 1976 年为纪念美国建国 200 周年而扩建的，全部投资 9.05 亿美元，由安德鲁·梅隆的亲属和子女及梅隆基金会捐款。这是一座现代派建筑，以几何形的简洁线条为其特色。整个东楼建筑的外墙也都采用玫瑰红与乳白色大理石作建材，与原馆的色彩保持一致。精美的艺术收藏和典雅气派的建筑，使得每年前来国家美术馆东西楼参观的人数高达 250 多万。

三是免费参观或从低收费。美国很多博物馆是免费参观的，有的博物馆即使卖门票价格也很低，或由参观者自愿买票。博物馆属于公益性文化机构，免费参观或低价门票符合博物馆的性质。根据国际博物馆协会 1989 年修订的关于"博物馆"的最新定义，"博物馆是不以营利为目的、为社会及其发展服务、对公众开放的永久性公共机构"。可见，"不以营利为目的"是构成博物馆的一项十分重要的条件，那些营利性"博物馆"只是打着博物馆旗号的企业，不能算是真正的博物馆。

四是以私人捐赠和创立为主。美国博物馆无论是国立、州立，还是市立、县立，绝大部分是在私人藏品捐赠或信托基础上建立的。据美国博物馆协会的分类，在美国 6600 多家博物馆中，有 65% 是私立非营利性博物馆；23.6% 是政府办博物馆，高校博物馆占 10.4%，另外 0.7% 是营利性"博物馆"。博物馆由私人捐赠、私立机构创立是美国博物馆的重要特征。但是，一旦博物馆建立之后，不论是国立还是私立，都变成事实上的非营利性公共文化机构。

五是馆藏数量大、品位高。这次我们没能参观纽约大都会艺术博物馆等美国其他著名博物馆，仅从华盛顿三家博物馆浏览到的藏品，就感到非常丰富和珍贵。据有关资料介绍，纽约大都会艺术博物馆共有 200 多万件藏品，堪称美术馆中的百科全书。馆内收藏了从史前至今 5000 年间的约 36.5 万件艺术品，分为古代艺术品、东方艺术品、欧洲艺术品和美国艺术品四大类。这些艺术品包罗万象，有建筑、雕刻、绘画、素描、版画、陶瓷、玻璃器皿、金属制品、纺织品、古代房间、家具、武器、盔甲和乐器等，每件都是无价之宝。

六是社会功能多、影响大。美国博物馆不但供人们参观，还成为男女老幼学习、娱乐和休息的场所，如经常举办音乐会、朗诵会和各种讲座。面向中小学，在馆内举办业余学校和培训班，辅导学生开展丰富多彩的课外文学、艺术和科技活动。所以，当代美国博物馆不仅是收藏中心，也是文化中心、教育中心、学术中心，还是休闲中心和娱乐中心。正如国际博物馆协会所倡导的："博物馆不仅是旧遗产的投影机，还应成为新文化的发生器。"

"博物馆"在美国已经成为一个很有吸引力的招牌，它代表着优雅的品位和高贵的档次。美国政府和社会各界极为重视博物馆的建设、收藏和利用，博物馆对美利坚民族特别是青少年文化艺术素质的熏陶及科学精神的培养产生了巨大的、潜移默化的作用。不但美国人喜欢光顾博物馆，近年来，来自亚洲尤其是中国的游客已成为美国各大博物馆观众人数增长最快的族群之一。

一点希冀

我国的博物馆起步较晚，发展较慢，受欧美国家的影响，我国在 19 世纪末、20 世纪初先后开办过一些博物馆，并将西方近代博物馆模式引入国内。

但是，从 1840 年到新中国成立，整整一百多年间，中国一直处于战乱动荡之中。鸦片战争、太平天国起义、中日甲午战争、八国联军侵略……腐败无能的清王朝签订一连串的丧权辱国条约，不但让西方列强割疆裂土，还掠夺和骗取了中华民族无数的文物宝藏。据不完全统计，现有一百多万件中华珍宝被收藏在世界近 50 个国家的 200 多个博物馆中。中国人到欧美国家访问，看到自己国家的稀世珍宝成为人家的藏品，无不深感痛惜。

"盛世文物、乱世黄金"，积贫积弱的旧中国是无暇顾及博物馆事业的。新中国成立后迎来了博物馆发展的好时期，但"文化大革命"一场浩劫，既毁掉了大量的文物典籍，又中断了博物馆事业的发展。改革开放之后，我国博物馆事业总算获得了迅猛发展，从中央到地方，从政府到民间都纷纷筹资建立各类博物馆，收集整理文化遗产，弘扬展示民族文化。近些年，借出差开会之机，作者也参观过国内不少或建筑宏伟、馆藏丰富，或规模不大但别具特色的博物馆，如陕西省博物馆、河南省博物馆、天津市博物馆、

早年流失海外的圆明园生肖铜兽头

西藏自治区博物馆、新疆自治区博物馆、西夏王陵博物馆、赤峰市博物馆、邯郸市博物馆、黄骅市博物馆、内蒙鄂温克族博物馆等等，每次参观都是在享受一次丰盛的历史文化大餐。

到目前为止，我国共有各类博物馆约 2300 多家，其中 80% 是在近 20 年内先后建成的，而且全国各地的博物馆建设方兴未艾。短短 20 多年的时间，应当说我们博物馆事业取得了历史性进步，但比起西方各国特别是美国，无论是博物馆收藏、展示，还是经营管理，我们都存在着很大差距。尤其是专业和管理人才短缺，管理体制落后，博物馆建得多看得少，不能充分发挥其应有的文化教育功能。因此，我国博物馆亟需学习借鉴美国等国家的先进经验，如鼓励私人捐赠和创立博物馆、建立博物馆发展基金、推行董事会制度、强化藏品意识、扩大展览内容，增强博物馆的教育、文化、旅游和娱乐功能等等。

中国作为有着 5000 年文明史的东方大国，发展博物馆事业具备得天独厚的条件，经过改革开放近 30 年的发展，国家、地方及民间经济实力大增，国民文化需求凸显，进一步加快发展我国的博物馆事业，尤其是提高博物馆的经营管理、收藏展出水平，充分发挥博物馆在培养民族科学文化素质、涵养民族精神气质方面的作用，是一个需要各级政府和社会各界认真思考的重大问题。

Las Vegas: A Reality and Mirage

Las Vegas attracts nearly 40 million tourists every year. They come to this mysterious and recreational place to hunt for novelty and gamble,speculating to hit the jackpot. The thing the tourists leave behind in Las Vegas is usually their money. But what they take away is the excitement and the psychological satisfaction or the thrill of gambling. Perhaps this is the reason for its enduring appeal and increasing prosperity.

Whenever Vegas is mentioned, it is evokes a sense of mystery and curiosity. How can one imagine that a mirage-like city that never sleeps could arise out of the Gobi desert of the west in the United States! Vegas attracts nearly 40 million visitors every year. Gambling tourism alone can create income of more than 40 billion dollars. Therefore, Las Vegas is considered to be the "miracle" of the world.

Rise of the Gambling Industry

The history of Las Vegas is really something of a legend. As early as 1905 before the construction of it, Las Vegas had already been the intersection of the western expedition routes and the later railways. In 1829, a young man named Raphael Riviera was exploring the route for his Spanish caravan when he accidentally discovered an artesian spring in this valley and its surrounding oasis. He named what he found in Spanish LASVEGAS (which means the fertile plain.) In 1905, the completion of the railway line connecting Southern California and Salt Lake City helped the Las Vegas area change from the tent stationed gradually into a railway town.

The early growth of Las Vegas was not always smooth. With the Great Depression of the U.S. economy, the development of the city was put on hold. It did not recover until the construction of the Hoover Dam 45 kilometers away in 1931. The Hoover Dam helped to expand employment opportunities and consumption demand in Las Vegas for thousands of

Street View of Las Vagas

workers who worked on the construction site, and who would come to Las Vegas to gamble and for entertainment when they had nothing to do on the weekends.

As early as in 1911, the state of Nevada where Las Vegas is located passed a very strict law to prohibit gambling as well as any games or activities related to it. However, gambling did not disappear as a result. Instead it quietly turned underground. Twenty years later, a man named Phil Tobin launched a legislative initiative to legalize underground gambling. He justified this by purporting to tax gambling as a means to raise funds for public schools. Although Tobin as a farmer had never gone to Las Vegas, in 1913, the laws put forward by him and later passed by the Nevada Parliament not only legalized gambling, but also loosened the control of trafficking in booze and prostitution. The implementation of these laws fundamentally changed the history of Las Vegas, leading it to become the world's primary gambling spot.

From the middle of the twentieth century, the convenient transportation and lenient laws enabled more and more wealthy people to build luxury houses and hotels in the center of the city. Especially after World War

II, among many large U.S. companies, there was a stirring of interest in mergers and acquisitions and hotel construction. Many large and luxury casinos and hotels sprang up in Las Vegas. At this time, gambling was no longer a recreational form of entertainment. Just like Hollywood and Disney, it had become a legitimate profiteering industry.

After half a century, Las Vegas has developed into the capital of the world hotel industry. In Las Vegas, on both sides of the roads, there are over 20 large and luxury hotels, which are all the most costly and most beautiful in the world. The most famous ones are Treasure Island, Pyramid, MGM, The Mirage, Caesars, Bellagio, Wynn, New York, Paris, etc, all very magnificent and luxurious.

Father of Las Vegas

Speaking of the casino hotel industry in Las Vegas, we cannot forget a legendary figure, Stephen Wynn, who is the "father of Las Vegas". Wynn was a giant of the American gaming industry, famous for being keen on adventures and challenges. His biggest hobby was to build more and more luxury casino hotels. The Golden Nugget Hotel in 1984, the Mirage in 1989, the Caesar in 1996, and the White Le Palace in 1998 are all Wynn's finest creations. With each endeavor, Wynn gave Las Vegas a new look.

Down on the bustling Fremont Street lies the Golden Nugget Hotel, where the natural nugget weighing 61 pounds is displayed for visitors to

MGM Grand Hotel

Luxor Hotel

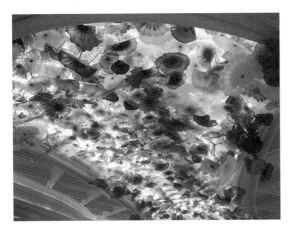

Glass Ceiling

The Mirage & Casino

appreciate.

The White Le Palace Resort Hotel is the most luxurious casino hotel on the Las Vegas Strip, with a lobby floor made of high-grade marble and on the ceiling a colorful design decorated by over 2000 glass vases. This glass design has been listed in the Guinness Book of World Records.

The Mirage Hotel open in 1989, represents a new peak for Wynn in his hotel construction history, with a cost of 6.3 billion dollars. In front of the hotel lies a model of an active volcano, which erupts in front of raging flames every 15 minutes. It has become one of the great wonders here in Las Vegas and also the ideal film location of Hollywood.

Wynn's latest masterpiece is a new landmark in — Wynn Las Vegas. It cost him 2.7 billion dollars and five years to accomplish this extremely large and ultra-luxury casino hotel of 2,700 rooms and 6,000 employees. The outer-layer construction of the hotel is inlaid with copper-colored glasses in the shape of a round arch. It is 50-stories high, and looks very dazzling. On April 28, 2005, the opening of Wynn created another mythical feat of Las Vegas. It is not only the world's most luxurious casino, but also the newest, highest and most legendary building in Las Vegas.

In the staff meeting before the opening of the hotel, Wynn encouraged all his employees not to worry about making mistakes or losing money, since they are unavoidable for a new casino or a new hotel. He only asked his staff to do one thing: "Let all the guests be happy here and enjoy themselves." for the future of the hotel "does not depend on us, but on them."

Luxury of Las Vegas

Most of the visitors to Vegas like to stroll around the charming streets and take in the sights.

On the afternoon of May 22, we flew from Washington Dulles International Airport to Las Vegas and checked into the Circus Hotel. After quickly settling in, we hurried to see the streetscape and performances. While walking along Las Vegas Avenue, I indeed got a kind of strange feeling. Although this place was a desert, it is now covered with flowers and trees. But the difference is that all the plants and even the soil were purchased from other places. A palm tree is worth ten thousand dollars, and the growth of every kind of plant is maintained by costly drip irrigation. Las Vegas is short of rain and water, but never short of money. Every day more than 900 flights and thousands of vehicles arrive here and most people are not tight with their money.

At night, the varied performances started in front of the casino hotels one after another. The famous ones are Buccaneer Bay Pirate Battle ship, Mirage Volcano and Fountains at Bellagio, etc. Besides appreciating the Volcano show at the Mirage Hotel, the dancing fountains in front of the Bellagio Hotel is another big feast for the tourists. Different types of water nozzles respond to the Bellagio Fountain music in a span of over 2 hectares in length. Some of the water choreography swings back and forth, creating the illusion of dancing water, some continuous, in response to the smooth, legato musical passages. Other water jets pulse rapidly in response to music that is lively and staccato, or send a water blast upward in the sky. Tourists cannot help being fascinated by the fantastic dancing fountain against the night of gambling city. I had seen a lot of music fountains, but it was the first time for me to see such wonderful scene. There is a Bellagio Fountain

Palms

Music Fountain

show every 15 minutes and at every turn the audience would flock to it. It is said that every fountain show will cost the hotel ten thousand dollars, and it plays 20 times every night.

The shows outside the hotel are exciting and impressive, but the scenes indoors are much more beautiful. When we stepped into the Venetian hotel, the beautiful replication of the canals of Venice, the artificial urban streetscape and sky in the hall of the hotel make you feel like you were in Venice. We were wandering under the "blue sky" in the Leisure Square, when the small band of the hotel started to play Italian songs. A lady in our group called Shi Li from Beijing sang her ad-lib song "O sole mio" with the band singer and won rounds of applause. This warm and cheerful scene was really unforgettable.

Trying the Pleasure from Gambling

Nearly all the visitors coming to Las Vegas will gamble once or more in the hotel casinos everywhere. Some gamble with millions of dollars; some just have a try with a bit of money and take a chance. In Las Vegas, people under the age of 21 are not allowed to enter the casino unsupervised and are not allowed to gamble. Many tourists come with their families. Parents will take their kids to see the beauty of Las Vegas at night. You can smoke parts of the casino, taking photos is seriously forbidden, since most of the gamblers who are there to enjoy themselves don't necessarily want other people to know they are there. Moreover, there are no windows and clocks in the casinos, so that gamblers forget the time and everything else, and just concentrate on gambling and enjoying themselves. In the casino, all sorts of people can be seen gambling, killing time in a peaceful and leisurely way.

If Disney is children's paradise, then Las Vegas is a paradise for young people, middle-aged and old people to be entertained. When night fell, the streets of Las Vegas were ablaze with lights and full of tourists. All year round, almost all of the casinos are full with large number of tourists, to play slot machines, roulette, or blackjack. When they not in the casinos, they may reflect on their luck. In a word, most of the visitors come here in

Shi Li Singing on the Stage

The Venetian Las Vegas

high spirits and go away with their money lost.

Vegas meets people's need to be lucky in gambling and hitting the jackpot. The success of it seems to be accidental but actually it is calculated. The mystery of it will continuously arouse the curious minds of tourists from all around the world just like a magnet, and stimulate them to put large amounts of money into thousands of slot machines and on roulette wheels in Las Vegas.

Although, the tourists usually leave their money in Vegas, they take away memories and a sense of satisfaction from all the exciting things it has to offer. Perhaps this is the secret of its thriving and prosperous gambling industry.

Gambling with Enthusiasm

Today, Las Vegas has developed its single gambling industry into a complex of lottery, performances, tourism and fairs and exhibitions. Every year, the 40 million visitors who come to Las Vegas contribute more than 40 billion dollars to this city, among which the income of gambling is only 12 billion dollars. That is to say, the average cost of the tourists here is 1,000 dollars, with 300 dollars being gambled away.

The popular and prosperous gambling entertainment industry is not a Las Vegas monopoly. Other states also followed suit to pan gold in sand. In the past, gambling was only allowed in Nevada and New Jersey, however, now it has spread to 48 states in the United States. Experts predict that, in the next few years, with the rapid expansion of the gambling industry, American people will be more likely to go to the casinos.

According to the media reports, with the access of foreign capital from the United States and Hong Kong, the gambling town of Macau opened several new casinos last year, among which there is the Wynn Casino constructed by Stephen Wynn. This casino was opened in September and

caused a sensation. Since the new casino was built, the gambling income was up to 39.252 billion dollars in the first nine months of 2006, which surpassed Las Vegas and made Macau rank above Las Vegas to be the world's No. 1 gambling town.

Luxurious Casino

亦真亦幻看赌城

拉斯维加斯每年吸引着近 4000 万游客来这里娱乐观光，它的神秘色彩和娱乐内涵，正好满足了人们猎奇、豪赌、撞大运的侥幸心理。游客留给拉斯维加斯的是金钱，带走的是刺激后的心理满足，这也许正是赌博业经久不衰、而且日益兴旺的奥妙所在。

提起拉斯维加斯，就会让人感到神秘和好奇，有谁会想到，在美国西部这片戈壁荒漠上，竟然崛起了一座海市蜃楼般的不夜城。它每年吸引着近 4000 万游客来这里娱乐观光，仅靠博彩旅游业就创造了 400 多亿美元的收入。因此，拉斯维加斯被认为是世界的"奇迹"。

赌业兴起

说起拉斯维加斯的发迹史，还颇有点传奇色彩。早在 1905 年建市之前，拉斯维加斯就已经是西部探险路线及后来铁路铺设的交汇点。 1829 年，一位名叫拉菲尔·利维拉的年轻人在给西班牙商队探路时，偶然发现了这片峡谷地带的自流泉水及周边的绿洲。于是，他便以西班牙语 LASVEGAS（拉斯维加斯，意为肥沃的平原）称呼他所发现的这个地方。1905 年，连接南加州和盐湖城两地的铁路干线完工，使拉斯维加斯一带从帐篷的驻扎地，逐步变成铁路沿线的一个城镇。

早期拉斯维加斯的成长并非一帆风顺，随着美国经济的大萧条，拉市的发展也曾一度陷入低谷。直到 1931 年，距离拉市 45 公里的胡佛大坝的兴建才给这座小镇带来新的生机。修建胡佛大坝带动了拉市的就业与消费，特别是在大坝工地施工的几千名工人，周末无所事事便纷纷来到拉斯维加斯赌博消遣。

早在 1911 年，拉市所在的内华达州通过了一项非常严厉的法律，限制赌博以及任何有赌博味道的游戏活动。但赌博并没有因法律的严厉而销声匿迹，只是悄悄转入地下。20 年后，一位名叫费尔·托宾的人，发起了让地下赌博合法化的立法动议，目的是对赌博名正言顺地课税，借此为公共学校筹集经费。尽管身为农场主的托宾一生从未到过拉斯维加斯，但 1931 年由他动议在内华达州议会通过的相关法律，不但使赌博合法化，而且也放松了对贩酒、卖淫等行业的管制。这些法律条文的实施从根本上改写了拉斯维加斯的历史，使拉斯维加斯走上了世界赌城的不归路。

从 20 世纪中期开始，便利的交通和宽松的法律，让越来越多的有钱人开始在市中心建造豪华住宅和酒店。特别是二战结束以后，很多美国大公司在拉市掀起了企业并购和建造酒店的热潮，一座座大型豪华赌场酒店如雨后春笋般在拉斯维加斯拔地而起。而这时的赌博已经不再是小打小闹的耍钱娱乐活动，如同好莱坞、迪斯尼一样，它已经成为合法的暴利产业。

经过半个世纪的发展，如今的拉斯维加斯已成为名冠全球的头号赌城，同时也是世界酒店业之都。拉斯维加斯大道两旁，各种豪华酒店鳞次栉比，集聚了全球造价最高、造型最美的 20 多家大型豪华酒店。最著名的有金银岛、金字塔、米高梅、金殿、凯撒、百乐宫、温恩、纽约、巴黎等等，一个比一个富丽堂皇、豪华气派。

赌城之父

说起拉斯维加斯的赌场酒店业，有一位传奇人物不能不提起，那就是有"赌城之父"之称的斯蒂芬·温恩。温恩是美国博彩业的巨擘，以酷爱冒险、热衷挑战自我著称，他最大的爱好就是建造一座比一座更豪华的赌场酒店。无论是 1984 年的金砖，1989 年的金殿，1996 年的凯撒，还是 1998 年的白乐宫，都是温恩的得意之作，温恩每出一张牌就能让拉斯维加斯变一次脸。

金砖酒店坐落在繁华的福瑞蒙特大街，重达 61 磅的天然金块一直存放在酒店内展示，供游客欣赏。

白乐宫度假村酒店是拉斯维加斯大道上最豪华的赌场酒店，大堂地板采用豪华高档的大理石，天花板上用 2000 多个玻璃花瓶装饰了一个五彩缤纷的图案，该玻璃装饰已被列入吉尼斯世界纪录。

1989 年开业的金殿酒店，使温恩创造了其赌场酒店建造史上的一个巅峰。这家酒店耗资 63 亿美元，耸立在酒店门口的活火山模型每隔 15 分钟便自动喷出熊熊的火焰，成为赌城一大奇景，也成为许多好莱坞电影的拍摄地。

温恩最新建造的是拉斯维加斯的新地标——温恩拉斯维加斯酒店 (Wynn)，他斥资 27 亿美元、耗时五年时间建造了这座拥有 2700 间客房，雇员达 6000 人的超大型、超豪华的赌场酒店。酒店外层建筑由铜色玻璃墙镶嵌，整体造型似圆形拱门，高 50 层，显得格外耀眼夺目。2005 年 4 月 28 日，温恩拉斯维加斯酒店的开业，再次造就了赌城神话。它不仅是世界上最豪华的赌场，也是赌城里最新、最高、最具传奇色彩的建筑。

在温恩酒店开业前的员工大会上，温恩对他的全体雇员鼓劲说，不要担心犯错误或亏钱，因为要开办新赌场，建造新酒店，这样的事根本无法避免。他只要求员工做好一件事，那就是"让所有来到此地的客人开心，玩得尽兴"。因为酒店的前途"不在于我们，而在于他们"。

赌城奢华

来到拉斯维加斯的游客，大多带着好奇的心情，逛一逛迷人的街景，体尝一下新奇的快乐。

22 日下午，我们从华盛顿杜勒斯机场飞抵拉斯维加斯，入住马戏 (Circus) 饭店，进房间稍作整理后，就赶紧乘车去看街景和表演。沿着拉斯维加斯大道流连徜徉，的确有一种异样的感觉，此地虽是沙漠戈壁，但处处却是花红树绿。这里的一草一木，甚至连土壤都是从外地购运来的，一棵棕榈树就要上万美元，各种植物生长均靠昂贵的滴灌工程来维持。虽说昂贵，但拉斯维加斯缺水少雨就是不缺钱，每天有 900 多次航班和数以千计的车辆抵达这里，到访的游客每年将近 4000 万人次，多数人来到这里都不吝啬花钱。

当夜幕快要降临时，各大赌场酒店门前的表演纷纷登台亮相。著名的有海盗船表演、火山喷发、音乐喷泉等等。除了远看金殿酒店火山喷发的奇特景观外，百乐宫酒店门前的音乐舞蹈喷泉让游客大饱眼福。在大约两公顷的水面上，伴随着空中优美的音乐旋律，水池中喷出的各种水花翩翩起舞，或婀娜多姿，或激流飞溅，或低缓漫步，或激昂冲天，在赌城夜色的衬映下，喷泉舞蹈妙不可言，游人看得如痴如醉。在国内也见过不少音乐喷泉，但如此美妙绝伦的场景还是第一次。喷泉每隔 15 分钟表演一次，每次表演游客都蜂拥而至。据说，音乐喷泉每表演一次酒店就耗费一万美元，每晚表演 20 次。

酒店外的表演刺激动人，酒店内的场景更是美轮美奂。当我们一行人走进威尼斯大酒店，酒店大堂内的人造城市街景、人造天空和人造运河，使你恍若进入真实场景。当我们逛到"蓝天"下的休闲广场时，酒店小乐队正在演奏意大利歌曲，来自北京的女同胞石丽即兴登台，与乐队男演员共同演唱《我的太阳》，赢得周围顾客的阵阵掌声，温馨欢快的场面令人难忘。

一赌为快

来到拉斯维加斯的游客，几乎都会在赌场林立的饭店中赌上一把，有的豪赌成性，一掷千金；有的小试身手，碰碰运气。在拉斯维加斯，21 岁以下的人是不准进入赌场的，许多携家带口的游客，家长多是陪孩子专程目睹夜幕中拉斯维加斯风采的。在赌场内可以抽烟，但不准照相，更不准摄像，因为豪赌的人比比皆是，但大多数人都不愿意让自己正在赌博时的尊容流传出去。赌场没有窗户，也没有钟表，是为了让赌客忘掉白天黑夜，忘掉时间钟点，尽情地玩个痛快。在赌场里，不光是青年人激情赌耍，不少中老年人也在老虎机前尽情搏杀，并不断地变换机位，心定气闲地消遣时光。

如果说，迪斯尼是孩子们的乐园，那么拉斯维加斯则是年轻人的天堂，同时也是中老年人消遣的地方。每当夜幕降临，拉斯维加斯大街上灯火辉煌，游人如织，在几乎所有的赌场内，一年四季，似乎永远充斥着比肩接踵、熙熙攘攘的游客。他们或玩老虎机，或耍轮盘赌，或拼比 21 点，当他们离开这里时，或得到了好奇心的满足，或对自己的运气感到失望，多数人都是乘兴而来，输钱而归。

拉斯维加斯的神秘色彩和娱乐内涵，正好满足了人们猎奇、豪赌、撞大运的侥幸心理。它的幸运和成功看似有很大的偶然性，实则蕴含着必然性。拉斯维加斯的神秘色彩将继续像磁铁一样，不断吸引着世界各地游人的好奇心和侥幸心，刺激着他们将大把大把的钞票兴奋地塞进拉斯维加斯成千上万个老虎机和轮盘赌里。

游客留给拉斯维加斯的是金钱，带走的是刺激后的心理满足，这也许正是赌博业经久不衰、而且日益兴旺的奥妙所在。

赌兴正浓

如今的拉斯维加斯已从单一的赌博业发展到博彩、表演、旅游和会展四业并举的格局。每年来拉市的 4000 万游客为该市创造 400 多亿美元的收入，而赌博收入只有 120 亿美元，平均每个游客花费 1000 美元，其中输掉 300 美元。

人气、财气如此兴旺的赌博娱乐业，不应只属于拉斯维加斯的专利和魅力。拉斯维加斯能在沙里淘金，自然有人效仿。过去在美国只有内华达州和新泽西州允许赌博，而今已扩展到美国 48 个州。专家预测，未来数年，随着赌博业在全美快速扩展，民众将比以往更容易去赌场。

据媒体报道，随着美国、香港等外资的进入，去年赌城澳门又开张了几家新赌场，其中就有"拉斯维加斯赌王"斯蒂芬·温恩 9 月份建成开业并引起轰动的永利赌场。新赌场的加入使澳门 2006 年头九个月的博彩业收入高达 392.52 亿澳元，超过拉斯维加斯成为全球第一赌城。

The Magnificent Grand Canyon

On the rim of the canyon, gazing at its humongous body, overwhelmed by its breathtaking majestic charm, I truly understood what the Grand Canyon represented. It says that what you saw is not as good as what you heard.Because what you saw is not as touching as what you heard. But Grand Canyon Colorado is different, the scenery here is ten times and even a hundred times more miraculous than anything you have heard about it.

If I am asked which natural landscape is most shocking and memorable, the Colorado Grand Canyon will surely be my first choice. On the morning of May 24, we started early from Las Vegas to visit this world famous wonder.

A Leisured Mood

We traveled over five hours and more than 500 kilometers from Las Vegas to the Grand Canyon. From our Toyota station wagon, we happily enjoyed the beauty of western America on the way. At first, we saw the winding hills and the desert wastelands with thorns and weeds. After about one-third of the way, flat wilderness and yellowish grasslands appeared. Clusters of village farmhouses were scattered on the grassland, three or five here, a dozen there, all built in the American western style.

As we approached the Grand Canyon, rows of dense forest belts appeared on both sides of the road. We were amazed by the Colorado Plateau, which was so fertile and beautiful, full of endless ups and downs

Tree Belt on the Plateau

that it seemed like we were traveling across China's northeastern hilly forest belt. It could be seen that the geomorphic environment of the American west is protected quite well. The original ecosystem is kept unharmed and a large area is given aerial seeding. The plateau seemed rough but not desolate. Seldom can people see the sandstorm or dust all over the sky.

Under the clear blue sky, in the vast boundless wilderness, appreciating the enchanting scenery of a foreign country, listening to the familiar music in the car, I suddenly felt that the sky was boundless and I got in a relaxed mood. On an impulse of emotion, I created a poem:

At dawn I left Vegas and to Arizona made my way,
To see and watch the canyon a thousand miles away,
Travelling under the blue sky with white clouds,
Listening to Dao Lang's singing all my way.

At noon, we arrived at a gas station, and then we rested and had lunch. Soon after, we got to the Grand Canyon Park. When the car drove to the entrance of the park, a young man in uniform wearing a cowboy hat said in American English with a prolonged end, "Twenty five dolla-r-s-!" I was amused and so I repeated it in his tone. The young lad might have heard

Desert

that, for he looked into the car when delivering the tickets, and said,
"Everyone is good!"

The Magic Blossom

Before visiting the Grand Canyon, it is necessary to know first the natural
conditions where the Grand Canyon was formed and its human allusions.

The Grand Canyon is located in the midstream of the Colorado River in
the northwest of Arizona and in the southwest of Colorado Plateau. The
Colorado River, a main river in North America, originates from the Rocky
Mountains and flows to the southwest, through 7 states, namely Wyoming,
Colorado, Utah, New Mexico, Nevada, Arizona and California, with a total
length of 2233 km. During a period of hundreds of millions of years, the
Colorado River cut out 19 canyons in the mainstream and the upstream
tributary of the river, and finally completed its world famous masterpiece,
the Grand Canyon, the King of the Canyons, in Arizona Plateau. The total
length of the Grand Canyon is 446 kilometers with a range of width on the
top between 6 and 28 km and an average width is 16 km; the deepest place
is 1800 meters and its average depth is more than 1500 meters. It would
take you 3 to 4 hours to walk from the top of the canyon to the bottom
of the canyon on the trails. The Colorado River flows through the bottom
of the Grand Canyon. The width of the river can reach 700 meters and
the narrowest place can be only 120 meters. At ordinary times the river is
narrow and shallow, while in summer, the snow in the upstream melts and
the water flows down, so the depth of the water can reach 18 meters.

The Canyon is full of mostly red rock textured to the bottom of the canyon,
colorful and varied in the form of the Cambrian period to Cenozoic
period. It is called "the Living Geological History Textbook" because of the
representative fossils of various geological ages found in the rocks.

The Grand Canyon was first discovered by a Spanish expedition in 1540. In
1869, an Artillery Major called Powell who had lost his left arm in the Civil
War, with his self-taught geographical knowledge and passion for science

Canyon Landscape

and adventure, led nine soldiers to drift on this unexplored river without the help of any modern instrumentation. The result was predictable: The ship hit a reef, crashed and was swept away by the torrent. After hiking to land, three soldiers escaped and three others were killed by the Indians. Finally only Powell himself climbed to the top of the cliff with one arm and survived. Later he published his diary of this 98-day adventure, which contributed to the passing of the bill by Congress to establish the Grand Canyon National Park. In 1919, when Wilson was the President, he named a section of the deepest canyon, which is 170 km long and covers an area of 2728 square kilometers, "The Grand Canyon National Park".

The Grand Canyon is the wonder of nature, and one of the most magnificent scenes on the Earth. It is said that in space it is the only natural landscape that can be seen with the naked eye, a huge rift lying in the Arizona plateau, tearing apart the surface of the earth. Someone once claimed that the Grand Canyon can only be the masterpiece of God. In fact, it is the result of hundreds of millions of years' diastrophism and the erosion of river, wind and rain. On the edge of the canyon, overlooking the flickering river at the bottom, you it is hard to imagine how mountains and streams could have such divine power to leave such a long, wide crack deep into the earth! You see, constant dropping really wears the stone! The magic of nature tells us: though human beings, the "paragon of animals," are wise and capable enough to change the world by miracles, we must show our respect to and awe for nature. Besides the recognition and reconstruction of nature, we should protect our own peace and security, and protect the earth on which people survive in the first place.

The Grand Canyon has come to be known as the symbol of America and the favor of God, since He bestowed this new land not only with scenic magnificence, but also with great spirits of exploring and enterprising as magnificent as the canyon.

Now, the Grand Canyon attracts five million tourists every year, to appreciate the uncanny workmanship of nature and magical changes of the

Buildings in the Park

Earth through billions of years.

Fantasy and Reverie

Before the visit, I had seen the picture of the Grand Canyon on TV several times, but I wasn't that impressed. But, when I finally stood on the rim of the canyon, gazing at its size and breathtaking charm, I was stunned and amazed. A kind of indescribable shock swept through my body and into my heart. It is incredible that the Earth has such spectacular landscape, which seems to come from the outer space. Just as the American writer John Muir said: "No matter how many roads you have walked and how many mountains and rivers you have seen, you will still feel that the Grand Canyon can only exist in another world and another planet."

It says that what you saw is not as good as what you heard. Because what you saw is not as touching as what you heard. But Grand Canyon Colorado is different, the magnificent beauty of the Grand Canyon defies all description. Only when you face the Grand Canyon in person can you experience that kind of psychological shock; listen to the call of the heart from the ancient, the universe and the nature. It is really a story of the end of time, a telling from the vast space and time, and indescribable awe and fear.

In 1903, when President Theodore Roosevelt came to visit it, he also said emotionally, "The Grand Canyon fills me with awe and fear. It is incomparable and indescribable, and in this vast world, it is unique."

Which is the First?

For over a century, the Grand Canyon has always been recognized as "The World's First Grand Canyon". In recent years, some countries have gradually realized the value of having the world's best geographical landscape. As a result, they launched their own Grand Canyons to challenge the one in Colorado, such as the 3200 meters deep Colca Canyon in Peru, which claims to be the world's deepest, and the Kali Gandaki Gorge in Nepal, which was located between two peaks more than 8000 meters high, and regards itself

Yarlung Zangbo Grand Canyon

as the world's deepest canyon. However, in the eyes of those familiar with the three canyons, the above two are deep enough, but far less majestic than the Colorado big brother.

In the world, perhaps only the Chinese Yarlung Zangbo Grand Canyon can be matched with the Grand Canyon.

The Yarlung Zangbo Grand Canyon is located in the Qinghai-Tibet Plateau, "the roof of the world." Its erosion and incision depth is 5382 meters, even beyond the world's deepest canyon, the Colca Canyon in Peru, which in length is 496 kilometers, longer than the Grand Canyon. What's more, the Yarlung Zangbo Grand Canyon can be called the best in the world with its nine vertical natural zones from the mountain snow to the low valley tropical monsoon rainforest, where most of the known higher plants, mammals, and all kinds of insects and Macro-fungi of the Qinghai-Tibet Plateau are located. The most dangerous and spectacular place in the canyon is the river section nearly a hundred kilometers down from the Whitehorse bear, where the clear and blue river roars violently deep between the mountains. The two sides are steep and mysterious, lush and green. No one can pass through here. Its danger and magic can be called "The Last Secret Place in the World."

In 1994, an expedition of Chinese scientists went to the Yarlung Zangbo Grand Canyon to carry out their research and uncovered a slice of its mystery. Now, the spectacular landscape of the Grand Canyon has been gradually known by the world. However, to become widely acknowledged as world famous or to rank the first depends not only on the natural wonders it possesses, but also the appreciation and recognition of the people on the Earth.

雄伟壮丽大峡谷

站在峡谷边缘，举目凝望它那巨大无比的躯壳，感受它摄人心魄的魅力，才真正体会到什么才是大峡谷。人们常讲，看景不如听景，那是因为你看到的往往不如听到的动人。但是，科罗拉多大峡谷就不同了，你亲眼看到的一定要比你听到的神奇十倍、百倍。

如果说地球上有哪处自然景观使人震撼、令人难忘，依我来看，首选非科罗拉多大峡谷莫属了。5 月 24 日，我们一早从拉斯维加斯出发，前去探访这个名扬天下的地球奇观。

心境悠悠

从拉斯维加斯到大峡谷，全程五百多公里，行车五个多小时。坐在丰田旅行车上，我们兴致勃勃地观赏前方的景色，尽情饱览美国西部风光。开始，沿途都是蜿蜒起伏的丘陵山脉和戈壁荒滩，荒滩上生长着一些荆棘和杂草。行程过了大约三分之一，开始出现平坦的原野和干黄的草滩，草滩上散落着一簇簇村庄农舍，或三五户，或十几家，别具西部风情。

当离大峡谷越来越近时，公路两旁呈现出成排连片的茂密林带。真是意想不到，科罗拉多高原竟如此丰满秀丽，波澜起伏，一望无际，真有行驶在我国东北丘陵林带的那种感觉。看来，美国西部地貌环境保护得相当不错，既没有破坏原始生态，又进行了大面积的飞播造林，戈壁高原虽显粗犷但并不荒凉，更没有看到风沙迷漫、尘暴飞扬的天气。

驰骋在晴空万里的蓝天下，纵横在广袤无际的原野上，欣赏着异国他乡的迷人风光，聆听着车内熟悉的歌声，顿觉天际苍远，心境悠悠，一时情动，诌诗摇首：

早发赌城驰梦乡，峡谷千里来探访，

蓝天白云伴我行，一路欢歌听刀郎。

中午 12 点，我们赶到一家加油站休息用餐，饭后动身，很快就到了大峡谷公园。当汽车行进到公园门口交费时，有位头戴牛仔帽、身穿制服的小伙子，用拖长了尾音的美式英语说道 "Twenty five dollars（25 美元）!" 我听着耳熟，也学着他的音调重复了一句。小伙子可能听到了，递门票时探头往车里瞅了瞅，跟着来了一句："Everyone is good（各位走好）!"

神奇绽放

前来探访大峡谷，得首先了解一下大峡谷形成的自然条件和人文典故。

大峡谷位于美国亚利桑那州西北部科罗拉多河中游，科罗拉多高原西南部。科罗拉多河是北美洲主要河流，它从落基山脉发源流向西南，进入墨西哥西北部，流经怀俄明、科罗拉多、犹他、新墨西哥、内华达、亚利桑那、加利福尼亚 7 个州，全长 2233 公里。在亿万年的漫长岁月中，科罗拉多河一路洪流奔泻，开山劈道，在主流与上游支流河段就已切割出 19 条峡谷，最后在亚利桑那高原完成了它的绝世之作，开凿出了这条惊世骇俗的"峡谷之王"：全长 446 公里，顶宽 6 至 28 公里，平均宽度为 16 公里；最深处 1800 米，平均深度超过 1500 米，从谷顶走到谷底需要 3 到 4 个时。科罗拉多河从大峡谷谷底流过，河面宽处 700 多米，窄处仅有 120 米。平时河窄水浅，到了夏季，上游冰雪融水下注，水深达到 18 米。

大峡谷山石多为红色，从谷底到顶部分布着从寒武纪到新生代各个时期的岩层，层次清晰，多姿多彩，并含有各个地质年代的代表性生物化石，故有"活的地质史教科书"之称。

大峡谷最初于 1540 年被西班牙一支探险队发现。1869 年，在美国南北战争中失去左臂的炮兵少校鲍威尔，酷爱科学和探险，他凭着自学的地理知识，在没有任何复杂仪器帮助的情况下，就带着 9 个弟兄在这条未经勘测的河流上进行漂流。结果可想而知：船被暗礁撞碎，人被激流卷走。在此后的徒步探险中，三个副手逃跑，三个弟兄被印第安人杀死，他本人独臂攀上崖顶死里逃生。

鲍威尔这次历时 98 天的历险日记发表后，促成了国会通过建立大峡谷国家公园的法案。1919 年，在威尔逊担任总统时，将其中长约 170 公里、面积 2728 平方公里的最深一段峡谷辟为"大峡谷国家公园"。

科罗拉多大峡谷是大自然的奇迹，是地球上最为壮丽的景色之一。有人说，在太空唯一可以用肉眼看到的自然景观就是科罗拉多大峡谷。从空中望去，一条巨大的裂痕横亘在亚利桑那高原上，像是地球表面被撕开一般。有人感叹，大峡谷只能是上帝的杰作，实际上它是亿万年地壳变动、河水冲刷和风雨侵蚀的结果。站在峡谷边上，遥望谷底忽隐忽现的河流，难以想象高山流水会有如此神力，竟给地球来了个开膛破肚，豁开了一道既长、又宽、又深的大口子，真可谓滴水穿石，铁棒磨针。大自然的神奇力量启示我们：有着万物灵长之称的人类，虽然拥有改天换地、创造奇迹的智慧和力量，但是，在大自然面前，一定要存有敬畏之心。人类在认识自然、改造自然的同时，首先应当保护好自身的和平与安全，保护好地球人赖以生存的这个星球。

大峡谷也被誉为美国的象征，是说上帝偏爱美利坚，在赐予它如此壮丽山河的同时，又赋予了它如此伟大的探索和进取精神，如同峡谷一般雄伟壮阔。

现在，大峡谷每年吸引着 500 万游客来到这里参观游览，欣赏大自然的鬼斧神工，认识地球亿万年的神奇变化。

神思遐想

参观大峡谷之前，曾在电视和图片上见过几次大峡谷的模样，当时并没有特别的感觉。可是，当我亲身走近大峡谷，站在峡谷边缘，举目凝望它那巨大无比的躯壳，感受它摄人心魄的魅力，才真正体会到什么才是大峡谷。那种强烈的心理震撼简直没法形容，可以说是惊呆了，叹服了！让人不可思议的是，地球上竟有这样似乎来自天外的壮丽景观。正如美国作家约翰·缪尔所说："不管你走过多少路，看过多少名山大川，你都会觉得大峡谷仿佛只能存在于另一个世界，另一个星球。"

人们常讲，看景不如听景，那是因为你看到的往往不如听到的动人。但是，科罗拉多大峡谷就不同了，你亲眼看到的一定要比你听到的神奇十倍、百倍。大峡谷那种雄伟险峻、纵横叠嶂、色彩斑斓、瑰丽动人、惊天地、泣鬼神的伟岸雄姿，是难以用语言来表述的。尤其是当你面对大峡谷所受到的那种心理冲击，只能靠你自己身临其境去体验，去倾听那来自远古的、宇宙的、大自然的、心灵深处的呼唤。这真是一个地老天荒的故事，是一个来自茫茫宇宙、浩瀚时空的诉说，这是一种难以名状的震慑和敬畏。

1903年，美国总统西奥多·罗斯福来此游览时，也曾发出过感慨，他说："大峡谷使我充满了敬畏，它无可比拟，无法形容，在这辽阔的世界上，绝无仅有。"

谁是第一

百余年来，科罗拉多大峡谷一直以"世界第一大峡谷"的名声享誉全球。近年来，一些国家逐渐认识到世界地理景观之最的价值，相继推出了自己国家的大峡谷，并向科罗拉多大峡谷发出了挑战。如秘鲁推出了科尔卡大峡谷，因其深度达到3200米，自称是世界最深的大峡谷。尼伯尔则推出由两座海拔8000米以上的高峰所夹持的谷地——喀利根德格大峡谷，也自认为是世界第一深峡谷。但是，据考察过这三条峡谷的人士比较，后两者虽深邃有余，然雄伟壮观不足，在科罗拉多大峡谷面前只能拱手称弟。

当今世界上唯一可以向科罗拉多大峡谷提出挑战的只能是中国雅鲁藏布大峡谷了。

雅鲁藏布大峡谷位于"世界屋脊"青藏高原上，平均海拔3000米以上，侵蚀下切深达5382米，长度为496公里，不但深度超过号称世界之最的秘鲁科尔卡大峡谷，长度也超过科罗拉多大峡谷。而且雅鲁藏布大峡谷具有从高山冰雪带到低河谷热带季风雨林等九个垂直自然带，麇集了青藏高原大部分已知的高等植物、哺乳动物、各类昆虫和大型真菌，堪称世界之最。峡谷最险峻、最壮观的地段，是从白马狗熊往下长约近百公里的河段，该处江水激流咆哮，清澈碧蓝；两岸险峻幽深，郁郁葱葱，至今还无人能够通过此地，其艰险与神奇，堪称"人类最后的秘境"。

1994年，由我国科学家组成一支考察队，对雅鲁藏布大峡谷进行了科学考察，才揭开了它神秘面纱的一角。现在，雅鲁藏布大峡谷的壮丽景观逐渐为世人所了解，然而，要成为举世公认的世界著名或第一大峡谷，不但要具备大自然的神奇造化，还要赢得地球人的赏识与共鸣。

Disputes over the Dam Project's Advantages and Disadvantages

Hoover Dam is the first super dam in the world, which is rated one of the seven miracles in modern American civil works. The Three Gorges Project is a century-old dream of the Chinese nation, and it is "China's most magnificent project since the Great Wall." The debate about the construction of the dam has lasted long. People who support the construction of the dam think that development and protection should coexist, while people who oppose it believe that we should retain one or two "original" rivers.

On the way from Las Vegas to the Grand Canyon, there is another magnificent landscape — the Hoover Dam. Located on the Colorado River, it is the first super-large dam in the world, the largest water conservancy project in the southwest of the United States, and is named one of the Seven Wonders of the American modern civil engineering. On May 24, on our way to the Grand Canyon, we fortunately witnessed its grandness.

A Miracle Made Out of Stones

The Colorado River, which is 2233 kilometers long, with the basin area of 630,000 square kilometers, originates in the Rocky Mountains, flows across seven states in America and Mexico before it arrives at the Gulf of California. For thousands of years, in the spring and early summer, because a lot of snow drifts melt into the Colorado River, the low-lying areas on both sides of the river flood with water and people's lives and property suffer serious losses. However, in the late summer and early autumn, the

Herbert Clark Hoover

Hoover Dam

river dries up like a stream and cannot irrigate the farmland. For a long time, there have been controversies on the rights of the water between the United States and Mexico, even among the seven states inside the U.S. , which use the river as their borderline. In 1922, the delegates of every state and the federal government held a meeting to discuss issues of water rights, and signed the Colorado River Agreement of shared interests and obligations in July of that year.

In order to control this calamitous river, in 1928, the Congress passed the stone canyon engineering bill and authorized the construction of the stone dam. Herbert Hoover who was the finance minister then and later was elected the 31st President of the United States played an important role in coordinating the seven states to reach the agreement of flood control and dam construction. He strongly supported the construction of the project and advocated that the construction funds be repaid by the energy income from the sale of electricity. To honor his pursuit, the U.S. Congress later permanently named the stone dam Hoover Dam.

It is interesting to know that Hoover lived in China for nearly 3 years from early 1899 to the end of 1900s. His Chinese name was Hu Hua.

In February 1899, the 24-year-old Hoover was sent to China, and he worked as the manager and coal mine technician in Moline — China Machine Mining Company. On July 30, 1900, Hoover, De Cuilin and Mo Lin conspired and secretly bought Kaiping Mines from Zhang Yi who was the Qing Government's direct governor of the Rehe Mine. In February 1901, due to his efforts in taking the Kaiping Mines by fraud, Hoover was promoted to the general manager of the Sino-British Kaiping Mines Ltd. But the good time did not last long. In the fall of that year, the Belgian shareholders bought a majority of the company's shares from other European and Chinese counterparts, and sent their own people to manage the company. Because of a disagreement with the new manager, Hoover resigned and went to London with his family in November of the same year.

The three years' experiences of being engineer and management in China was the start-up stage in Hoover's life, and this experience enabled him to get ready to make good use of his wisdom and talent to control the flood and construct the dam. He developed his knowledge in China and accumulated a large amount of money which laid a solid material foundation for his later pursuit in politics. In his memoirs, after being away from China for more than 10 years, Hoover devoted a whole chapter to describe his experiences in China and to express his praise of and admiration for the Chinese people.

The construction of Hoover dam was started in January 1931 and was completed in 1935. It began to generate electricity for the first time in October 1936, two years ahead of the schedule. The dam has a concrete arch which is 221 meters high, 379 meters long, the width of the dam crest is 14 meters, the width of the bottom of the dam is 201 meters, and the amount of concrete poured is 2.6 million cubic meters.

The reservoir formed by the Hoover Dam is called Lake Mead. It is named after Elwood Mead, who was the Director of the U.S. Bureau of Reclamation. Lake Mead has an area of 593 square kilometers, whose water storage capacity is 38.3 billion cubic meters, with a maximum depth of 180 meters, and it is one of the world's largest artificial lakes. Due to the global warming, less snow and reduced rainfall, the current storage capacity of Lake Mead has obviously decreased. When we visited the dam, the water mark line in front of the dam seemed to have reduced several meters.

The Hoover hydroelectric power plant is located behind the dam. There are 19 units, with a total installed capacity of 2.08 million kilowatts, and its annual generation capacity is 4 billion kilowatts per hour, which was the best functioning hydroelectric power plant in the world at that time.

The Hoover Dam project has multiple economic and social benefits, such as irrigation, water supply, electricity, leisure, etc. When the construction of the dam was completed and it started to generate electricity, every year it provided 4 billion KW of electricity for midwestern states, such as California, Nevada and Arizona, and it also provided one billion gallons of water for Los Angeles and San Diego. It not only solved the plight of the energy shortage for the development of the western region in the United States, but also solved the problem of severe water shortage. It played an extremely important role in the development of the coastal zone in the western United States.

The Hoover Dam has existed for 70 years. Through the sale of electrical energy, the original cost of the construction of the dam, 175 million dollars, has already been recovered by the federal government, even with the interest paid on it. Today, the annual pure income of the hydropower station is 700,000,000 dollars.

"A Placid Lake Between Cliffs Steep"

One thing often coincides with another. On May 20, when we were visiting the Hoover Dam in the United States, the construction of the Three Gorges Dam in China was also completed.

The construction of the Three Gorges Project is a century-old dream of the Chinese nation, and the relentless pursuit of several generations. As early as 1919, Sun Yat-sen put forward the strategy of building the Three

Mao Zedong Inspecting the Three Gorges

Gorges Dam in the *The Outline of the Founding of the Country*. In 1945, the Nanjing KMT government set up a Technical Research Council of the Three Gorges hydroelectric scheme, chaired by the notable Qian Changzhao. It also hired Savannah, who was the chief engineer of the U.S. Bureau of Reclamation, as the technical adviser. The survey and design of the Three Gorges Project entered the operation stage. However, due to lack of funds and political disputes, the preparatory work of the Three Gorges Project was abandoned halfway through.

After the founding of New China, Mao Zedong, Zhou Enlai and other leaders were very concerned about the Three Gorges Project. In July 1949, when Mao Zedong met Qian Changzhao (who served as the vice chairman of the CPPCC national committee in 1980), they talked about the Yangtze River Water Resources Development Plan. Mao said "In the future, this thing is still to be finished." In March 1958, Mao Zedong made a special effort to visit the Three Gorges in the Yangtze River and studied the construction of the Project. But because of the problems in funds, technology and political movements, the construction was delayed again.

Until the 1980s, the Construction Program of Three Gorges Project was officially considered an item on the agenda of the country. After several arguments and repeated demonstration, on April 3, 1992, the Fifth Session of the Seventh NPC officially passed the *Resolution on the Construction of the Three Gorges Project*. After a hundred years' ups and downs, the Three Gorges Project finally officially started in December 1994. After nearly 12 years' construction, the main part of the Three Gorges Project — Three

Distant View of Three Gorges Dam

Gorges Dam — was totally completed in the Yangtze Xiling Gorge on May 20, 2006.

The main building of the Three Gorges Projects is composed of three parts, namely the dam, hydropower station and navigation structures. So far, it is the world's largest water conservancy project. The Three Gorges Dam is the world's largest Concrete Gravity Dam, and the amount of concrete pouring reaches more than 16 million cubic meters, six times more than the Hoover Dam. The top of the Three Gorges Dam is 185 meters high, and the total length of the dam is 2335 meters, which can be called the first dam in the world.

In 1965, Chairman Mao Zedong described what he imagined for the future of the Three Gorges Dam in his poem *Prelude to Water · Swimming*:

Stone walls will stand in the waters west,
To block clouds and rains from Wushan's crest,
To make a placid lake between cliffs steep.
Mount Goddess should be well and sound today,
But she'd marvel at the world's new array.

The Three Gorges Dam is indeed a miracle of the modern world. Foreign reports praised that the Three Gorges Project is "China's most magnificent project since the Great Wall." and is the source and symbol of the strength of China, which reflects the Chinese strength and vitality.

In the flood season of 2006, the Three Gorges Dam started to fully retain water. By October 27, the Three Gorges Reservoir successfully achieved its 156 meters' water storage target, which made the flood control standard of the middle and lower reaches of the Yangtze River increase from once in 10 years to once in a hundred years. Since then, the 15 million people and 23 million mu of fertile farmland there were relieved from the threat of flooding.

The total investment of the Three Gorges Project will be more than 200 billion Yuan and the project will be completed in 2009. By the end of the first half of 2006, the Three Gorges Project had completed an investment of 126 billion Yuan, and the electricity generation project installed 26 mega units of 700,000 kilowatts, with an annual generating maximum capacity of 84.7 billion degrees, which is more than 21 times that of the Hoover Dam hydropower. On the American media,it is reported that the generating capacity of Three Gorges hydroelectric power station equals to 18 nuclear power stations,which will satisfy 5% power demand of China. On the American media,it is reported that the generating capacity of Three Gorges hydroelectric power station equals to 18 nuclear power stations,which will satisfy 5% power demand of China.

Advantages and Disadvantages of Building the Dam

The construction of dams is one of the projects that can evoke people's passions. It also reflects that the will and creativity of human beings have reached the pinnacle. From the point of the international dam construction process, over the past century, almost every day there appears a dam on the earth. The whole world has already spent two trillion dollars and built 45,000 dams.

Since the 1930s, the construction of the dam developed very fast. The U.S. Hoover Dam first opened the construction of the world's large dams. In the 1970s, the completion of the Egyptian Aswan Dam which cost 1 billion dollars symbolized that dam construction reached its peak. In the 1980s, the construction of the dam began to decline. As people became more environmentally and ecologically aware and concerned, they began to reflect on the negative effects which were caused by the dams. In the 1990s, the anti-dam organizations and many people in the United States and other developed countries thought that we should end the dam age.

The debate on the construction of the dam lasted for a long time, and it has become more and more severe in the last decade. The supporters of dam construction think that the dam has a wide range of comprehensive benefits in the aspect of flood control, irrigation, power generation, water supply, fishing, shipping, tourism, etc., that the dam is essential to developing the economy and improving people's living conditions. The development of hydropower is conducive to reducing greenhouse gas emissions, and is also conducive to the sustainable use of energy. Compared with the negative impact of the dam on the ecological environment, the advantages of the dam far outweigh its disadvantages.

People against dam construction have a long list of adverse effects of the dam on the social and ecological environment: Flooding farmland, mineral resources, forests, grasslands, and wildlife habitats; flooding the natural landscape and cultural relics; causing a large number of involuntary immigrants; blocking rivers, and affecting shipping and fish migration; affecting terrestrial and aquatic ecosystems, damaging the biodiversity; hindering the free-flowing of the rivers, even causing discontinuous flow, and damaging the health of the river; endangering people if there is a huge dam failure, and especially, in the times of war, allowing easy access to the land and making it vulnerable to attack, which is a "time bomb" hanging over people's heads, etc.

In a word, people who support dam construction think that development and protection should coexist, and people who oppose it think that we should retain one or two "original" rivers, and pass them on to the next generation. We are better off letting every river flow freely.

With the changing of time and the development of society, human beings are becoming more and more aware of the importance of environmental issues. If we do not pay attention to environmental protection in the construction of the dam and destroy the ecological balance, we will accept severe punishment from nature in the future. But the energy problem is also important. For many developing countries, the industrial demand for energy and agricultural demand for water conservancy are both very urgent. Moreover, the hydropower development degree of the developed countries had generally been more than 50%. For example, the water power resources of the United States had been developed and used for 80%, and the dam sites which could be used for the development of economy had been almost fully developed. Although China has 86,000 dams which makes it the largest number in the world, the development and utilization of water power resources in China is less than 25%. Therefore, the hydropower construction is still an inevitable choice for China to solve the bottleneck problems of floods, drought and power shortage.

It should be said that the concern of the dam and ecological issue is the reflection of human progress. The fierce debate of the international community on the issue of the construction of the dam should arouse much attention. It warns the dam builders and managers that in the development of every river and the planning and design of every dam, we should treat the potential for ecological problems very carefully. We should run the ideas of people-oriented and harmony between people and water through the whole process of planning and design, construction and operation management so that the construction of the dam can not only meet the demand of flood control, water supply, food and energy security which is brought by the population growth and the development of the economic society, but also achieves the win-win goal of protecting the ecological environment.

水坝工程与利弊之争

胡佛大坝是世界上第一座超大型水坝，被评为美国现代土木工程七大奇迹之一。三峡工程是中华民族的百年梦想，是"自长城以来中国最宏伟的工程"。关于大坝建设的争论由来已久，赞成建坝者认为开发和保护应该并存，反对建坝者认为应保留一两条"原汁原味"的河流。

从拉斯维加斯通往科罗拉多大峡谷的路上，还有一处壮丽景观，那就是胡佛大坝。这座位于科罗拉多河上的胡佛大坝是世界上第一座超大型水坝，是美国西南地区最大的水利枢纽工程，被评为美国现代土木工程七大奇迹之一。5 月 24 日，在参观大峡谷的途中，我们有幸目睹了它的容姿。

顽石变奇迹

发源于落基山脉、全长 2233 公里的科罗拉多河，流域面积达 63 万平方公里，跨越美国 7 个州，经墨西哥，流入加利福尼亚湾。千百年来科罗拉多河每年春季和夏初，由于大量的融雪径流汇入，致使河流两岸的低洼地区泛滥成灾，民众生命财产遭受严重损失。但到了夏末秋初，河流干涸得像一条溪流，无法引水灌溉农田。长期以来，为了该河流的水权，美国与墨西哥之间和以河流为边界的美国七个州之间，曾存在着激烈的争议。到了 1922 年，各州派代表与联邦政府开会讨论水权问题，并于该年 7 月签署了利益共享和义务分担的科罗拉多河协议。

为了治理这条多灾多难的河流，1928 年，国会通过了顽石峡谷工程法案，授权建设顽石大坝。时任财政部长后又当选美国第 31 任总统的赫伯特·胡佛，在协调 7 个州达成治水建坝协议中发挥了重大作用，他强烈支持该工程建设，并主张建设资金完全由销售电力的能源收入来偿还。因此，后来美国国会将顽石大坝永久命名为胡佛大坝。

作者在胡佛大坝留影

有意思的是，这位胡佛总统曾于 1899 年初至 1901 年底在中国生活了近 3 年，他的中文名字叫胡华。

1899 年 2 月，24 岁的胡佛奉派来到中国，在莫林公司——中国机矿公司任经理兼煤矿技师。1900 年 7 月 30 日，胡佛与德璀琳、墨林合谋从清政府直隶热河矿务督办张翼手中秘密买下了开平煤矿。1901 年 2 月，胡佛因骗占开平煤矿和秦皇岛港有功，被提升为中英合办的开平矿务有限公司总办。但是好景不长，同年秋，比利时股东从欧洲其他股东和中方股东手中买下了公司的大部分股份，并派自己的人来做公司经理。胡佛因同新任经理意见不合而辞职，同年 11 月，携眷属去了伦敦。

在中国的 3 年经历是胡佛人生的创业阶段，工程师和经理人的阅历，为他后来在协调治水、建设大坝方面发挥聪明才干积累了经验；他在中国发迹并积累了大量资本，为他以后步入政坛奠定了雄厚的物质基础。在离开中国 10 余年后撰写的回忆录中，胡佛以整整一章的篇幅描述了当年他在中国的经历，同时表达了对中国人民的赞美和崇敬。

胡佛大坝于 1931 年 1 月开工，1935 年完工，1936 年 10 月首次发电，比计划提前了两年。这是一座拱形混凝土大坝，坝高 221 米，坝顶长 379 米，坝顶宽 14 米，坝底宽 201 米，混凝土浇筑量为 260 万立方米。

由胡佛大坝而形成的水库叫米德湖，是以美国垦务局局长爱霍·米德的名字命名的。米德湖水库面积可达到 593 平方公里，蓄水量为 383 亿立方米，最大水深为 180 米，是世界最大的人工湖之一。由于全球变暖、雪线后退、降雨减少，目前米德湖的库容明显下降。当我们参观大坝时，大坝跟前的水痕线看上去降低了好几米。

胡佛水力发电厂位于大坝后面，共安装了 19 台机组，总装机容量为 208 万千瓦，年发电量 40 亿千瓦 / 时，为当时世界水力发电之最。

胡佛水利枢纽工程有灌溉、供水、电力、休闲等经济和社会多重效益。大坝建成发电后，每年为加利福尼亚、内华达、亚利桑那等美国中西部各州提供 40 亿度电，为洛杉矶和圣迭戈市供水 10 亿加仑。它不仅为美国西部开发解除了能源匮乏的困境，而且解决了西部城市严重缺水的问题，为美国西部海岸带的发展发挥了极为重要的作用。

胡佛大坝建成 70 年了，当年建坝投资的 1.75 亿美元，早已通过销售电力能源连本带利归还给联邦政府，如今水电站每年纯收入达 7 亿美元。

高峡出平湖

世事巧合，5 月 20 日，正当我们在美国访问即将参观胡佛大坝之时，也正是我国三峡大坝建成之日。

建设三峡工程，是中华民族的百年梦想，是中国几代人的不懈追求。早在 1919 年，孙中山在《建国大纲》中就提出建设三峡大坝的方略，1945 年，国民政府成立了三峡水力发电计划技术研究委员会，由著名人士钱昌照担任主任委员，并聘请美国垦务局总工程师萨凡奇做技术顾问，三峡工程的勘察设计也进入实际运作阶段。然而，由于缺少资金和政治纷争等原因，三峡工程筹备工作半途而废。

新中国成立后，毛泽东、周恩来等领导人非常关心三峡工程。1949 年 7 月，毛泽东在会见钱昌照（1980 年担任全国政协副主席）时，谈到长江水利开发计划，毛泽东说："将来这件事还是要办的。" 1958 年 3 月，毛泽东专门乘船视察长江三峡，研究三峡工程建设问题，但由于资金、技术和政治运动等原因，三峡工程一直被耽搁下来。

进入 20 世纪 80 年代，三峡工程建设方案才正式提到国家建设的议事日程，几经争论和反复论证，1992 年 4 月 3 日，七届全国人大五次会议正式通过《关于兴建三峡工程的决议》。历经上百年的风雨历程，三峡大坝终于在 1994 年 12 月正式开工。经过近 12 年的建设，三峡工程的主体工程——三峡大坝于 2006 年 5 月 20 日，终于在长江西陵峡全线建成。

三峡水利枢纽工程主要建筑物由大坝、水电站、通航建筑物三大部分组成，是迄今为止世界上最大的水利枢纽工程。三峡大坝也是世界上最大的混凝土重力坝，混凝土浇筑量达 1600 多万立方米，是胡佛大坝的 6 倍多。三峡大坝坝顶高 185 米，大坝全长 2335 米，堪称世界第一坝。

1965 年，毛泽东主席在《水调歌头·游泳》一词中，对未来的三峡大坝作了神思遐想的描写："更立西江石壁，截断巫山云雨，高峡出平湖。神女应无恙，当惊世界殊。"三峡大坝的建成的确是当今世界的奇迹，有外电赞叹，三峡工程是"自长城以来中国最宏伟的工程"，是中国力量的源泉和象征，体现了中国的实力和活力。

2006 年汛期，三峡大坝开始全面挡水，到 10 月 27 日，三峡水库成功实现 156 米蓄水目标，可使长江中下游的防洪标准从 10 年一遇提高到百年一遇，长江中下游 1500 万人、2300 万亩良田从此解除洪水威胁。

三峡工程全部投资将达到 2000 多亿元，全部竣工要到 2009 年。截止到 2006 年上半年，三峡工程已完成投资 1260 亿元，发电工程安装了 26 台 70 万千瓦的特大机组，年发电量可达 847 亿度，是胡佛大坝水电站的 21 倍多。美国媒体报道，三峡水电站发电量相当于 18 个核电站，将满足中国二十分之一的电力需求。

大坝利与弊

水坝建设是最能唤起人类激情的工程之一，更是人类意志和创造力登峰造极的表现。从国际水坝建设的进程来看，近百年来，地球上几乎每天出现一座大坝，全世界已花费了两万亿美元建造了 4.5 万座大坝。

从 20 世纪 30 年代开始，各国水坝建设发展得非常快，美国胡佛大坝首开世界大型水坝之先河。70 年代，耗资 10 亿美元的埃及阿斯旺大坝竣工后，水坝建设达到了顶峰。进入 80 年代，水坝建设开始衰退，随着人们对环境生态的认识，开始反思大坝带来的负面效应。到了 90 年代，美国等一些发达国家的反坝组织和人士认为，应该结束大坝时代。

关于大坝建设的争论由来已久，而且在近十几年来愈演愈烈。支持大坝建设的人认为，大坝具有防洪、灌溉、发电、供水、渔业、航运、旅游等多方面的综合效益，大坝是发展经济和改善人民生活条件的必需，开发水电有利于减排温室气体，有利于能源可持续利用，与大坝对生态环境的负面影响相比，大坝的利远远大于弊。

反对大坝建设的人则列出了一长串大坝对社会和生态环境的不利影响：淹没耕地和矿产资源，淹没森林、草原和野生动物栖息地；淹没自然景观和文物古迹；造成大批非自愿移民；阻断江河，影响航运和鱼类回游；影响陆生和水生生态系统，损害生物多样性；阻碍了河流的自由奔流，甚至造成河道断流，损害了河流的健康生命；大坝有巨大的溃坝风险，特别在战争时期是易受攻击的要害部位，是悬在人们头上的"定时炸弹"，等等。

总之，赞成建坝者认为开发和保护应该并存，反对建坝者认为应保留一两条"原汁原味"的河流，传给子孙后代，最好让每一条江河都自由地流淌。

随着时代变迁和社会进步，人类越来越意识到环境问题的重要，如果在水坝建设中不注意环境保护，破坏了生态平衡，未来大自然的惩罚将是严厉的。但能源问题同样重要，对于许多发展中国家来说，生存和发展是其面临的主要矛盾，工业对能源的需求，农业对水利的渴望十分迫切。而且，发达国家的水电开发程度一般都已超过50%，如美国水能资源已经开发利用了80%，经济可开发的坝址几乎已全部开发。而中国虽然有86000座水坝，是世界上水坝数量最多的国家，但中国的水能资源开发利用还不到25%。因此，水电建设仍是中国解决洪水、干旱和电力短缺等瓶颈问题的必然选择。

应当说，对大坝与生态问题的关注是人类进步的表现。国际社会对水坝建设的激烈争论应该引起我们的足够重视，它警示大坝的建设者和管理者，在对每一条河流进行开发、对每一座大坝进行规划设计时，都应当十分慎重地对待生态问题，要把以人为本和人水和谐的理念贯穿到规划设计、建筑施工和运行管理的全过程，从而使大坝建设既能满足人口增长和经济社会发展对防洪、供水、粮食和能源安全的需求，同时又能达到保护生态环境的双赢目标。

Los Angeles: The City of Angels

The world-renowned film kingdom Hollywood, the fascinating Disneyland, the elegant and graceful Beverly Hills and the bright and splendid coastal scenery all make Los Angeles a world-famous "Film City" and "Tourist City." Los Angeles seems destined to be closely related with China. Not only did the Los Angeles Olympic Games inspire the Chinese people, but also Chinese actors and directors achieved success again and again on the world's film stage of Hollywood.

I remember that, in the spring of 1999, at the crucial moment when China was negotiating with the United States for the issue of China's accession to the WTO, the former Chinese premier Zhu Rongji was invited to visit the United States. In a press conference held in Washington, Mr Zhu was relaxed and spoke with an air confidence. When he answered a reporter's question in English, he pronounced Los Angeles as "luo shan zhuo si." At that time I felt the Prime Minister's pronunciation was standard, so I regarded "luo shan zhuo si" as the accurate pronunciation of the English name of Los Angeles. It was not until this trip to the United States that I realized that, in fact, Los Angeles is pronounced the same as the Chinese transliteration of the Spanish (Los Angeles).

The city of Los Angeles, located along the Pacific coast in California, has a very beautiful knickname — "The City of Angels." On May 24, we started from Las Vegas to visit this pearl of a city on the West Coast.

Snapshots along the Way

On the way from Las Vegas to Los Angeles, we had to pass through a desert of more than two hundred kilometers. In fact, it was far from a typical desert since, except for several patches of bare desert which can occasionally be seen, most of the landscape of the vast expanse is green space. The annual rainfall here is only 100 millimeters and in May, the rainy

Panorama of Downtown

season has passed, but the plants in the desert are still thick green and lush.

The temperature of the desert was a little high. At 11 a.m., when we traveled to Baker County in California, we saw a tall thermometer on the roadside. We were able to see the temperature clearly at a distance of tens of meters: 96 degrees Fahrenheit (equivalent to 35 degrees Celsius). However, at that time the temperature in Los Angeles was about 27 degrees Celsius. Traveling in the United States, you have to consider the conversion of temperature and the change of time.

At noon, we arrived in Bastogne, a small town located in the middle of Los Angeles and Las Vegas, to have a rest. This town is a common half point between Los Angeles and Las Vegas, where many tourist groups stop to have a quick meal. At the door of a shop patronized by most tourists, an old Chinese lady was handing out some paper materials to the pedestrians. At the beginning, people did not pay much attention, but after a while, they came to her to ask for the material one after another. It turned out that this lady was a Christian from Hong Kong, who gave free Christian materials to the passing tourists all the year round, including a small map booklet introducing the biblical stories named *Look at this Piece of Good Land*, which was beautifully printed and informative, and always first to be taken by the tourists? was always the one first soon taken away.

Visit to the Pearl-like City

After the short delay for shopping in Bastogne, we arrived at Los Angeles around 6 o'clock in the afternoon. When the car drove near the city, the tour guide began to introduce us to the history of its development and describe its style.

As the second largest city in the United States, Los Angeles is a scenic and brilliant coastal city, on the verge of the vast Pacific Ocean and resting against the boundless San Gabriel Mountains. The city is located in a basin surrounded by the mountain on three sides and the sea on one side, and its terrain is mostly open and flat except for some local hills. The urban area is over 1,200 square kilometers and its population is nearly 4 million. The greater Los Angeles also includes the Los Angeles County, part of Orange and Ventura counties and more than 80 towns and cities such as Pasadena and Long Beach, with a total area of 10,576 square kilometers and a population of about 9.52 million.

Thermometer in Desert

Los Angeles used to be pastoral villages of the Indians. In 1769, the Spanish expedition came there to open new churches and built the town as a Spanish colony in 1781, naming it "The Town of the Angel Queen Santa Maria," in short, "The Town of Angels." Later it was occupied by Mexico, and after the Mexican War in 1846 it became the territory of the United States.

In the late 19th century and early 20th century, with the discovery of oil, Los Angeles began to thrive. Its commerce, finance and tourism industry gradually followed suit, with the number of immigrants surging and the city continuing to expand, making Los Angeles into the mega-city of the United States. Immigration has made Los Angeles a multi-ethnic and multi-cultural international metropolis. The ethnic minorities account for nearly half of its population, and have formed a large number of immigrant communities. In Los Angeles there are more than 400,000 Chinese.

Los Angeles has become the largest base of the American petroleum chemical industry, marine, aerospace industry and electronics industry, and is also the largest industrial center in the western United States, with its manufacturing output accounting for about half of all of California, and ranking third in the country. It is one of the major centers of American science and technology, its staff of scientists, engineers and technicians rank highest in the nation and it enjoys the reputation of being considered the "city of technology".

Coming from the eastern United States to the West Coast, we all felt the obvious differences between Los Angeles and the East Coast cities such as New York and Washington. First, the geography and climate is different. Los Angeles, which is next to the mountain and the sea, has more of a Mediterranean climate, sunny and mild all the year round, dry and with little rain. Its average temperature is about 12 degrees Celsius and the annual rainfall is about 350 mm.

Next, the road traffic is different. Los Angeles is famous for its wide roads and car congestion. With a total mileage of more than 700 kilometers, it has the most developed expressways and also the most cars in the United

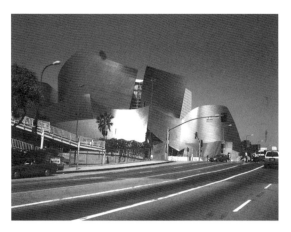

Walt Disney Concert Hall

The Guggenheim Museum Bilbao in Spain

States. It is reported that the United States with nearly three hundred million people has more than two hundred million vehicles, which means 0.7 cars per capita. Los Angeles has more than 9 million vehicles, of which 6 million are in use every single day, shuttling people back and forth between the city center and their living places in the suburb. More than 20 expressways and city streets are filled with the long lines of cars. Even the No. 5 and No.10 expressways with 10 lanes respectively often have to face traffic jams at rush hour.

Third, the urban layout and architecture are different. Los Angeles is located in the Pacific seismic belt. The earthquake in 1994 caused the collapse of its city expressways and the casualties of more than 70 people. Therefore, there are only about ten high-rises built in downtown city. The area of Los Angeles is vastly spread out and there are nearly a hundred suburban towns with tens of millions of families. There are rows upon rows of courtyard-styled buildings nestled throughout the greens of plains, valleys and hills, all with their own charm, and all elegant and exquisite.

Although Los Angeles does not have splendid skyscrapers like New York, it does boast of many famous buildings, all different in style and unique in features, such as the exotic Walt Disney concert hall, and the Kodak Theatre where the Academy Awards are held, etc. The Walt Disney concert hall, located in downtown Los Angeles, was built in 2003 and designed by the most influential contemporary American architect Frank Gehry. Of his architectural works, the most famous one is the Guggenheim Museum in Bilbao, Spain. As soon as it was completed in 1997, it immediately attracted the attention of the world with its strikingly beautiful shape, specific structure and new material, all of which came from the idea of his hometown concert hall, and was called "The world's most meaningful and most beautiful museum". The Disney concert hall which was built soon afterwards, had the same impact as the Guggenheim Museum. Covered by stainless steel cladding, the strange hall looks like its surrounded by a block of aluminum boards, flashing and dazzling in the sunlight. It has the most advanced audio equipment and is one of the top concert halls in the world today.

A City of Culture and Sports

The colorful Los Angeles is not only the industrial and financial center of the western United States, but also the cultural and entertainment center and the world tourist resort. The world-renowned film kingdom Hollywood, the fascinating Disneyland, the elegant and graceful Beverly Hills and the bright and splendid coastal scenery all make Los Angeles a world-famous "City of Film" and "City of Tourism."

As a metropolitan city, the media industry in Los Angeles is also very developed. The city has more than 70 radio stations, nearly 100 TV stations and the newspapers, radios and televisions are in English, Chinese, Spanish, Japanese, Vietnamese and other languages. The daily circulation of the famous *Los Angeles Times* is from 1 to 1.5 million copies. Its advertisement publishing revenue is the top among the nation's newspapers, and in terms of influence and status it ranks the third largest newspaper in the United States only after the *New York Times* and the *Washington Post*.

The next morning, when we were driving to visit the city, we passed the office building of *Los Angeles Times*. We were shocked to learn that the headquarters of this famous newspaper is actually a stocky rustic old building. Seeing this unremarkable office building, I was reminded of the simple and narrow Wall Street in New York and thought: The United States is not as what we usually imagine it to be. Not everything is modern, fashionable and magnificent. The Americans are pragmatic. In the process of modernization and urbanization, they did not throw away all the so-called out-of-date stuff and blindly pursue trendiness, modernness, luxury and style.

Los Angeles is also a famous city of sports. The infamous Los Angeles Lakers is the NBA's most influential team which had won the U.S. championship six times. What especially makes Los Angeles proud is that, it is one of a handful of cities which has held the Summer Olympic Games twice. In 1932, the tenth Olympic Games were held in Los Angeles. With Mr. Zhang Xueliang's fund, China sent a delegation to participate in the Olympic Games for the first time. Liu Changchun, a student of the Northeastern University, China's only athlete, attended the game. In the 100 and 200 meters dash preliminaries, he won the fifth and sixth prize.

In 1984, it was also in Los Angeles that the Chinese sports delegation returned to the Olympic Games. New China's athletes' debut in the Olympics demonstrated the elegant demeanor of an emerging sporting nation. On the first day of the game, the pistol shooting athlete Xu Haifeng

Old Building of *Los Angles Times*

Liu Changchun on the Starting Line

Li Ning in Gymnastics

won the first gold medal of the Olympic Games, which was China's "breakthrough of zero" in the history of the Olympic Games. In this Olympic Games, Chinese athletes won a total of 15 gold medals, 8 silver medals and 9 bronze medals, ranking fourth in the number of gold medals.

Los Angeles seems destined to share a bond with China. Not only did the Los Angeles Olympic Games make the Chinese nation wash the shame of the "sick man of Asia" and inspire the Chinese people. But also, in recent years, Chinese (including Hong Kong and Taiwan) actors and directors are continuously honored and respected by the film industry for their successful work. Therefore, we should be grateful to the Los Angeles.

天使之城洛杉矶

享誉全球的电影王国好莱坞、引人入胜的迪斯尼乐园、钟灵毓秀的贝佛利山庄、明媚灿烂的海滨风光等，使洛杉矶成为一座举世闻名的"电影城"和"旅游城"。洛杉矶似乎与中国有缘，不但洛杉矶奥运会振奋了国人士气，而且中国电影演员和导演也在好莱坞这个世界电影舞台上连连获得成功。

记得 1999 年春天，正值中国为加入世贸组织与美国谈判的关键时刻，朱镕基总理应邀访问美国。在华盛顿举行的记者招待会上，朱总理侃侃而谈、诙谐自如，一派大国总理的气度和风范。当他回答记者提问时，用英语将洛杉矶读为"落山卓思"。当时觉得总理的发音标准，便认定"落山卓思"才是洛杉矶英文地名的准确读法。这次去了美国才明白，洛杉矶其实是西班牙语 (Los Angeles) 的中文译音。

位于美国加利福尼亚州太平洋沿岸的洛杉矶市，有着"天使之城"的美称。5 月 24 日，我们从拉斯维加斯出发，前去访问这座西海岸明珠城市。

沿途掠影

从拉斯维加斯去洛杉矶的途中，须穿越两百多公里的戈壁沙漠。说是戈壁，实际上除偶尔见到几处光秃的沙漠外，沿途大多是一望无际的沙漠绿地。这里的年降雨量只有 100 多毫米，5 月份已经过了雨季，但沙漠上的植物依然是绿意浓浓，生命旺盛。

沙漠地带温度偏高，上午 11 点，当我们行进到加州小镇贝克郡时，看到路边竖立着一个高大的温度计标牌，距离几十米就能看清上面的温度：华氏 96 度（相当于摄氏 35 度），而此时洛杉矶的温度约在摄氏 27 度左右。在美国访问经常遇到气温的换算和时差的变更。

中午 12 点，我们赶到位于洛杉矶和拉斯维加斯中间的小城巴斯通，休息、用餐、逛店。这里是来往洛、拉两市的中途站，很多旅游团队都在这里打尖。在游客集中的商店门口，有位华人老太太正在给行人发放资料，开始大家没太在意，过了一会儿，游客都纷纷围上去索要。原来这位老太太是一位香港基督徒，常年在此地给过往旅客免费赠送基督教宣传材料，其中有本介绍圣经故事的地图小册子《看看这片美地》，印刷精美、知识性强，很快就被拿光。

明珠巡礼

由于在巴斯通购物耽搁，下午6点左右，我们才赶到洛杉矶。汽车驶近市区，导游开始给我们讲解洛杉矶的发展历史和城市风貌。

作为全美国第二大城市的洛杉矶，是一座风景秀丽、璀璨夺目的海滨城市。它濒临浩瀚的太平洋，背靠茫茫的圣加布里埃尔山，市区坐落在三面环山、一面环海的盆地中，除局部丘陵外，地势开阔平坦。市区面积1200多平方公里，人口近400万。大洛杉矶地区还包括洛杉矶县和奥兰治、文图拉两县的一部分，以及帕萨迪纳、长滩等80多个大小城镇，总面积达10576平方公里，人口约952万。

洛杉矶原为印第安人的牧区村落，1769年，西班牙远征队为开设新的教会地点来到这里，于1781年建镇，成为西班牙殖民地，并把这里称为"天使女王圣玛丽亚的城镇"，简称"天使之城"。后来被墨西哥占领，1846年美、墨战争后成为美国领土。

19世纪末20世纪初，随着石油的发现，洛杉矶开始崛起，商业、金融和旅游业逐渐兴旺，移民激增，城区不断向四周扩展，洛杉矶逐渐发展成为美国的特大城市。大量的移民使洛杉矶成为一个多民族、多种文化色彩的国际性城市，少数民族占全市人口的一半左右，并形成众多的移民社区，其中洛杉矶地区的华人约有40余万。

现在的洛杉矶已成为美国石油化工、海洋、航天工业和电子业的最大基地，是美国西部最大的工业中心，制造业产值约占加州的二分之一，居全国第三位。它是美国科技的主要中心之一，拥有科学家和工程技术人员的数量居全美第一，享有"科技之城"的美誉。

我们刚刚从美国东部来到西海岸，感觉洛杉矶与纽约、华盛顿等东海岸城市有明显的差异。首先是地理气候不同，依山傍海的洛杉矶属于地中海型气侯，一年四季阳光明媚，干燥少雨，气候温和宜人，年平均气温摄氏12度左右，年降雨约350毫米。

其次是道路交通状况不同。洛杉矶以道路宽阔、汽车拥堵而著称，境内高速公路总里程达700多公里，是美国高速公路最发达的城市，也是全美拥有汽车最多的城市。据介绍，近三亿人口的美国拥有汽车两亿多辆，人均0.7辆，其中仅洛杉矶市就拥有900多万辆。每天有600万辆汽车上下班，往返于市中心和郊区住地，汽车长龙把20多条高速公路和市区大街塞得满满的，即便是宽达10个车道的5号和10号高速公路，上下班也经常塞车。

第三是城市布局和建筑特色不同。洛杉矶处于太平洋地震带，1994年的大地震造成该市高速公路塌陷，70多人死亡，因此，市区商业中心仅建有十几栋高层建筑。洛杉矶区域广阔，布局分散，可以说，整座城市是由近百个城郊小镇和数千万个家庭住宅组成的，鳞次栉比的庭院式建筑掩映在绿荫丛中，色彩淡雅，造型精巧，风格各异，遍布于平地和山丘之上。

尽管没有纽约曼哈顿那样蔚为壮观的摩天大楼群，但洛杉矶却拥有许多风格迥异、独具特色的著名建筑，如造型奇特的迪斯尼音乐厅、举行奥斯卡颁奖典礼的柯达剧院等等。位于洛杉矶市中心的迪斯尼音乐厅，建于2003年，是由当代最具影响力的美国建筑师弗兰克·盖里设计的。在他的建筑作品中，最著名的是位于西班牙毕尔巴鄂市的古根海姆博物馆。建成于1997年的古根海姆博物馆甫一落成，便以它奇美的造型、特异的结构和崭新的材料引起举世瞩目，被誉为"世界上最有意义、最美丽的博物馆"。古根海姆博物馆的设计最初来源于盖里对家乡音乐厅的构思，其后几年建成的迪斯尼音乐厅与古根海姆博物馆一样惊世骇俗，这座稀奇古怪的建筑，由不锈钢材质覆面，其外形像是由一块块铝带板捆绑在一起，在阳光照射下，建筑物表面银光闪烁，耀眼夺目。音乐厅采用了最先进的音响设备，被喻为当今世界上最顶尖的音乐厅之一。

文体名城

丰富多彩的洛杉矶不但是美国西部的工业和金融中心，而且还是美国的文化娱乐中心和世界旅游胜地。享誉全球的电影王国好莱坞、引人入胜的迪斯尼乐园、钟灵毓秀的贝佛利山庄、明媚灿烂的海滨风光等，使洛杉矶成为一座举世闻名的"电影城"和"旅游城"。

作为大都会城市，洛杉矶的传媒业也非常发达，全市有 70 多家广播电台、近百家电视台，有英文、中文、西班牙文、日文、越南文等多种语言的报纸、广播和电视，著名的《洛杉矶时报》日发行量经常保持在 100 至 150 万份，而其广告登载量为全美报纸之冠，其影响与地位仅次于《纽约时报》和《华盛顿邮报》，被称为美国第三大报。

第二天上午，我们乘车参观市区时，恰好路过时报办公楼，出乎意料的是，这家大报的总部竟是一座敦实土气的旧式建筑。看到这座不太起眼的办公楼，联想起朴素狭窄的华尔街，令人心生感慨：美国并非我们通常想象的那样，一切东西都是现代的、摩登的、富丽堂皇的，美国人是讲究实际的，在它的现代化和城市化进程中，并非把所谓过时的东西统统拆掉，盲目地追求新潮、现代、豪华、气派。

洛杉矶也是一座体育名城，著名的洛杉矶湖人队是 NBA 中极具影响力的球队，曾 6 次获得全美总冠军。尤其令洛杉矶自豪的是，它还是世界上屈指可数的举办过两届夏季奥运会的城市。1932 年，第十届奥运会在洛杉矶举行，在张学良先生的资助下，中国派代表团第一次参加了奥运会，东北大学学生刘长春作为中国唯一的运动员代表参加了比赛，在 100 和 200 米短跑预赛中，刘长春分列第 5、第 6 名。

时光到了 1984 年，又是在洛杉矶，中国体育代表团重返奥运会，新中国运动员在奥运赛场首次亮相便展示出新兴体育大国的风采。开赛第一天，射击运动员许海峰就拿下了本届奥运会的第一块金牌，实现了中国人在奥运史上奖牌"零的突破"。在这届奥运会上，中国运动员共获得金牌 15 枚，银牌 8 枚，铜牌 9 枚，金牌数位居第四。

洛杉矶似乎与中国有缘，不但洛杉矶奥运会使中华民族洗刷了"东亚病夫"的耻辱，振奋了国人士气，而且近年来，中国（包括港、台）电影演员和导演也在好莱坞这个世界电影舞台上连连获得成功，为华人赢得了荣誉和尊敬，为此，我们应当感谢洛杉矶。

Hollywood: A Kingdom of Movies

The word "Hollywood" is not only a label of the world-famous Big Brother of movie-makers — the "American movie", but also used as a metonym of "American culture". By creating American storylines in the movies, Hollywood has successfully promoted. popularized and profited from Americans' values and lifestyle. In comparison in the eyes of many foreigners, the huge movie market of China is like the "Diamond Mine" needing to be developed.

When speaking of Hollywood, people will immediately associate it with American movies and the Oscar Awards. As for foreign newcomers to Los Angeles, Hollywood is a major attraction, with its great movie studios, blockbusters and shining stars.

A Centennial "Hollywood"

Hollywood is located on the northwestern part of Los Angles. The word Hollywood originally means holly trees,but now it becomes the word representing American Movies. In 1886, a real-estate developer Harvey Wilcox bought this area of land and his wife named it "Hollywood" in February 1887, to memorialize her holly-shaded manor in their hometown Illinois. Thus, the year 1887 has always been regarded as the birth year of "Hollywood" in the history of American movie.

However, Hollywood was known only as a tourist destination in north California from 1887 to 1902, before it had

Chinese Theatre

Hollywood Walk of Fame

anything to do with movies. The American movie industry witnessed its fast development with Edison's invention of the first movie machine in 1896. In October, 1911, a group of filmmakers from New Jersey came to Los Angeles and found it sunny and beautiful, perfect for their studios which depended largely on sunshine for shooting. In the 1930s and 1940s, Hollywood reached its golden age. Columbia Pictures, Metro–Goldwyn–Mayer, Paramount Pictures, 20th Century-Fox, Warner Bros., Universal Pictures, United Artists and RKO Radio Pictures — the eight major film studios and its subsidiaries were all located there. In 1923, to attract more investors, a real-estate company created the big advertisement sign "Hollywood Land" on the hillside, which became the synonymous with the Hollywood studio from then on. Later on, due to the deterioration, the 4 letters of "land" were removed, leaving "Hollywood" only.

Shaking Hands with "Chaplin"

There are many landmarks in Hollywood, such as Hollywood Walk of Fame, Universal Studios and Kodak Theatre, etc. The Hollywood Walk of Fame is one of the most popular attractions. It is located at the heart of Hollywood; which used to be the filmmaking center, and is now a place to commemorate the glamorous stars that made it famous. More than 5,000 five-pointed pink terrazzo stars are embedded in the sidewalk along the boulevard, and they are inlaid with five kinds of brass emblems indicating

Shaking Hands with "Charles Chaplin"

five categories of the honoree's outstanding contributions in film, TV, radio, phonograph record and comedy/tragedy masks. And 2,500 of them belong to film stars including both Hollywood hotshots and Hong Kong action movie star like Bruce Lee and Jackie Chan from China.

On the west side of the Hollywood Walk of Fame there is a theatre that built in Chinese style as that was a place to premiere movies that were candidates for Oscars. The architecture, with its distinctive Chinese wing-angled eaves against gaudy and showy colors, has become a landmark of Hollywood. Nearly 150 celebrities have left their handprints, footprints, or autographs on the cement of the theater's forecourt, including Hong Kong's director John Woo. What is more interesting, you can even find a "Duck Feet" print of Donald Duck.

The stars on the Hollywood Walk of Fame attract numerous movie fans. When we finally got to the Chinese Theatre by walking through blocks embedded with these stars, we found the front of its gates full with of tourists. Performers costumed as Chaplin and Spiderman were roaming around trying to get people to take photos with them. As I am an admirer of work of Charlie Chaplin, I enthusiastically went to shake hands with the Chaplin imitator and have a photo taken with him. "Chaplin" asked me if I was "from China?" I said, "Yes, I am from China." "Where?" "Hebei Province." and he replied, "Oh, thank you!"

Novelty and Excitement

We were feeling excited after visiting Hollywood Walk of Fame. Next stop was the theme park—Universal Studios Hollywood. It covers about 1200 square kilometers (1800 mu), with many avenues and architectures for location shooting. Since the 1950s, the American movie industry was on the wane due to the fierce competition of the TV industry. Many studios moved out and began to shoot on location around the world. Therefore, many studios were changed into shopping and entertainment centers or even rebuilt into residential zones. The Universal Studio Company was the original source behind transforming the huge studio into various popular amusement projects.

At the entrance of Universal Studios, a group of caricatured figure statues first greeted us: a director busy in shooting, a cameraman with an attentive look, a female assistant holding the megaphone high and others.

After passing by these statues, we got on the tourist car in the studio and headed for the park rides where we could personally experience the impressive special effects. When the ride drove across a wooden bridge, the bridge suddenly collapsed and the car fell down causing us to scream in fear. Then the ride moved into a cave, and a huge monster jumped out, roaring and howling as if it would swallow us. As soon as we landed safely on a hillside, the lightning flash and thunder rumbled in the sky. Immediately, rain poured down and violent floods rushed toward us. We hurriedly fled to a steam only to find the earth quaking, and huge stones rolling down from the split hill, which made our car almost overturn.

Soon we seemed to get used to these "adventures" and thought the next wouldn't be much different. However, we were surprised when the car

Universal Studio

Fighting over Water

drove to the side of a lake and the gas station in the middle of lake suddenly exploded into fire. At once, the water flooded the road while heavy smoke filled the air, and before we realized what had happened we were already in the lake. At this moment, a huge shark appeared and swallowed a boat? Blood bubbled out from the lake. Then the shark jumped out of the lake and opened its bloody mouth towards our car. Women were screaming, but in a minute we all were laughing when they thought about the thrilling and exciting scenes.

The next stop was the Water-world, where we sat in three-sided stands around a water stage against a castle background, to watch the special effect performance of the TV show, "Miami Vice." Before the performance, on each of the three sides, the actors playing sailors would encourage the audience to shout as loudly as possible. If the shout of one side was not loud enough, the sailor would pretend to lose his temper and pour water on the audience. Of course this was just a warming-up exercise to enliven the atmosphere. After that, the show began. A group of robbers rushed in by a motor yacht as they shot at the castle. The guards immediately fought back and started a series of breathtakingly intense scenes: the bloody wrestling, the exploding of oil tanks and the castle burst into flames. When the robbers took the upper hand, the castle's supporting forces arrived in time, which sank the motor yacht and brought airplanes down, and shot most of the robbers. With the chief robber being arrested, the show came to an end, but we were still overwhelmed with admiration for its vivid and superb performance.

Attractive and Applaudable

The change of Hollywood, from a remote village in the suburbs of Los Angeles at the beginning of the 20th century, to the modern movie kingdom in a matter of only 20 years, is nothing short of a miracle. Through the decades, Hollywood has established many classic genres, including westerns, comedies, musicals, romances, cops and robber movies, gangster movies, horror films, sci-fi and war movies, etc, all of which constitute the most popular cinematography.

Hollywood movies created not only an unprecedented record in global film distribution and box-office success, but also a world leading artistic quality. Many movies created in the early years of Hollywood such as *The Great Dictator*, *Gone with the Wind*, *Waterloo Bridge*, *Rebecca*, *Citizen Kane*, *Casablanca*, etc have become classics in their respective genres.

From the late 1940s to the mid-1950s, the Hollywood movie industry declined somewhat as some of the big movie companies stopped shooting and screening since they couldn't compete with television. But in the late 1960s, it began to revitalize. From the 1970s to the 1980s, young directors such as Coppola, Lucas and Spielberg brought new energy to Hollywood. These men had the sensitivity and talent to match art with great commercial value in movies such as *The Godfather*, *Kramer vs. Kramer* and *Star Wars*, *Jurassic Park* and so on.

The 1990s witnessed another flourishing age of Hollywood, with a list of globally famous blockbusters such as *Forrest Gump*, *Schindler's List*, *Titanic* and *Saving Private* Ryan which all enjoyed commercial and artistic success. Meanwhile, Hollywood became a place for innovation, a place to develop new technology. A new generation of sci-fi films like *Star Wars* and *Superman* born in this period, with their modern technique presenting spectacular and miraculous effects through combining scientific fantasy, disaster and adventure into one, brought Hollywood tremendous creative vitality and a rapid increase in the movie screening and box office returns. This is a great contribution to the development of the world movie industry.

The Metonym of "American Culture"

Since the 1930s and the 1940s, Hollywood has become more a metonym of "American culture" than a synonym of the world famous "American Movie". When it swept the world film market with its irresistible surges of shock being sustained by many countries, it has turned to be a trend of "Hollywood Phenomenon", which exerted influences on the global culture, economy and even politics, far beyond the limit of film industry.

However, the world was surprised that America managed to change movie entertainment into a huge lucrative cultural and economic industry. Statistics showed that in 2000, Hollywood movies' export revenues reached 12 billion dollars, and the total revenue of movies and its related industries were up to 60 billion dollars. Since the year of 2000, American movie and TV audio-visual products have preceded those of the Aerospace industry and now rank first in export products. Meanwhile, together with the movie products, Hollywood has been successfully exporting American culture, promoting American values, lifestyle, even munitions. It is said that Hollywood should owe the global popularity of blockbusters to its unshakable ties with American government, the Wall Street and gun sellers. Actually, Hollywood seems to have acted as the spokesman of the U.S. State Department and the outpost of the U.S. Department of Defense, "American blockbuster is a four-in-one big deal of culture, politics, military and economy."

The so-called Hollywood blockbuster is underpinned by a huge sum of money and much publicity. To make a blockbuster, tens of millions or even hundreds of millions are often needed, and to handle the marketing and publicity campaign costs another millions more. The investment is huge, but once the movie succeeds, a fat profit will be rewarded. Take *Titanic* as an example, with an investment of 200 million dollars, it made up to 1.83 billion dollars at the box-office, which set a record of the highest cost with the most return in movie history.

Film Still from Titanic

Film Still from Hero

Hollywood owes a big thanks to its huge domestic market. So far, Hollywood movies not only occupy 85% of the global box-office, but also hold 96% of the domestic market share. In 1999, the costs of what Americans spent on movie industry (including box-office, videotape and the Cinemax on TV) were up to 39 billion dollars, in which 35 billion dollars were spent on feature films made in the Unites States. In the total income of the American movie industry, the box-office receipts only account for about a quarter, while the "post-filming" products, such as related books, toys and games, clothing, shoes and hats, soundtrack, theme park and other merchandise, have the largest share, often several times higher than that of the box office.

Aside from the developed market, the relatively mature legal system and a huge audience, the prosperity of Hollywood movies also lies in the unit-producer system, the idol-shaping star system and a series of successful movie-making systems. In the U.S., the producer is the real master of the film, and also the key to its success. Producers are directing behind the scenes while movie stars performing on the screen, who, native-born or from abroad, are recognized as the trump card of American movies' success.

A Potential "Diamond Mine"

The movie business is largely dependent on the technology of the culture industry, to promote it, with its development of television, audio-video, publishing, toy production, tourism and other related culture industries. The entertainment features of film products and the public attribute of the cinematographic art determined movie industry to be the most energetic and dynamic part of the culture industry with unique developing advantages.

Movies are always a popular form of entertainment in any country, China is no exception. People like watching movies and therefore the movie industry has big potential. Experts say that there are 250-350 million people in China who can afford movie entertainment at present. With the development of the Chinese economy and the rise of per-capita income within the following ten years, this number may double. Therefore this huge movie market is treated as the undeveloped "diamond mine" by foreigners.

Although the potential is boundless, there are other forms of entertainments including TV, internet, etc. that rival the movie industry, causing a decrease in movie audiences and box office revenues. The Chinese moviegoer reached 27.9 billion in 1979 and decreased to 220 million in 2001, only one in two people went to the cinema per year, less than one tenth of that in the United States. There were five to six hundred movies produced in America which earned a box-office receipt of 9.5 billion in 2001, and each American went to the cinema an average of 5.7 times.

Since 2003, our country's movie production has increased steadily and successfully in quantity, quality, box-office receipt and export sales. The quantity of Chinese films was around 100 in previous years, while the amount reached 260 in 2005 and increased to 330 in 2006 (excluding 100 digital movies made for TV broadcasting). In 2003, the box-office receipts of Chinese films accounted for more than 50% of the total box-office receipt, and in 2005 this number reached 55.1%, breaking the long foreign movies' predominance. Meanwhile, the Chinese film has gotten the highest box-office for three years in a row. In 2003, the box-office receipt of the movie *Hero* was 250 million Yuan. In 2004, the movie *Kung Fu Hustle* got a box-office receipt of 170 million Yuan and in 2005, the movie *The Promise* earned 180 million Yuan. The export amount of Chinese movies increased from 25 in 2003 to 69 in 2005, and the revenue of export movies reached 1.6499 billion Yuan from 500 million Yuan. Among the 49 movies imported to China in 2005, 26 were American movies, accounting for 58.06% of the imported movies. Although the Chinese movies have made big progress, compared to the foreign movie industry, they still have obvious advantages in quantity and box-office receipt. Take the year 2005 as an example. The 260 Chinese movies produced a box-office receipt of 1.127 billion Yuan while the 49 foreign movies had produced a box-office receipt of 918 million Yuan, and the gap of the box-office receipt of a single movie between Chinese and foreign movies is huge, too. For every Chinese movie that earned 4.33 million Yuan, a single American movie reached 18.73 million Yuan.

This data suggests that in the recent years, the Chinese movie industry has made a big progress and has maintained a developed momentum. But generally speaking, the quality has yet to be improved, and the market competitiveness needs to be stronger, an industry with core competence and international competitiveness is about to formed, as the professors of Chinese movie industry said, movie is a product, and behind it formed an industry, while in China there is only product, the industry has not been formed yet.

电影王国好莱坞

好莱坞不仅仅是称霸世界的"美国电影"代名词，更是"美国文化"的同义语。好莱坞在拍摄美国电影、编造美国故事、赚取世界货币的同时，也成功地推销了美国人的价值观和生活方式。中国庞大的电影市场被外国人认为是有待开发的"钻石矿"。

提起好莱坞，人们会立刻联想到美国电影和奥斯卡金像奖。来到洛杉矶，首选好莱坞，对于外国游客来讲，好莱坞影城、好莱坞大片、好莱坞明星太有吸引力了。

百年"冬青林"

好莱坞位于洛杉矶西北部，英语 Hollywood，原是"冬青林"的意思，后来成为美国电影的代名词。1886 年，一个叫哈维·威尔科克斯的房地产商人买下了这块土地，1887 年 2 月，威尔科克斯夫人为了怀念她在伊利诺伊州故乡冬青树环抱的庄园，便把这块土地取名"好莱坞"，美国电影史通常把 1887 年定为"好莱坞"诞生年。

然而，从 1887 至 1902 年，这里是加州南部的一个旅游胜地，与电影毫无关系，1896 年爱迪生发明第一架电影机后，美国电影进入高速发展时期。1911 年 10 月一批从新泽西州来的电影工作者到达洛杉矶，发现这里日照充足，景色美丽，非常适合当时要全部靠阳光拍片的要求，就在此建立起第一个电影制片厂——"内斯特影片公司"。以后又有好多家制片公司来此设厂或拍片，到三四十年代达到好莱坞的鼎盛时期，哥伦比亚、米高梅、派拉蒙、二十世纪福克斯、华纳兄弟、环球、联美和雷尼屋等美国八大制片公司以及它们所属的电影制片厂、电影洗印厂和电影机械厂等绝大部分电影工业都集中在这里。1923 年一家房地产公司为了招揽生意，在山坡上树立起了巨大的

Hollywood Land 的广告牌，从此成为"好莱坞"电影城的标志。后来"Land"4 个字母标牌由于损坏被拆掉，只剩下 Hollywood 了。

握手"卓别林"

好莱坞影城有多处景观，主要有星光大道、环球影城、柯达剧场等，名声最大的当属星光大道。星光大道是好莱坞的心脏，曾经是电影制作中心，现在成为展示演艺界明星风采的地方。在星光大道两侧步行道上镶嵌着 5000 多颗粉红色大理石五角星，五角星里镶有五种青铜图案，分别代表电影、电视、广播、唱片和舞台等五个领域取得突出成就的明星，其中电影明星 2500 多名。他们当中不但有好莱坞大腕，也有中国香港武打影星李小龙和成龙的大名。

在星光大道偏西侧有一座中国剧院，作为奥斯卡参评影片的演出场所。这座飞檐凸翘、大红大绿的中国寺庙风格的建筑，几乎成了好莱坞的一种标志。在剧院门前的水泥地面上，印有 150 多个著名影星的手印、脚印和签名，其中有香港电影导演吴宇森的印记，更有趣的是，竟然还有"唐老鸭"的鸭掌。

星光大道的明星效应，吸引了无数的影迷、游客到此寻觅参观。当我们沿着镶满五星图案的人行道来到中国剧院时，只见剧院门前挤满了游人，卓别林和蜘蛛侠的装扮者在眼前晃来晃去，招徕游客与其拍照。看到扮相逼真的"卓别林"，我便上前与他热烈地握手拍照。"卓别林"高兴地问道：From China（来自中国）？我回答：Yes, I am from China（是的，我来自中国）。Where（什么地方）？ Hebei Province（河北省）。 Oh, thank you（噢，谢谢）！

新奇与刺激

参观完星光大道意犹未尽，又去体验主题公园——好莱坞环球影城(Universal Studios Hollywood)。环球影城占地约 1800 亩，有许多供拍摄外景的街道及建筑物。20 世纪 50 年代以后，由于电视的激烈竞争，美国电影业逐渐衰落，许多制片厂陆续迁出，到世界各地现场拍摄。这样，好莱坞的许多摄影设施便空闲起来，有的变为商场和娱乐中心，有的甚至拆建成新的住宅区，环球电影公司则别出心裁，把巨大的摄影场地改造成丰富多彩的游乐项目，结果大受欢迎。

来到环球影城入口处，首先看到矗立在广场上的一组人物雕塑：指挥拍片的导演、神情专注的摄影师和高举话筒的女助手，动作和表情极为夸张。

进入影城后，先是登上游览车，身临其境观看拍摄电影的各种精彩特技场面：当车子驶上木桥时，突然咔嚓一声，木桥断了，车子跌落，游客发出惊叫声。接着驶进山洞，一只巨大的怪兽出现在车旁，冲着你咆哮、嚎叫，似乎要把游客连同汽车一起抓过去、吞噬掉。刚来到山村野坡，马上电闪雷鸣，大雨倾盆，汹涌的洪水从山坡上滚滚冲来。行进到一座山涧，忽然大地震颤，山崩地裂，巨石滚下，车身倾斜。

几次"历险"后，觉得不会再有什么新奇好看的了。不然，当游览车刚行驶到一座湖边，湖中心的加油站立即爆炸起火，随着浓烟腾起，湖水流进车道，人车置身湖水。此时，一头巨大的鲨鱼游过来，掀翻了一只小船，水面上顿时冒出一股血水。接着，鲨鱼冲出水面，对着车厢张开血盆大口，吓得女士们失声喊叫，惊叫之后则是一片欢笑，让游客充分体验了惊险刺激的快乐。

环游摄影棚之后，便来到"水世界"，进入三面看台、一面城堡、中间水区的表演场，等待观看精彩的特技表演节目——"迈阿密罪恶"。演出开始前，靠近看台的三位水手分别指挥各自看台上的观众队伍齐声高喊，显示力量，如果哪方声音较弱被他方压倒，水手就会"大发雷霆"，提起水桶向观众泼去。当然，这是演出前的插曲，为了活跃全场气氛，调动观众情绪。表演开始了，一群强盗驾着摩托快艇闯入城堡，开枪射击，守卫者与匪徒展开枪战和格斗，打斗动作特技高难，场面激烈火爆。在强盗得势、耀武扬威之际，城堡支援部队到了，摩托艇冲击，飞机坠落，油灌爆炸，城堡燃起熊熊大火……最后匪徒大部被击毙，匪首束手就擒，整场表演形象逼真，奇妙险绝，感觉畅快淋漓。

叫座又叫好

好莱坞这个20世纪初洛杉矶郊外的荒凉小村，在短短二三十年的时间里，就神话般地崛起一座世界上最大的现代化电影城，并蔚然成为一片茂密不衰的"常青树"，这不能不说是一个奇迹。在几十年创作和生产实践中，好莱坞逐步形成了许多经典的影片类型，如西部片、喜剧片、歌舞片、爱情片、强盗片、警匪片、恐怖片、科幻片、战争片等等，各种类别的影片构成了好莱坞深受观众欢迎的电影艺术。

好莱坞电影不但创造了在全球影片发行量和卖座率的空前纪录，而且在艺术质量上也达到了世界领先水平，早年好莱坞的很多影片，如《大独裁者》、《乱世佳人》、《魂断蓝桥》、《蝴蝶梦》、《公民凯恩》、《卡萨布兰卡》等，都成为世界电影史上的经典作品。

从 20 世纪 40 年代末到 50 年代中期，好莱坞电影因为遭受到诸如大制片公司被迫放弃电影和发行放映业务以及电视冲击等，曾经一度走向衰落，60 年代中后期又开始振兴。到了七八十年代，好莱坞成长起了像科波拉、卢卡斯、斯皮尔伯格等一批著名青年导演，他们恰当地把握了商业价值与艺术追求之间的微妙关系，先后拍出了像《教父》、《克莱默夫妇》、《星球大战》、《侏罗纪公园》等一批既叫座又叫好的影片。

进入 90 年代，好莱坞佳作迭出，陆续推出了像《阿甘正传》《辛德勒名单》、《泰坦尼克号》、《拯救大兵瑞恩》等一批享誉全球的影片，使美国电影真正走向商业与艺术的双重成功，再创辉煌盛世。同时，好莱坞影片在技术上不断创新和发展，像《星球大战》、《超人》等新一代科幻片，采用现代制作技术，集科幻片、灾难片、惊险片之大成，场面壮观、惊险神奇，它们的出现，激发了好莱坞巨大的创造活力，并直接导致了美国影片制作和票房收入的直线上升，同时也对世界电影事业的发展作出了贡献。

"美国文化"的同义语

从 20 世纪三四十年代开始，好莱坞就不仅仅是称霸世界的"美国电影"代名词，更是"美国文化"的同义语。当它以汹涌之势席卷世界电影市场，被许多国家视作洪水猛兽而想方设法予以抵挡的时候，它也就超越了电影的界限，成为影响世界文化、经济乃至政治的好莱坞现象。

然而，不得不令人叹服的是，美国人成功地运用商业法则和工业化生产模式，把电影娱乐业搞成了文化经济的大产业。据统计，2000 年好莱坞大片出口收入达到 120 亿美元，影视业和相关产业的总收入高达 600 亿美元。2000 年以后，美国影视和音像产品超过航空航天业，成为第一大出口产品。不仅是出口电影产品，而且是出口美国文化，好莱坞在拍摄美国电影、编造美国故事、赚取世界货币的同时，也成功地推销了美国人的价值观、生活方式及军火商品。有人讲，美国大片盛行全球，独步天下，靠的就是好莱坞跟美国政府、华尔街及军火商的铁关系，好莱坞事实上充当了美国国务院的代言人和国防部的前哨兵，"美国大片就是文化、政治、军事、经济四位一体的大买卖"。

所谓好莱坞大片，都是用巨额美金堆出来的，靠现代传媒吹出来的。现在拍制一部大片动辄几千万甚至上亿美元，另外还要拿出几千万美元用于市场营销、宣传造势。虽然投资巨大，一旦成功，回报率很高，如《泰坦尼克号》，投资 2 亿美元，票房收入 18.3 亿美元，创造了电影史上投资最多、票房收入最高的纪录。

好莱坞电影能够称霸世界，首先是因为美国拥有巨大的国内市场。目前，不但全球影院 85% 的片源来自好莱坞，而且好莱坞电影还牢牢控制着美国本土 96% 的市场份额。1999 年美国人花费在电影上（含票房、录像带和电视频道电影）的支出为 390 亿美元，其中 350 亿美元是花费在了美国国产故事片上。在美国全部电影产业收入中，票房收入仅占四分之一强，而录像带、电视频道以及与影片内容相关的图书出版、游戏玩具、服装鞋帽、原声音乐和主题公园等其他相关收入，即"电影后"产品开发的收入则是大头，往往是一部电影票房收入的几倍。

好莱坞电影的成功，除了成熟的市场经济、法制环境和庞大的国内观众群外，还有统一专权的制片人制度、塑造大众偶像的明星制度等一系列成功的好莱坞制片制度。在美国，影片真正的主人是制片人，制片人是决定影片成败的关键。在幕后指挥的是制片人，在前台表演的则是好莱坞明星，这一大批来自美国本土和世界各国的好莱坞明星成了美国电影征服世界的杀手锏。

有待开发的"钻石矿"

电影是以高新技术为支撑的高智能、高投入、高产出的文化产业，对于带动电视业、音像业、出版业、玩具业、旅游业等相关文化产业的发展具有重要的拉动作用。电影产品的娱乐功能，电影艺术的大众属性，决定了电影产业是文化产业中最具活力与生命力的部分，具有独特的发展优势。

不论在哪个国家，电影总是人们喜闻乐见的娱乐方式。在中国，电影艺术深受国民大众的欢迎，电影产业有着巨大的发展潜力。据专家测算，目前有电影消费能力的中国人口已经达到 2.5 至 3.5 亿，而且未来十年，随着中国经济的发展和人均收入的提高，这一数字有可能会翻一番，这一庞大的电影市场被外国人认为是有待开发的"钻石矿"。

虽然发展前景广阔，但是近年来，由于电视、互联网及其他娱乐方式的冲击，使我国电影观众人数明显下降，票房收入大幅度下滑。1979 年，我国电影观众曾经达到 279 亿人次，而 2001 年则降到 2.2 亿人次，人均到影院看电影仅为 0.5 人次，不足美国的十分之一。美国每年生产电影五六百部，2001年创造了 95 亿美元的票房收入，人均进影院看电影 5.7 次。

2003 年以来，我国电影生产的数量、质量、票房收入和出口销售稳定攀升，连创佳绩。国产影片的数量前几年一直徘徊在每年 100 部左右，2005 年达到 260 部，2006 年增长到 330 部（这不包括为电视播放拍摄的数字电影 100部）。2003 年国产影片的票房收入占票房总收入的比例突破 50%，2005 年达到 55.1%，打破了多年来外国影片票房收入领先的局面。同时，连续三年，单片最高票房均为国产影片，2003 年为《英雄》2.5 亿元，2004 年为《功夫》1.7亿元，2005 年为《无极》1.8 亿元。国产影片的出口数量也由 2003 年的 25 部上升到 2005 年的 69 部，出口收入由 5 亿元提高到 16.499 亿元。2005 年进口影片为 49 部，其中美国影片为 26 部，占当年进口影片的 53.06%。尽管国产影片有了很大进步，但是，从影片数量与票房收入的比例看，外国影片仍占有明显优势，如 2005 年 260 部国产影片的票房收入为 11.27 亿元，49 部外国影片的票房收入为 9.18 亿元，从单片平均票房看，国产影片为 433 万元人民币，外国影片则为 1873 万元人民币。

以上数据表明，近几年中国电影业取得了突破性进展，呈现出良好的发展势头。但是，总体上看，国产影片质量不高，市场竞争力不强，尚未形成具有核心竞争力和国际竞争力的产业，正如中国电影界人士所指出的，电影是一个产品，电影后边是一个产业，目前中国电影只有产品没有产业。

Disney: A Paradise of Recreation

Disney is a place that not only brings joy to children, but also takes adults back to their childhood. "Disney has shown the world a new way of profit-making, that is, to change laughter into dollars, and build profit by the pursuit of joy rather than the deprivation of it". By contrast, the theme parks in our country are always found to be lacking creativity and full of repetition. Some are poorly managed and roughly manufactured. Some are bizarre and motley and some are overpriced.

The culture of Disneyland as created by Americans is more of a miracle than a fairy tale, which is epitomized in its slogan: "Disneyland provides mankind with the best recreation form".

Happy Moments

We came to visit Disneyland on Friday, May 26, together with thousands of visitors who were crowded on the square, lining up to enter the park. Finally it was our turn. As we entered, we noticed a slope decorated with yellow flowers in the shape of the word "50" — Disneyland was celebrating its 50th birthday.

We strolled down Main Street enjoying the colorful scenery which went from the entrance to the furthermost part of the park. Both sides of the street had structures which were representative of American landmarks in the 19th century. We came to the center of the park and photographed each other with the statue of Disney's founder — Walt Disney. To enjoy all fun of Disneyland — more than 60 sorts of entertainments — would take three days, but we had only half a day. So we followed the advice of the guide and only chose a few rides to experience, such as "Indiana Jones Adventure," "Jungle Cruise," "Future Time and Space." "3D Movie" and "A Small World," etc.

Logo of 50 Years Anniversary

Small World

Jungle Cruise was both exciting and enjoyable, but before you can get on the ride, you need to wait in line. Once we were in, we entered a castle, and went through many different houses before we finally set out on an adventure boat. The boat bounced up and down, left and right, across a jungle. We saw things like elephants with their trunks popping out of the woods and Indians dancing around the campfire. The boat went slowly through the water as tourists leisurely enjoyed various performances and the scenery. Suddenly the boat lifted onto a rail and driven through a dark tunnel. After a sharp turn came the most exciting moment: when the boat gradually emerged from the tunnel, we found that we were hanging in the air! We screamed as our boat fell into the water!

The Future Time and Space was my favorite exhibit, far more exciting than the roller coaster. It was a combination of a ride with electric seats and an elaborate movie. It's different from the outdoor roller coaster in which you can see what is going to happen, The Future Time and Space creates virtual scenes in which the sights, sounds and movements are replicated to make the experience feel real. In a dark room, we were fastened to a computer-controlled electric seat of a spaceship. The screen around us constantly changed as the spaceship took off; there was speeding up and rolling around to make you feel like you are travelling through the space:

sometimes just floating in the sky, or rushing into the star and then blasting into pieces; sometimes falling into an abyss, crossing through a tunnel, or fighting against the alien chariot in fierce gunfire... You never knew what would happen next but you knew it would be suspenseful and tense, so you were always surprised and on the edge of your seat.

Next we went to a 3D Disney movie which was very interesting. We were seated in special chairs and given 3D glasses to wear. Everything was rigged up to make coincide with the movie and, even though you knew it wasn't real, you would still get scared because it felt like it was. Suddenly the man fighting in the screen might take a strike at you, and then "Bang" when you were about to hide from him, you found yourself right in his trap; then something would explode loudly as if it was the end of the world and the scene would become chaotic. At that moment, hundreds of thousands of rats ran toward the audience, and it felt as if they were scuttling up your trousers. The girls were scared to death, screaming and smacking at their legs. Later we found out that to enhance the experience, cool air was blown from under the seat, making you feel like rats were running around beneath you. At one point, a huge dog leaned its head out of the screen and sneezed, and we immediately felt spit on our face, which was achieved by another special device tied to the seat.

The parade float at 5 o'clock every afternoon might be the highlight program in Disneyland, or it could be called the Disney Carnival. Many children took their seats by the roadside early, waiting for the floats to come. When the music sounded, all the children sprang up to their feet, jumping and cheering. The float drove forward slowly and many cartoon characters in colorful costumes ran back and forth around it, waving

Float Performance

to the visitors. The cartoon figures were the most eye-catching, expecially Mickey. The floats went by at great speed and it almost made you wish that time could stand still so you enjoy all the performance leisurely. Cameras were constantly flashing at the smiling faces: there came the humorous Donald Duck, cheerful Bambi, beautiful Snow White, and elegant Cinderella, glittering Bolton, robust Tarzan...The huge caravan brought the day to a climatic close.

A Talented Creation

Disneyland was the brilliant creation of Walt Disney, whose biggest dream was to make an amazing paradise, a miraculous amusement park for children and their parents to have fun together.

Walt Disney was an early American film producer and famous animator in Hollywood. The fictional characters he created—Mickey Mouse and Donald Duck—were popularized around the world since they first appeared in the cartoon *Steamboat Willie* in 1928. Mickey Mouse has almost replaced Uncle Sam as the symbol of the U.S.

To meet the audience's demand and accomplish his own dream, Walt Disney founded The Walt Disney Company in 1952 and started the construction of Disneyland. His dream came true in the year 1955, when the first Disneyland was opened in Anaheim, Southern California. At that time America was in a period of economic prosperity after the ending of WW II and the Korean War. Disneyland appeared just in time to satisfy the entertainment need of American's young generation.

After the popularity of the first Disneyland, the company built a second park in Orlando, Florida in 1971. The park occupied 111 square kilometers, several times bigger than the former one, with 3 theme parks, 18 restaurants, 3 golf courses, a night club, a water park, a camp site and some large conference halls, at a cost of 766 million dollars.

At the beginning of 1980s, Disney began its business expansion abroad, bringing its prototype to Tokyo and Paris. On April 15, 1983, when the cherry was blooming, Tokyo Disneyland had its grand opening with an investment of 150 billion yen. Since then, the park has received 260 million visitors, and created a big profit several times higher than the investment.

In 1992, Disney Company invested its fourth park in Paris. Disneyland had once been regarded as the invasion of American culture and resisted by France, but Mickey Mouse and Donald Duck was too compelling to be refused, and ultimately the ancient European culture had to give way.

As Disneyland was about to celebrate its 50th birthday in 2005, a fifth park on a global scale was opened in Hong Kong. On July 17, Disneyland held its birthday celebration in California. Arnold Schwarzenegger, the former U.S. television action-movie star and Governor of California and some other stars attended the ceremony.

Within half a century since its opening, California Disneyland has received 500 million tourists, about 10 million tourists average per year. In 2004, the previous 4 Disneylands attracted a total of 30 million tourists, and in 2005, with the newly-joined Hong Kong Disneyland, the number reached 35 million. Statistics show that every year tourists might eat 4 million hamburgers, 1.6 million hot-dogs and 3.2 million ice-creams in each park. The ticket price of Los Angeles Disneyland was 59 dollars, and with 35

50 Years Anniversary of Disney Land

Arnold Schwarzenegger on the Anniversary Celebration

million tourists coming to the global 5 parks, the annual ticket income of Disneyland Company, in average, would be up to 2 billion dollars. In addition, other consumptions in food, housing, transportation, travel, shopping and entertainment, together with the revenue of film and television industry, and the income from the trademark licensing of Disney animated images, constituted a total of 28.4 billion dollars for Walt Disney Company in 2003. With such a high income, no wonder that the former CEO of the Walt Disney Company, Mr. Eisner's annual salary plus stock option income reached 575.6 million dollars, listed on the top among the biggest 365 public companies in America.

The Key to Success

For more than 50 years, Disneyland has attracted tens of thousands of visitors. What, then, made it so fascinating? The exciting entertainments or the lovely cartoon characters? At least one thing is clear: this is a place which can bring laughter to children, bring childhood memories to adults, and a escape away from strife and sadness. "Here you can step forward to the future, to your dream world, or fly back to the past, no bother what is happening at present."

The key to Disney's success is its brilliant and innovative ideas in meeting people's needs and bringing comfort to the human soul. When Disney's founder Walt Disney died on December 15, 1966, Americans found it hard to find the words to describe him. In the eulogy of its Evening News, CBS said, "Disney was a creative genius, who brought laughter to the whole world...whose contributions in healing and comforting human soul might be bigger than any psychiatrist in the world."

Someone said with emotion, "Disney has demonstrated a new way to make profit, that is, to convert laughter into money, and build profit upon the pursuit of joy instead of depriving it from people."

In management, the Disney mission statement can be defined as "Customer first & Service in detail", and each employee is trained to follow this credo.

Disney felt that to make the customers happy meant that they would come back. So, for instance, the corporation takes great pains in training the cleaning staff, because they come into contact with the tourists most often. In Tokyo Disneyland some cleaners were students working on their vocation. Although they work only for two months, they must go through a 3-day specialized training before they start. Besides cleaning, they also learn to take pictures, give directions, and even change a diaper for a baby.

For 20 years since the grand opening, Tokyo Disneyland helped 20 thousand lost children to find their parents, although they did not make this information public for fear that it would keep people away. Instead, they set up 10 Child-care Centers, where the lost child would be sent as soon as they were discovered, and the staff there would try to connect with the parents. When parents arrived, they always found their children drinking Cola, eating chips and hamburgers happily.

As a model for the global theme parks, Disneyland has brought laughter and sweet memories to 500 million people around the world for 50 years. However, confronted with an "electronic age" of internet and computer

Statue of Walt Disney

games in the present changing society, will Disney be prosperous forever? Eisner, the former CEO of Disney answered confidently, "Disney will never come to an end, as long as imagination exists in the world, Disney will keep growing."

What to Learn?

Since the middle of 1980s, China has seen a trend of theme parks popping up all over. But they have not been as profitable as one would expect with such rapid development of the tourist industry. Data show that for the latest 20 years, 2500 sorts of various man-made sceneries such as "palace", "town" or "garden" were built in a frenzy, with a total investment of 150 billion Yuan. Some parks lack creation and are too similar to others. Some are poorly managed and roughly manufactured, and some are wired and overpriced. Of the 2500 parks, 70% are in deficit, 20% break even; only the 10% left have made a profit. With the exception of the success of "Splendid China", "Window of the World" in Shenzhen, "The World Park" in Beijing, "The World Expo" in Kunming, "Suzhou Amusement Land" and "Wuxi Movie and TV Base" in Jiangsu Province, "the Town of the Song Dynasty" in Hangzhou and over 20 others, the rest of the theme parks are all in a poor condition, not only wasting a huge amount of land and investments, but are also disrespectful to Chinese culture and Chinese spirit.

It is a popular saying in the domestic tourist industry that the lifespan of Chinese theme park is only about three to four years, which, according to the experts, results from hasty investment and construction without sufficient discussion and detailed researches, unhealthy competition due to blind imitation and duplication. Aimlessly following suit and building at their will might be one of the main evidence for the fickleness of some Chinese, who rushed for a quick success. Entertainment need to be created, and parks to be built, but the point is that we should put our time and energy in content innovation, preserving cultural identity and refined management.

娱乐天堂迪斯尼

这是一个能够让孩子欢笑、让成人找回童真的地方。"迪斯尼为全世界示范了一种新的生财模式：将欢乐换算成金币，将利润构筑在追求快乐，而不是剥夺之上。"比较而言，国内主题公园有的内容重复，缺乏创意；有的粗制滥造，经营不善；有的光怪陆离，坑人骗钱。

迪斯尼乐园是美国人创造的文化，它不仅创造了一个童话，而且创造了一个奇迹，那就是它提出的口号："迪斯尼给人类提供最好的娱乐方式。"

欢乐时光

5月26日，星期五，当我们来到迪斯尼乐园门外广场时，只见人山人海，数以千计的游客汇聚在广场上，等待入园。我们随着排队的人流依次入园后，看到对面的堤坡上用菊黄色的鲜花装饰成的"50"字样格外鲜艳醒目，这是迪斯尼乐园在纪念它的50岁生日。

进入乐园后，先是在中央大街上漫步，观看眼花缭乱的街景，中央大街从大门口一直伸展到园内深处，两侧都是模仿美国19世纪最有代表性的街道建筑，在东园中央，竖立着创始人沃尔特·迪斯尼的雕像，大家挨个上前拍照留念，随后去参观体验精彩的娱乐项目。迪斯尼乐园共有60多个娱乐项目，全部游玩需要三天时间，我们仅有半天多时间，只能按导游的介绍，选择了印第安部落、激流探险、未来时空、动感电影、小小世界等几个项目。

急流探险是个既刺激又愉快的游戏，但需要排队等候。当我们进入一个城堡后，在不同的房子里绕来绕去，最终坐上探险船启航出发。小船忽上忽下，忽左忽右，在一片丛林中穿行，两边时而是大象从丛林中伸出鼻子，时而是印第安人在篝火旁载歌载舞。小船慢悠悠地行进，游人可以轻松地观看各种表演和风光。当小船咔咔地被推上链条时，最刺激惊险的一幕来临了：穿过一个漆黑的过道，一个猛的转弯，当你感到有明显亮光继而是刺眼的阳光时，你已经被悬在空中，随着一声声尖叫，小船和乘客几乎是自由落体般从洞口跌落到水面。

未来时空是一项最富刺激性的游戏，比坐过山车还要惊险。它是一个由电动座椅与星空影片结合起来的项目。与坐过山车感觉不同的是，过山车是在空旷的室外真实地高速翻滚，你能知道将面临的是什么。而未来时空则是用一种虚拟的场景，模拟真实的感觉。在一间漆黑的屋子里，你被固定在电动车上，座椅由电脑操纵，随着银幕上情景的变幻，太空船在起飞、加速、翻滚，使人好似进入太空，忽而在星空中遨游、一跃千里；忽而冲向星体、炸得粉碎；忽而跌入深渊、穿越隧道，忽而遭遇外星战车，炮火激射、火光飞溅……你不知道下一步会出现什么，一切都充满了悬念和紧张，其惊奇场面与恐惧心理跟真实情景一样。

迪斯尼的动感电影非常有意思。戴上立体眼镜，坐在特制的椅子上，心里明明知道美国人是在利用声、光、电来吓唬你，但还是被银幕里一次次逼真的景象欺骗了。突然，正在影片中打斗的那个人向你迎面一击，"啪！"你本能地一扭头，想躲过去，结果，上当了。一声巨大的爆炸，仿佛是世界末日，人群乱成一锅粥。突然，千千万万个小老鼠从银幕中跑出来，跑到你的座位上，好像顺着你的裤腿钻了进去，吓得女孩子哇哇大叫，照着裤子噼啪乱打。原来，那是配合剧中情节，座位下面突然喷出一团团冷气，让你感觉到有老鼠进去。接下来，一只大狗从银幕中伸长脖子，冲着你打了个喷嚏，唾沫星子仿佛溅了你一头一脸，那也是座位上的喷水装置制造的效果。

每天下午5点举行的花车表演是迪斯尼乐园的重头戏，堪称迪斯尼狂欢节。5点钟之前，许多小朋友就耐心地坐在大道旁等待花车的到来。当音乐声响起，小朋友们纷纷站立起来，花车缓缓地向前移动，一个个装扮鲜艳的动画角色跑前跑后，向游客致意。花车最醒目的地方站着米老鼠，还有其他动画角色。一车过去，又来一车，你就觉得，时间最好停滞，使你能够从容地欣赏他们的表演。相机在不断地闪光，镜头在捕捉他们的笑脸。幽默的唐老鸭来了，欢快的小鹿班比来了，美丽优雅的白雪公主来了，气质高贵的灰姑娘来了，金光闪闪的小象波顿来了，好奇健壮的人猿泰山来了……一场盛大的狂欢，将迪斯尼乐园全天的游戏推向了高潮。

天才创意

迪斯尼乐园是沃尔特·迪斯尼的天才创意，他一生中最伟大的设想就是建造一座神奇的乐园，一个可以使孩子和父母都感兴趣的娱乐场所。

沃尔特·迪斯尼是早期好莱坞的电影制片人、著名的动画片艺术家。他创作的动物角色米老鼠和唐老鸭，自 1928 年在《威利号汽船》动画片中问世以来，流行全球，米老鼠几乎代替了山姆大叔的形象，成为美国的象征。

为了满足观众的要求，实现自己的梦想，1952 年沃尔特组建了迪斯尼公司，开始筹建迪斯尼乐园，结果梦想成真，位于南加州阿纳海姆市的第一座迪斯尼乐园于 1955 年建成开业。当时正值二战和朝鲜战争结束后，美国经济处于繁荣期，迪斯尼乐园应运而生，恰好满足了美国"婴儿潮"一代的青少年对娱乐文化的消费需求。

第一座乐园火爆之后，迪斯尼公司 1971 年又在佛罗里达州奥兰多市建成开张了第二座乐园。该园占地 111 平方公里，比洛杉矶迪斯尼乐园面积大数倍，拥有 3 个主题公园、18 家饭店、1 个夜总会、3 个高尔夫球场、1 个水上公园、1 个野营地以及一些大规模的会议设施，总投资 7.66 亿美元。

进入 20 世纪 80 年代，迪斯尼开始向海外扩展，先后把乐园模式复制到东京和巴黎。1983 年 4 月 15 日，正当樱花盛开的时节，耗资 1500 亿日元的东京迪斯尼乐园正式开张。自开业以来，该园已接待游客 2.6 亿人次，创下了数倍于投资的巨额利润。

1992 年，迪斯尼公司又投巨资，在巴黎建成了第 4 座乐园。迪斯尼在法国曾因被认为是美国文化的入侵而受到抵制，然而，古老的欧洲文化终究没能抵挡住新生代米老鼠和唐老鸭的魅力，最后还是俯首就范。

2005 年，在迪斯尼乐园迎来 50 岁生日之际，全球第 5 家迪斯尼乐园在香港开园，这年 7 月 17 日，迪斯尼公司在美国加州迪斯尼乐园举行了生日典礼，美国前影视动作巨星、现任加州州长施瓦辛格及众多明星出席了庆典仪式。

自开业 50 年来，加州迪斯尼乐园共接待游客 5 亿人次，平均每年 1000 万。2004 年全球 4 家迪斯尼乐园吸引了 3000 万游客前去参观，2005 年加上新开业的香港迪斯尼乐园，游客增加到 3500 万。据统计，游客每年在一座园内要吃掉 400 万个汉堡包、160 万个热狗和 320 万只冰激凌。洛杉矶迪斯尼乐园每张门票 59 美元，全球五家迪斯尼乐园、3500 万游客，平均算起来，迪斯尼公司每年门票收入就有 20 亿美元，加上吃、住、行、游、购、娱等其他消费以及电影电视业收入，还有迪斯尼动画形象产品商标使用许可收入，迪斯尼公司 2003 年的营业收入达到 284 亿美元。肉肥汤也肥，难怪迪斯尼公司前总裁艾斯纳先生的年薪加股票期权收入高达 5.7560 亿美元，为 1998 年美国最大的 365 家上市公司 CEO 年收入之最。

成功奥秘

50 多年来，迪斯尼乐园以其经久不衰的魅力吸引全球数以万计的游客慕名而至，它的魅力究竟在哪里？是惊险刺激的娱乐节目？还是惹人喜爱的拟人动物？至少有一点可以肯定：这是一个能够让孩子欢笑、让成人找回童真的地方，这也是一片远离纷争、没有悲伤的净土。"在这里，你可以暂时抛开今天，走进昨日、明日和梦想的世界。"

迪斯尼成功的真谛，是它在满足人类天性、安慰人类心灵方面的天才创意和不断创新。1966 年 12 月 15 日，当迪斯尼创始人沃尔特·迪斯尼病逝时，美国人一时找不到合适的词来形容他，哥伦比亚广播公司在晚间新闻的颂词中说："迪斯尼是一位富有创造性的天才，他为全世界的人带来了欢乐，……他在医治、安慰人类心灵方面所作的贡献，也许比世界上任何一位心理医生都要大。"

分析迪斯尼成功的原因，有人感慨地说："迪斯尼为全世界示范了一种新的生财模式：将欢乐换算成金币，将利润构筑在追求快乐而不是剥夺之上。"

在经营上，迪斯尼将"顾客至上、以人为本、细致入微"的服务理念深深植入员工的灵魂并将其转化为实际行动。为了让顾客满意和回头，迪斯尼动了很多脑筋。他们发现，客人来到迪斯尼游玩，碰到最多的是普通的清洁工，所以他们非常重视对清洁工的培训。比如东京迪斯尼一些扫地的员工是假期打工的学生，虽然他们只干两个月，但依然要进行 3 天的专门训练，除了扫地之外，还要让他们学会照相、辨别方向，甚至学会换尿布。

从开业到现在 20 多年里，东京迪斯尼就曾为被丢失的 2 万多名小孩找到他们的家人。难能可贵的是，他们在发现有小孩走失后从不广播，认为广播找人会让顾客有一种不安全感。他们在乐园里设置了 10 个托儿中心，只要发现有小孩与大人走散，就用最快的速度把小孩送到托儿中心，然后想尽办法与大人取得联系，当父母乘坐电车来到托儿中心时，会发现孩子们正开心地喝着可乐、吃着薯条或汉堡包呢。

作为全球主题公园的典范，迪斯尼乐园已经度过了 50 个辉煌春秋，为全世界 5 亿人带来欢笑和记忆，但是，随着社会的变迁，面临互联网、电子游戏等"电子时代"的挑战，未来的迪斯尼还会长盛不衰吗？对此，迪斯尼前总裁艾斯纳充满自信，他说："迪斯尼永远不会完结，世界上只要还有想象力，迪斯尼就会继续成长和改变。"

如何借鉴

从 20 世纪 80 年代中期开始，中国大地上也刮起了投资兴建主题公园的热潮，但是，该热潮并没有随着旅游业的快速发展而带来丰厚的回报。有资料显示，至今 20 余年间，全国各地陆续兴建的各种"宫"、"城"、"园"等人造景观共计 2500 多处，总投资达 1500 亿元。这些主题公园有的内容重复，缺乏创意；有的粗制滥造，经营不善；有的光怪陆离，坑人骗钱。其中 70%处于亏损状态，20% 持平，只有 10% 左右盈利。据了解，除深圳的"锦绣中华"、"世界之窗"，北京的"世界公园"，昆明的"世博园"，江苏的"苏州乐园"、"无锡太湖影视基地"，杭州的"宋城"等二三十家水平较高的主题公园获得成功外，其他绝大多数人造公园门可罗雀，惨淡经营，不仅造成土地、资金的巨大浪费，也是对中华文化的亵渎，对国人精神的污染。

"国内的主题公园只有 3 年到 4 年的生命周期"，这是近年来国内旅游业界的流行说法；投资上马未作详细论证和研究，就匆匆开工建设，简单模仿，内容重复导致恶性竞争，这是专家分析中国主题公园短命的主要原因。盲目跟风、乱造景观，这也是近些年国人心态浮躁、急功近利的突出表现之一。国人需要娱乐，公园需要建造，但关键要在内容创新、文化特色、精细管理等方面动脑筋、下功夫。

Tramps and Millionaires

Bill Gates and Warren Buffett's charitable contributions have shocked the world and set a good example for the global millionaires. I hope Chinese millionaires, with the growth of the society and their personal wealth, will learn more from them, and will devote more to establish a higher realm of life.

In Los Angeles, there is a fashionable residential area that is known as the place where movie stars live. This is Beverly Hills. It is quite cozy to take a long drive along the Sunset Boulevard to Beverly Hills. The scenery along the way is fascinating. Beverly Hills is beautiful and elegant. However, tourists are not encouraged to get out of the car when visiting here, and, for the most part, they can only get a glance of the celebrities' residents through trees and flowers.

Our tourist guide told us that these superior villas were all made of the finest wood. The price of each resident could be above 10 million dollars. Even if an ordinary person could afford to buy one of these houses, the real estate tax on each would be astronomical. Beverly Hills is definitely a paradise for the rich. Not only are the villas luxurious, but also the surroundings are very beauteous and tranquil, in particular, the palm trees along the streets are nationally famous and unique to the area.

Palm Street

In sharp contrast to the luxury of millionaires is the life of the homeless, the tramps. Los Angeles has a reputation of "Skid Row". According to a research, in 2005, there were 48 thousand homeless people living around downtown Los Angeles, and, in addition to those in the suburbs, the number was up to 82 thousand, ranking it the highest in the United States. A survey made by the U.S. Department of Housing and Urban Development in February 28, 2007 showed that on average 754 thousand people were homeless in the United States every night, among whom 20% were teenagers below 18 years old, 29% with families, 18% were retired soldiers, and 9% were women escaping from domestic violence. It also indicated that in the same group of people, 46% were drug addicts and 36% suffered from mental disease.

The Los Angeles government has set up the Los Angeles Homeless Services Authority (LAHSA) for the homeless people. To give relief to the poor and the homeless, they offer three meals a day, a subsidy per month, and also new clothes for Christmas or New Year. Thus, except for the state of homelessness, the tramps live a relatively comfortable life. But the huge amount of homelessness has brought trouble to the environment and social security. Most office workers did not want to live in the downtown. So the city often became empty in the evening.

The Vagrant on Hollywood Walk of Fame

It can be seen that the United States is not the paradise for everyone, though it ranks No.1 in the global economy. Like other countries, the gap between the rich and the poor also exists in the United States, and the homelessness has been an issue with the U.S. federal government for a long time as one of the most significant social problems. To help alleviate this problem, the government

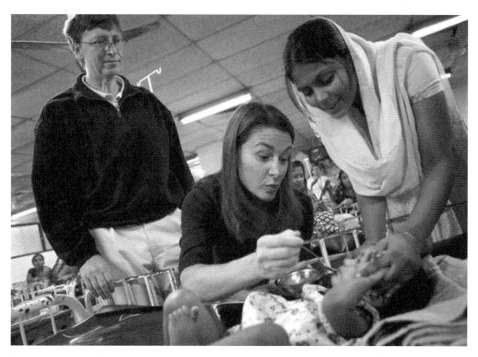

Bill and Melinda Gates Helping the Poor

offers a relief fund of 1.5 billion dollars to the homeless populations every year. Because of this, dozens of cities in the United States scramble each year to inflate their count of the homeless population in order to be eligible to receive more funding. In 2005, LAHSA listed No. 1 and received a relief fund of 55.6 million dollars from the U.S. Department of Housing and Urban Development.

After all, it is not possible to eliminate homelessness in any country or society. It will always be a problem as long as the human society exists, since any social system has its own defect. In addition, the differences between individuals, smart and clumsy, industrious and lazy, rich and poor, officials and civilians, celebrities and ordinary people, etc. all result in the fact that there is no complete equality between people. People's family background might be different; their property might be different; their social status might also be different especially in some countries with backward economic and social system. The biggest difference is the disparity in opportunity, which refers to education opportunity, job opportunity, lucrative opportunity and promotion opportunity.

Nobles grow up by being sheltered while civilians depend on themselves. Compared with the descendants of the bigwigs, common people are obviously inferior in managing power, wealth and human relations, and their life will be much tougher. If they try to be somebody, they need to make a conceted effort and need talent as well as opportunity, which are the keys to success. Therefore, young people are always encouraged in this way: work hard, your fate will lie in your own hands! This idea was definitely right, but it dodged a crucial fact that except personal efforts, power and wealth can also decide the possibility of success. Moreover, because of these differences and actual disparities, it is difficult for any country or society to achieve absolute equality.

In today's civilized nations, under the premise of maintaining the rules of the market, focusing on efficiency, the government adopts secondary allocation to shorten the gap between the rich and poor, providing necessary social security and life relief to the vulnerable groups, trying their best to achieve relative equivalence. As the society has developed nowadays, the gap between the rich and poor is not that insurmountable. In a relatively healthy market economy and legal society, there are numerous people who achieve success through industrious attitude, intelligence and opportunity. In the United States, there are countless inaccuracies about the founders of industries such as Microsoft and Wal-Mart. China also has a lot of nouveaux riches, although some of them might have started out in an unsavory manner.

Everybody admires Bill Gate's success and envies his great fortune. Many people dream of living the same life as his. But after he made his fortune, he did something astonishing: he retired from his position and set up the Bill & Melinda Gates Foundation to support the world medical and health services especially for the prevention and treatment of AIDs. Bill Gates gradually gave up daily management of Microsoft to focus on the management of the charity foundation.

And recently another person surprised people in the United States with his generosity. That was Warren Buffett, Bill Gates' friend, the world's second

Business Magnate Warren Buffett

richest person who is nicknamed the "Oracle of Omaha." He announced that of his 44 billion dollars fortune, he would donate 85% to charity from July, 2006, and most of his endowment would go to Bill Gates' charity fund.

Bill Gates had donated 29 billion dollars to his charity fund. This time, Buffett would donate 37 billion dollars to the charity fund, which would become the largest amount of personal donation.

Bill Gates said that he would leave 10 million dollars to his children, and donate the rest of his property to charity. So people predict that Bill Gates' donation will be larger than Buffett's.

Gates' and Buffett's behavior set a good example for the world, giving people a glimpse of the most remarkable side of human beings. I wonder how the Chinese millionaire's feel about this? Was it peer pressure or did they do this kind deed for themselves? I think as a successful entrepreneur, except for the issue of inheritance tax, they regard charity as a career which can help others as well as being self-satisfying. Achieved new great career and life pursuit.

According to the 2006 Forbes China Rich List, there are more and more billionaires in China. Over 400 billionaires have a possession of more than 0.8 billion Yuan, and 15 of them possess more than 8 billion Yuan, and the richest person has a possession of 18.09 billion Yuan. It is a small amount compared with Bill Gates' 50 billion dollars and Buffett's 44 billion dollars. But the more billionaires China has, the richer and stronger our country has become. And the rising of billionaires and wealth is good for the country and society. As China has practiced the market-oriented policy, we should change our attitude towards the rich and accept their social status and positive influence.

But the overall image of the rich is not that good. Some were suspicious about where they got their money from, while others were considered to be lacking in social responsibility and sympathy, living in a life of luxury illegally. Just as the foreigners said, although the Chinese rich know how to make money, they may not know how to spend money. We should know that rich is more than a representation of wealth and social status. It also represents diligence, knowledge, achievement, accomplishment, responsibility and courtesy. And in this way the rich will be seen with respect rather than mistrusted.

Although there is much criticism, the public has expected more of the rich in developing China, hoping that they can follow the example of Bill Gates and Buffett, make more contribution and get a higher level in their state of life with the development of the society and the growth of their personal wealth.

流浪汉和大富豪

　　盖茨和巴菲特的举动轰动了世界，震撼了世人，他们给全世界的富豪树立了慈善济世的榜样。期待中国的富豪们也能像盖茨和巴菲特那样，随着社会的进步和个人财富的增长，涵养起更高的人生境界，有更多的济世善举和社会贡献。

　　洛杉矶有处以影视界名流为主要居民的高级住宅区，那就是贝佛利山庄(Beverly Hills)。沿着日落大道去贝佛利山庄兜上一圈是件很惬意的事。长长的日落大道景色迷人，贝佛利山庄优美高雅。但游人到了贝佛利山庄却不能下车参观，只能从车上透过绿荫花丛浏览名人豪宅。

　　导游介绍，这里的高级别墅都是用上等木料修建的，每座价格都在千万美元以上，甭说普通人买不起，就是买得起，房地产税也缴不起。贝佛利山庄的确是富人的天堂，不仅别墅高级，而且周围环境非常美丽和幽静，特别是街道两旁的棕榈树名冠全美，风景独特。

　　与富豪生活形成鲜明对比的是洛杉矶的无家可归者，即流浪汉。洛杉矶有"无家可归者之都"的美称，据调查，2005 年，在洛杉矶市区游荡着近 4.8万名流浪汉，加上郊区高达 8.2 万人，居美国各大城市之冠。据美国住房和城市发展部 2007 年 2 月 28 日公布的一项调查显示，平均每个夜晚全美境内有75.4 万人无家可归。在这些无家可归者当中，20% 是 18 岁以下的未成年人，29% 的人有家庭，18% 的人是退伍老兵，9% 的人是逃避家庭暴力的妇女。在这些人中，46% 有毒瘾，36% 有精神疾病。

　　洛杉矶市政府设有无家可归者服务局，由服务局开办的贫民救济中心每日为流浪者提供三餐，每月还发给零用钱，过圣诞新年还要发放新衣服。除了居无定所，这些流浪汉倒也过着无忧无虑的生活。由于大批流浪汉的占领，市区的环境卫生和社会治安就成了问题，在市区上班的大多数人不愿在市内居住，到了晚上，整个市中心就成了一座空城。

看来，尽管美国拥有世界第一的经济实力，但美国并不是所有人的"天堂"。和许多国家一样，美国也存在着严重的贫富差距问题，无家可归者一直就是困扰美国政府的突出社会问题之一。为此，美国联邦政府每年要给无家可归者提供近 15 亿美元的救济。为争夺这笔可观的资金，美国数十个城市争先恐后地清点统计街头流浪者的数目，希望人数越多越好。2005 年，拔得头筹的洛杉矶市流浪者服务局获得美国住房和城市发展部 5560 万美元的拨款。

可话又说回来，流浪汉现象在任何国家、任何社会都不可能完全消除，有人类社会存在，就有类似的社会问题存在。因为任何社会制度都不可能是没有缺陷的，人与人也是有差别的，有聪明与愚笨的差别，勤劳与懒惰的差别，富人与穷人的差别，官员与平民的差别，名人和普通人的差别，等等。人与人不可能是完全平等的，有先天出身的不平等，拥有财富的不平等，社会地位的不平等，特别在一些经济社会制度落后的国家，各个阶层的人之间存在的最大的不平等是机会上的不平等，即教育机会的不平等，就业机会的不平等，发财机会的不平等，升迁机会的不平等。

平民靠奋斗，贵族靠庇荫。比起官宦富家子弟，平民阶层出身的人在权力、财富、人脉等方面处于明显劣势，人生的路要艰难得多，要想出人头地，就要靠拼搏、靠才能、靠机遇。勤奋、才能加机遇，是人生成功的三大要素，因此，励志者总是鼓励青年人：努力吧，命运掌握在你自己手里！这话无疑是正确的，但它却回避了一个至关重要的问题，那就是个人努力以外的因素——权力、财富对人生成功机会的重要影响。因为有差别，因为存在事实上的不平等，所以，任何国家和社会都难以做到绝对公平。

当今文明国家，政府在维护市场规则、注重效率的前提下，采取二次分配的办法解决贫富悬殊的问题，尤其是给弱势群体提供必要的社会保障和生活救济，力求相对公平，维持社会稳定。人类社会走到今天，贫富差距也不是不可逾越的鸿沟，在比较健全的市场经济和法制社会，凭着勤劳智慧，凭着善抓机遇，一举成功的例子比比皆是，在美国，软件帝国微软、零售王国沃尔玛等类似的创业神话数不胜数。在当今中国，一夜暴富的现象更不少见，只是有些人淘取的第一桶金不那么干净，也有些人暴富之后为富不仁，令人不齿。

世人都羡慕比尔·盖茨的成功人生，羡慕他拥有富可敌国的巨大财富，许多人都在做着同样的梦。但是，比尔盖茨在取得巨大成功、拥有巨大财富之后，竟做出了超出常人想象的惊人之举：功成身退、奉献社会。他把自己积累的几百亿美元拿出来,和他夫人梅琳达·盖茨一起建立"比尔和梅琳达·盖茨基金会"，用于资助全世界医疗卫生事业特别是艾滋病的防治，盖茨还宣布从 2008 年起逐渐淡出微软日常管理工作，将主要精力放在经营慈善基金会上。

最近，美国又发生了一件同样令世界轰动的消息：全球第二大富豪，也是比尔·盖茨的好友，素有"股神"之称的沃伦·巴菲特最近宣布从 2006 年7 月开始，把自己 440 亿美元财产的 85% 捐献给慈善事业，而其中大部分将投向盖茨所创立的基金会。

盖茨对自己慈善基金会的捐款总额已达到 290 亿美元，但这次巴菲特的捐赠将达 370 亿美元，成为有史以来最大一笔个人慈善捐款。比尔·盖茨表示将来只给子女留下 1000 万美元，其余将全部捐献给慈善事业，因此预料巴菲特的记录将来还会被盖茨超过。

盖茨和巴菲特的举动轰动了世界,震撼了世人，他们给全世界的富豪树立了慈善济世的榜样，让世人看到了人性最灿烂的一面。对他们的做法，不知中国的富豪们作何感想，盖茨和巴菲特为什么要这么做？他们的行为是社会制度使然，还是自身素质使然？我想，除了遗产税等外在因素外，作为获得巨大成功的企业家，盖茨和巴菲特是把慈善作为一种事业，把捐赠作为一种追求，既帮助了他人，也完善了自我，成就了新的伟大事业和人生追求。

据《2006 福布斯中国富豪榜》公布的名单和数据表明，目前中国的亿万富翁越来越多了，个人或家族资产超过 8 亿元人民币的富豪多达 400 名，80亿元人民币以上的富豪有 15 位，夺得富豪冠军的资产为 180. 9 亿元人民币。虽然比起盖茨的 500 多亿美元和巴菲特的 440 亿美元，中国的富豪依然是小巫见大巫，但中国的亿万富翁多了，说明我们国家的财富多了，实力强了。富豪数量和财富增加对国家和社会是个利好消息，中国发展市场经济，需要转变对富人的观念和态度，应当承认富人的社会地位和积极作用。

但是，目前中国的富人阶层总体形象欠佳，有些富人不但在财富来源、致富手段上受到公众质疑，而且有的富人因没有社会责任感，缺乏同情心，奢侈挥霍，甚至行为不法而受到社会舆论的谴责。正如外国朋友所指出的，中国的富人"虽然学会了赚钱,却未必知道该如何花钱。"要知道,富人不仅仅是金钱、财富与身份地位的代名词,更是勤奋、智慧、成就、修养、责任与绅士的同义语,如此,富人才会是一个受人尊敬的阶层,而不应成为舆论谴责的对象。

尽管有不少批评的声音,但正在崛起的中国,社会公众对富人阶层也抱有更多的期待,期待中国的富豪们也能像盖茨和巴菲特那样,随着社会的进步和个人财富的增长,涵养起更高的人生境界,有更多的济世善举和社会贡献。

Beauty of San Francisco

If you are alive, you will not feel bored in San Francisco. If you are dead, San Francisco will bring you to life.

Old Gold Mountain, "Jiu Jin Shan" in Chinese language, or "Sanfan City" in Cantonese, known as the most beautiful city in the United States, is the last stop of our journey. We came to this fascinating coastal city on May 28, 2006.

Old Gold Mountain arouses different emotions in the Chinese people. The official English name of this place is San Francisco, which was given to it by the early Spanish colonizers in Spanish language. Later it was named Old Gold Mountain by the Chinese to commemorate the tragic history of the Chinese workers there. At the beginning of the 19th century, there were only a few hundred residents in San Francisco, but after its discovery of the gold fields in 1848, immigrants flocked to this land in great numbers, which was termed as "the Gold Rush" in history. Many Chinese at that time were sent there as "contract laborers" to mine gold and build the railway, which proved to be a tough life. But many Chinese laborers from Guangdong settled there and they first named it Old Gold Mountain, to distinguish it from the then newly-found gold hills in Australia.

San Francisco is located in the northwest California, on the peninsula between the Pacific Ocean and the San Francisco Bay. The flight from Los Angeles to San Francisco was slightly over an hour. At noon on a sunny day, we flew to the north along the coastline. The clear sky extended infinitely before us, colorful clouds floating above sometimes over the winding and rolling mountain ranges, sometimes over the calm and bright blue sea. Between the mountains and the sea, a line of golden beaches and breaking waves ran through. When the plane circled round over the airport, a panoramic view of San Francisco came into view, and appeared just like a

Distant View of San Francisco

beautiful Taiji picture, inlaid among the green mountains and rivers.

San Francisco was surrounded by the sea on three sides with picturesque scenery. It is rainy in spring and winter, cool and foggy in summer and autumn. The lowest temperature is 11°C and the highest temperature reached 17°C perennially and there is no clear division of seasons. The average rainfall is 790 mm mainly from November to April. Because of the good environment, cool climate, beautiful scenery, coupled with the multicultural tolerance, San Francisco has become one of the most livable cities and biggest tourist destinations.

With the topography of peninsula and hills, the city of San Francisco is built upon 42 rolling slopes. Since driving in the downtown steep streets would be very dangerous, people prefer to choose subway, bus and the ancient tramcar as tools of public transport. The ancient tramcar, also named "tinkle car" by local people, has a history of more than 120 years, has become a symbol of the city's culture and remains very popular among the residents there.

Along the streets of San Francisco, another thing worthy of noticing is the wooden telegraph poles on both sides. Through a history of about 60 to 70 years, the wooden poles have been dotted with a web of electric wires, which bring a unique perspective to the city.

Although San Francisco is so picturesque, it is unfortunate to be located at the pacific seismic zone. A sudden earthquake attacked the city on April 18, 1906, and more than 3000 people lost their lives. The ruptured gas lines ignited fires and ruined almost all the buildings in this city. After that, the city suffered six other earthquakes, but it recovered quickly after each strike and developed faster. The new residence were mainly built put of wood and laid out distinctively along the ups and downs of the hills in Victorian style. To prevent destruction from the earthquake, only about 10 high buildings were erected downtown, among which stands the most unique building designed by Ieoh Ming Pei—the Transamerica Pyramid—with a height of 260 meters and 48 stories, and a Catholic Church with a nontraditional appearance of both elegance and modernity, whose beauty changes depending on where you look at it but is always in the shape of a cross.

There are many scenic spots in San Francisco, such as Fisherman's Wharf, Golden Gate Bridge and Chinatown, etc. Fisherman's Wharf used to be a wharf for Italian fisherman to berth their fishing boat, and now it has become the most popular place in San Francisco. On the shore of the wharf you have a full view of the beautiful San Francisco Bay, with the freighters sailing, seagulls hovering and yachts cruising in the distance where the sea and the sky merge into one.

Pier 39 and Fisherman's Wharf are connected by a bustling commercial street, with some two-story wooden buildings of fashionable stores and restaurants on both sides, among which the sidewalk seafood stalls are particularly popular. When tourists come to the south of the Pier 39, they are immediately drawn to the hundreds of seals crowding the deck of the wharf, enjoying the sunshine, playing with each other, or scrambling for territory, attract the tourists taking lots of photos.

San Francisco Bay is one of the busiest international harbors in America. The mountains on the California coast sink into the seabed of Golden Gate, to connect the Bay with the Pacific Ocean and form a natural harbor. To the west bank of the harbor is located the downtown of San Francisco, and to the east is Auckland City. Four bridges were built across the two sides, one of each stretching across the Golden Gate — this is the world famous Gold Gate Bridge.

It took four years, from January, 1933 to May, 1937, more than 0.1 million tons of steels and 35.5 million dollars to build the Golden Gate Bridge. The total length of the bridge is 2737 meters and the two main bridge piers are about 65-stories high with a distance between them of 1280 meters. When the construction of the huge bridge was completed, the German chief engineer, Joseph Strauss, wrote a poem to express his happiness, "Resplendent in the western sun, the Bridge looms mountain high; its titan piers grip ocean floor, its great steel arms link shore with shore, and its towers pierce the sky." But Strauss did not foresee that his masterpiece

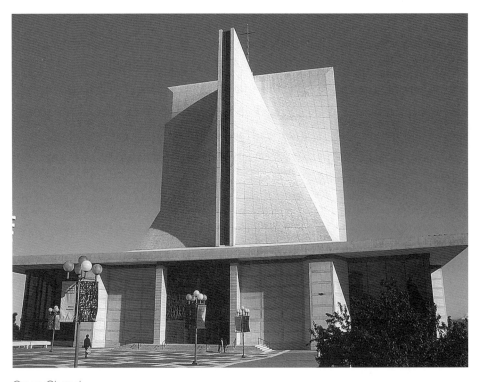

Cross Chapel

Trolley

would become a diving platform by those who committed suicide. For fifty year since its completion, suicides happen almost every mouth; therefore the most beautiful bridge in the world is also called the Bridge of Death. To memorize Strauss's contribution to the United States, people set up a statue of him beside the bridge.

The Golden Gate Bridge, with its splendid appearance and unique color, has become the symbol of San Francisco. Stretching over the roaring Golden Gate straits, the bridge looks like a gorgeous dragon flying in the sky especially when it is lit up, with its partly hidden red silhouette against the sunset. Walking on the bridge in the wind, and looking westward to the Pacific Ocean, you will find the sky and the sea melt into one, eastward to the San Francisco Bay, the white boats sailing on the quiet water in the embrace of blue mountains, and far into the direction of the downtown, the city flickering more like a mirage than an aircraft.

The scenery of Golden Gate Bridge and its surroundings enchanted me so much that I couldn't help writing a poem on it:

A rainbow flies to span the ocean banks
A huge dragon spans two green hills.
On the west, waves of the Pacific kiss the sky,
On the east, bay water mirrors the white sails.
Bathed in the sunset is the reddish bridge,

Veiled in high clouds and mist of twilight.
However enchanted San Francisco is,
The Golden Gate Bridge remains best

A Bird Standing on the Head of Statue of Joseph Strauss

San Francisco is also a cultural metropolis, where world famous theatres like Curran Theatre and Golden Gate Theatre are located. In the north of the San Francisco Bay lies a beach of 9 kilometers long. Beside it some luxury residential areas were built, which later became a haunt for artists. The former residence of the modern American writer Jack London is here, and now is a memorial.

San Francisco is also diverse, with a population composed of various ethnic groups, mainly from Asia, Italy, France, Mexico and Spain, all of which have their own community. In the downtown area of San Francisco live 0.2 million Chinese, which makes it the second largest city of Chinese residents besides New York.

As the Chinese residents in San Francisco are mainly Cantonese, the Chinese community there has made a special request to the Chinese government to select an ambassador who can speak both English and Cantonese. The Chinatown has a population of 80 thousand and is the biggest in America, and also the largest Chinese community out of Asia. The streets in the Chinatown are small and narrow, but crowded with cars and people all the time. There are many bristly shops that appear prominently with different

Red Bridge over Azure Water

China Town

Chinese or English signs throughout a symbolized Chinese–style arch and many red lanterns hanging on the buildings — all immersed in a strong atmosphere of traditional Chinese commercial culture.

San Francisco was the last stop of our visit to the United States, we were there for less than one day, which was not enough for us to fully enjoy the beauty and charm of it, but American writer William Saroyan's words might help to further our imagination of San Francisco:

If you are alive, you will not feel bored in San Francisco.
If you are dead, San Francisco will bring you to life.

旧金山之美

如果你还活着，旧金山不会使你厌烦；如果你已经死了，那旧金山会让你再度起死回生。

旧金山，又称三藩市，被誉为全美国最漂亮的城市。2006 年 5 月 28 日，作为访美的最后一站，我们来到了这座迷人的滨海城市。

提起旧金山，华人似乎对它有种特殊的情结。原本旧金山的正式名称叫圣弗朗西斯科 (San Francisco)，是早年西班牙人来到此地后，以西班牙语命名的。中国人之所以把它叫旧金山，其中饱含着华人劳工的血泪史。19 世纪初，这里的居民只有几百人，1848 年此地发现金矿后，移民蜂拥而至，掀起了淘金热，许多华人作为"契约劳工"来这里挖金矿，修铁路，备尝艰辛。此后，以广东移民为主的大批华工在这里安家落户，繁衍发展，他们称先前在美国挖掘金矿的这个地方为旧金山，以区别后来在澳大利亚发现的新金山。

旧金山地处加利福尼亚州西北部，太平洋和旧金山湾之间的半岛上，从洛杉矶到旧金山，坐飞机只需一个多小时。那天中午，我们乘坐的航班沿着海岸线向北飞去，透过窗口，可以看到机舱外面是万里晴空，彩云飘动，山峦蜿蜒起伏，海面湛蓝如镜，山海之间流淌着一条由白色浪花和金色沙滩组成的海岸线。当飞机抵达旧金山、在机场上空盘旋时，旧金山半岛就立刻呈现在眼前，整座城市就像是一幅美丽的太极画卷，镶嵌在青山绿水间。

旧金山三面环海，风景独秀，这里冬春温和多雨，夏秋凉爽多雾，常年气温最低摄氏 11 度，最高摄氏 17 度，无明显的四季之分。年平均降雨 790 毫米，而且集中在 11 至 4 月份。因为环境优美，气候凉爽，风光明媚，加上文化多元、包容大度，旧金山成为最适宜居住和旅游的城市。

旧金山属于半岛丘陵地形，整座城市建在 42 座高低起伏的山丘上。市区街道非常陡斜，行车比较惊险，市内公共交通工具除地铁和巴士外，还在使用古老美观的有轨电车，也就是人们俗称的叮当车。古色古香的叮当车已有

渔人码头

货轮启航

海豹嬉戏

120多年的历史，作为一种城市文化象征，叮当车至今依然是旧金山市民喜欢乘坐的交通工具。

漫步旧金山街头，还有一个现象很特别，那就是矗立在街道两旁的一排排木质电线杆。这些电线杆已有六七十年的历史，捆架在木杆上的各种线路像蜘蛛网一样密密麻麻，成为一道独特风景线。

美丽的旧金山虽然占尽人间春色，但不幸的是，它与洛杉矶一样处于太平洋地震断裂带。1906年4月18日，一场突如其来的大地震造成三千多人死亡，地震破坏加上由地震引发的煤气大火几乎毁掉了城市的所有建筑。以后又经历过6次地震，但每次地震后，旧金山都迅速恢复重建，浴火重生。新建的居民住宅多为木质结构，维多利亚式房屋随着起伏的山丘地形依次摆开，风格别具。为了防震，市中心仅建有十来栋高楼，其中由贝聿铭设计的环美金字塔大楼高48层、260米，是旧金山最高也是最具特色的建筑。还有造型独特的天主教堂，打破传统的设计模式，外观典雅靓丽，极富现代艺术感，无论从哪个方向看去都成十字架形状。

　　旧金山风景名胜众多，其中最著名的有渔人码头、金门大桥和中国城等景点。渔人码头过去曾是意大利渔夫停泊渔船的地方，如今却是旧金山最热闹的去处。当我们走进渔人码头，但见游人如织，热闹非凡。来到码头岸边，凭栏眺望旧金山海湾，眼前货轮启航，游艇冲浪，海天一色，海鸥翱翔，美不胜收。

　　39号码头和渔人码头连接在一起，两个码头中央是一条繁华热闹的商业街，两旁都是二层木结构建筑，当中有许多别致、时髦的商店和餐馆，香气袭人的海鲜大排档是这里的一大特色。当你转到39号码头的南侧，只见港湾内的木筏上簇拥着几百只海豹，它们一边晒着日光，一边打斗戏嬉，争夺配偶和地盘，引得游人纷纷围观拍照。

　　旧金山港湾是美国最繁忙的国际港口之一，因加利福尼亚海岸山脉在金门海峡处陷落海底，旧金山湾与太平洋贯通，这里便成了天然良港。海湾西岸是旧金山市区所在地，东岸是奥克兰市，东西两岸建有4座大桥，其中一座大桥横跨金门海峡，就是著名的金门大桥。

　　金门大桥于1933年1月动工，1937年5月建成，用了四年时间，耗费钢材10万多吨，总投资3550万美元。大桥总长2737米，两个主桥墩约为65层楼高，主桥墩之间的距离为1280米。大桥落成时，首席设计师德国人约瑟夫·斯特劳斯曾赋诗一首，表达他的喜悦之情："我用钢缆为天堂之风织成一把竖琴，在日落之门为人类修建通途。"令约瑟夫没有想到的是，他的杰作竟会成为自杀者的跳台，大桥建成50年来，几乎每个月都有人在金门大桥结束生命，因此，人们又把这座世界上最美丽的桥称为死亡之桥。为了纪念约瑟夫对美国作出的贡献，后来人们把他的全身铜雕像安放在桥畔。

　　金门大桥外形壮观，气势雄伟，色调独特，成为旧金山的象征。大桥横跨于波涛汹涌、两岸陡峭的金门海峡之上，当华灯初放，犹如巨龙凌空；当晚霞初上，红色的桥身，高耸的钢塔，若隐若现，极其美丽。当你迎风走上金门桥头，西望太平洋，但见碧海连天，无涯浩瀚；东观旧金山海湾，又见碧波如镜，白帆点点，群山叠翠，气象万千；再从此处眺望旧金山市区，整座城市恍若海市蜃楼，又恰似航空母舰。

　　金门大桥和周围景观使人陶醉，让人留恋，令我心潮涌动，不禁赋诗赞叹：

彩虹飞架大洋边，
巨龙街起两岸山；
西海波涛连天际，
东湾碧水映白帆。
红桥出浴晚霞落，
轻纱薄雾彩云端；
三藩景色处妖娆，
金门桥头别样观。

旧金山也是一座文化都市，这里有举世闻名的柯伦剧院和金门剧院。旧金山北海湾有一条长约9公里的海滩，岸边是豪华住宅区，全美艺术家云集于此，美国近代作家杰克·伦敦在这里的故居，已被辟为纪念馆。

旧金山更是一座国际化城市，人口构成复杂，其中为数众多的是亚洲人、意大利人、法国人、墨西哥人、西班牙人，这些族群都有自己的社区。在旧金山都市区的华人约有20万，是美国除纽约之外华人最集中的城市。

因旧金山华人以广东人居多，所以，近年华人社团特别要求中国政府选派驻旧金山的领事既要会英语又要懂粤语。华人集聚的唐人街即中国城人口达8万之众，规模为美国各城市之冠，也是亚洲以外最大的华人社区。当我们乘车穿过中国城，只见狭窄的街道上中式店铺林立，中英文招牌醒目，象征中国城的中式牌楼在街头耸立，街上车水马龙，红灯高悬，浸透出浓厚的中国传统商业文化氛围。

旧金山是我们访美的最后一站，不足一天的行程，没有时间让我们尽情饱览它的美丽，感受它的迷人，还是让美国作家威廉·萨罗扬的描述来丰富人们对旧金山的想象吧："如果你还活着，旧金山不会使你厌烦；如果你已经死了，那旧金山会让你再度起死回生。"

Charms of Stanford and University-Related Topics

If Harvard and Yale represent the traditional humanity of the United States, Stanford University might be the symbol of the modern technology of the 21st century. Universities should be not only the basis for cultivating talents, but also the think tank of national strategies, the storage of the ideological innovation, the assistant of the technology improvement and the cradle of the national spirit. Thus for China, the reform of the university mechanism, of college entrance examination and the innovation in running schools should be put on the agenda as soon as possible.

The last day of our visit in the United States came on May 27, and our plane would take off for China at twelve o'clock. At our request, the guide agreed to take us to Stanford University near the San Francisco Bay that morning.

Sketches of Stanford

Stanford University is as famous as Harvard and Yale in the United States. In its history of more than one hundred years, one president (the 31st President Hoover), 25 Nobel Prize winners, 142 academicians of American Academy of Arts and Sciences, 84 academicians of the National Academy of Sciences, 14 National Medal of Science winners and numerous entrepreneurs graduated from here. Rice, the present U.S. Secretary of State, was once a lecturer and researcher at Stanford.

There is no gate leading into Stanford University, no logo or bounding walls around

Campus of Stanford University

Hoover Tower

it. Only the two towers you see along the way to the campus can help to identify it.

The campus of Stanford University is just like a big park, flourishing with exuberant greens dotted with blooming flowers, spacious and beautiful. The sandstone buildings appear to be more ancient and elegant with red roofs and yellow walls, and the famous Hoover Tower stands among them, high and graceful.

Statues of *the Burghers of Calais*

Hoover Tower holds the valuable hand written diary of Chiang Kai-shek (Jiang Jieshi) which had recorded his inner feeling between 1917 and 1973. Jiang's diary was made known to public on March 31, 2006 by the Hoover Institution of Stanford University. Because of its great value in understanding the major events in China of the last century as well as inner thoughts of Jiang, the document has drawn great attention both home and abroad.

Beside the Hoover Tower is the Stanford Memorial Church, solemn and elegant, built in memory of the old Stanford, the interior of which was adorned profusely with mosaics on walls. Since it was Sunday, many people were there to worship. Our guide explained that people outside Stanford could also hold a wedding here as long as one of the couple was an alumni of the university.

The church covers a large space with several courtyards. In the first yard, a collection of black sculptures stands at the center, which is *The Burghers of Calais* made by the world famous artist Auguste Rodin. There is also an art gallery in Stanford, displaying many other exquisite sculptures of Rodin. This collection depicts the situation in Calais—the northern city of France during the Hundred Years' War in the 14th century, when it was surrounded by the English army at that time and about to be captured. After bilateral negotiations, Edward III, the King of England, agreed to spare the people of the city if any six of its top leaders would surrender themselves to him, presumably to be hanged. Six burghers volunteered to sacrifice themselves for the sake of all the citizens. In his sculpture, Rodin captured vividly the inner emotion, outer expression, and the action of the moment: each of them looking grave, some determined and resolute, some indignant with tears, some staggering in panic and helplessness in reaction to the face of imminent death are real masterpieces.

Splendors of Stanford

Stanford University, also called the "Harvard of the West", was founded in 1891, under the donation of the railroad tycoon Leland Stanford. It was not that prestigious at the beginning, but with the open-minded school spirit and the optimistic attitude of the west-coast Americans, it has gradually combined into one the western American culture and the essence of the high-technology, to have made numerous achievements in research and academic.

Stanford University has 14,000 students at present, possessing 30 libraries with a collection of more than 6.5 million books in its database. The university runs under sufficient fee and is equipped with all modern technology. The sports facility is also very modern, with a gymnasium holding 85,000 people, a golf course and a natatorium.

Stanford is a comprehensive university mainly focusing on science, engineering and medicine, and many of its engineering, medical and science subjects are ranked top ten among American Universities. Its Law, Social Sciences and Humanities also have good reputations and their English, psychology, politics and history departments are also among the top ranking of American universities. Subjects such as mass media, drama, economics and MBA are ranked the top six among the American universities. Stanford University requires students to be all-round, good at both art and science.

Just like the Harvard Business School, Stanford Graduate School of Business is also considered one of the best business schools in the United States. But their standards are quite different. Harvard adopts the tradition of cultivating "talents in suits" for big enterprises, while Stanford University emphasizes more on training "T-shirt generation," the innovating spirit led by the newly emerging small entrepreneurs.

It is well known that Stanford University has a close relation with Silicon Valley. The "Father of Silicon Valley", Fred Terman helped his student to build the world famous Hewlett Packard Company when he was the Dean of Electronic Engineering Department at Stanford. In 1951, Terman and Wallace, the university president at that time, decided to rent 655 acres of the campus to some high-tech companies to set up the Stanford Research Park, which was the precursor to Silicon Valley.

Between China and Stanford University there were deep historical roots. Many Chinese scholars and scientists graduated from there, including the famous botanist Pei Jian, the medical scientist Zhang Xiaoqian, the internationally famous mathematician Li Jun, and the academician of Chinese Academy of Sciences Xie Jialin, etc. Among the newly emerging overseas students, a talent boy named Zou Qiuzhen is very outstanding. He is the chief engineer of CDMA, the top technology of global communication. Zou used to be a member of the "Gifted Class" at Southeast University in Nanjing and entered college directly at the age of 15 when he graduated from the middle school. In 1992, he was accepted to Stanford and after only 8 and a half months, he got his master's degree in electronic engineering from Stanford.

What Can Be Called a University?

Due to the short stay, we could not see the whole Stanford University, but it still left a deep impression on us. Besides Stanford, there are many other world top-rank universities in the United States, such as Harvard, Yale, MIT, Princeton, Columbia, Pennsylvania University, etc, where a large number of elites proficient in ideology, economy, science and technology gather. These universities have not only cultivated tens of thousands of talents for both the United States and the world (currently 30% of American Ph.D. degrees have been gained by overseas students), but also produced a huge amount of scientific achievements. It can be said that American universities have made a great contribution to American economy and social development, technology innovation, ideological and cultural progress and cultural exchange with foreign countries. Just as the president of Yale University Richard Levin had said, "As never before in their long history, universities have become instruments of national competition as well as instruments of peace. They are the locus of the scientific discoveries that move economies forward, and the primary means of educating the talent required to obtain and maintain competitive advantage."

American universities are all famous because of the cultivate many Nobel Prize winners, celebrities, political leaders and entrepreneurs. Although most of the universities are not as big as Stanford in terms of campus space, they all have top-class faculties, outstanding achievements and great vitality. Just as Mei Yiqi, the former president of Tsinghai University, said,

"What can be called a university? Not in possession of high buildings, but in possession of great masters."

Where are Chinese Universities Heading for?

Thirty years have passed since the reform and opening-up, and the higher education in China has a completely new look. The general size and level of universities have improved significantly. By the end of 2005, the number of undergraduate college students has exceeded 2.3 million with a gross entrance rate of 21%.

But in recent years the social trend of profit-seeking is also factor in the university. In our country many universities lay more emphasis on the result than the process of education, more on the size over the quality, more on the modernization than the utilization of the campus, all of which have led to the problems at present—the unreasonable increase of the loan rate and tuition feel but at the same time, the decrease of educational quality and job opportunity. The declining quality of China's higher education and the loss of university spirit is highlighted as the hotspot and criticized in the press both at home and abroad. Actually in China now neither common universities nor prestigious ones can compete with foreign counterparts in America and Europe. In addition, they have left far behind the humanistic spirit advocated by Chinese traditional education. Particularly in over ten years since the end of 1990s, the universities have gotten larger; the facilities have improved; the investment has been doubled and redoubled, and the income of teachers' has been raised greatly. However, the general quality of the graduates has not been enhanced accordingly. On the contrary, quality of the graduates has become even worse than in the 1980s.

Recently I read a report from *Semimonthly* Reading entitled "Chinese and Foreign University Presidents on China's Higher Education". It is about the remarks given by different university leaders on "The 3rd Chinese-foreign University Presidents Forum," which questions and criticizes China's current higher education in a self-reflexive manner, and appeals for reforms and

Richard C. Levin, the President of Yale University

innovations on university mechanism and teaching mode.

Wang Shuguo, president of Harbin Institute of Technology said humorously, "my research is about robot, and I hope the robot can be more like human beings. But as the university president, I am worried about cultivating human beings like robots."

Wang Zuwen, president of Dalian Maritime University said with emotion, "the former Southwest Associated University cultivated great ideologists and Nobel Prize winner under a very difficult circumstance, while in the recent 50 years of higher education in China, among tens of thousands of graduates, why is there nobody as great at all?"

Li Jian, president of Northeast Forestry University expressed his confusion directly, "the IQ of Chinese scholars is not lower than that of the foreigners, and the annual income of the outstanding professors keeps rising up to 200,000 Yuan, but why is there not any top-class talents cultivated in China?"

Qian Xuhong, president of East China University of Science and Technology jokingly termed the students, who have grown up in the examination-oriented education, as "the standardized generation," with no spare time to play, no time to dream, with only creative ideas killed by test papers.

In one voice the university presidents chastised the current education system for putting too much emphasis on cramming knowledge and repeatedly testing student's mastery of the book knowledge, but killing the students' interest and curiosity. "This might be the biggest difference between us and the foreign counterparts."

Qin Shaode, Party Secretary of Fudan University pointed out that as long as the college entrance exam exists, the quality-oriented education will be merely a phase. "There are no papers that are qualified to testify students' comprehensive quality."

Zhu Qingshi, president of China Scientific and Technical University attacked the phenomenon of plagiarism and other academic frauds, which have lingered on in recent years: "the academic atmosphere has reached its nadir in all Chinese universities." University is no longer the ivory tower for those in pursuit of academic spirit, and the faculties including younger teachers appear to be fatigue and sluggish. "Their topics of conversation are generally house, child, or how to publish essays with shortcuts, nothing about learning."

"To run a university well is to follow the eight words, 'self-government of university and freedom of academic research'", said by Zheng Xiangrong, president of Hunan Normal University. "Behind this perhaps lies more essential difference between us and the foreign universities."

All these thoughts and ideas represent the voices of conscience, of anxieties about the future of higher education in China, and of penetrating insights into the problems. Neither the university presidents nor the students are to be blame for the decline of education quality. It is the wrongs in the education system, the abuses in social circumstances, the shackles in the history and the government-run nature of universities that lead to it.

With public criticism, the appeals from the university presidents and the expectation on higher education from a prosperous country, China must consider putting on agenda reforming the education system and the university entrance examination system as soon as possible. If they do so, the second spring of Chinese higher education after the 1977's restoration of the college entrance examination system is about to come and Chinese prestigious universities will soon catch up with the world famous top class counterparts.

斯坦福魅力与大学话题

如果说，哈佛和耶鲁代表着美国传统的人文精神，斯坦福大学则是
21 世纪科技精神的象征。大学不仅是培养人才的高地，而且是国家战略
的智囊库、思想创新的蓄水池、科技进步的助推器、民族精神的涵养园。
我国必须将变革大学体制、改革高考制度、创新办学方式等实际举措提到
议事日程。

5 月 27 日是访美的最后一天，中午 12 点就要乘班机回国了。一大早起来，
觉得上午还有点时间可以出去看看。在我们的要求下，导游临时安排参观位
于旧金山湾附近的斯坦福大学 (Stanford University)。

校园剪影

在美国，斯坦福是与哈佛、耶鲁齐名的著名学府。在该校 100 多年的历
史中，已培养出 1 位总统（第 31 任总统胡佛），25 位诺贝尔奖获得者，142
位美国艺术科学院院士，84 位国家科学院院士，14 位国家科学奖得主以及数
不胜数的企业家。现任美国国务卿赖斯女士曾在该校担任讲师和研究员。

走近斯坦福，看不到大学校门，没有校牌标识，也没有校园围墙，校园
直通公路入口处的两座门亭，算是斯坦福大学唯一的标识了吧。

走进斯坦福，如同置身一座大公园，院落宽阔、树木繁茂，草地葱绿花
丛点缀，给人一种粗犷、开阔的美感。校园内一座座红瓦黄墙的砂岩建筑显
得古朴典雅，著名的胡佛塔高高耸立，优雅迷人。

胡佛塔内藏有非常珍贵的蒋介石日记手稿，记载了 1917 至 1973 年之间
蒋介石的心路历程。斯坦福大学胡佛研究中心于 2006 年 3 月 31 日对公众公
开蒋介石日记，因为手稿对于解读上个世纪围绕中国发生的一系列重大历史
事件，同时了解蒋介石的内心世界具有重要的参考价值，所以引起了海内外

学者的广泛关注。

胡佛塔旁边是庄重典雅、饰满壁画的大教堂，它是为纪念老斯坦福而建的。我们参观的这天上午恰逢星期日，前来做礼拜的人络绎不绝，晚点的人行色匆匆。导游介绍，学校外面的人也可以在这座教堂举行婚礼，但男女双方其中一个必须是斯坦福的毕业生。

教堂占地面积很大，分好几个院落，在第一层庭院中央平地上，矗立着一组黑色雕塑，它是世界著名雕塑大师罗丹的作品《加莱义民》。斯坦福大学建有一座艺术馆，陈列着很多罗丹的精美雕塑作品。这组雕像表现的是 14 世纪英法百年战争期间，法国北方城市加莱遭英军围困，破城在即，经过谈判，英王爱德华三世同意不屠城，但必须以市民推举 6 名代表受绞刑作为条件，危难时刻，6 名义士为拯救加莱挺身而出、甘愿赴死的情景。6 个人物雕像，个个面色凝重，或果敢坚定、或悲愤流泪、或蹒跚恐慌、或绝望无助，神态各异，形象逼真，把他们临危赴难时的心理表情和形体动作刻画得惟妙惟肖，不愧是大师的杰作。

名校风采

有着"西部哈佛"之称的斯坦福大学创建于 1891 年，是由当时的美国"铁路大王"斯坦福捐建的。建校初期斯坦福并不十分有名，但在开明校风和美国西海岸乐观主义精神的熏陶下，融合了西部文化和高科技的精髓，在科研和学术领域都取得骄人的成就。

目前，斯坦福大学共有在校生 1.4 万人，设有 30 个图书馆，藏书 650 多万册，全是电脑化管理。斯坦福大学基金雄厚，经费充足，教学设备一流。学校的体育设施也很先进，有能容纳 8.5 万人的体育馆、高尔夫球场和游泳馆等。

如果说，哈佛和耶鲁代表着美国传统的人文精神，那么，斯坦福大学则是 21 世纪科技精神的象征。斯坦福是一所注重理、工、医学科的综合大学，该校的许多工程学科、医科和数理化基础学科都排在全美大学前 10 名。该校的法学、社会科学系和人文科学系也毫不逊色，在美国名气很大。它的英语、心理学、政治和历史系在全美名列前茅，大众传播、戏剧、经济学、工商管理(MBA)等学科在美国大学排名中位居前 6 名。斯坦福大学要求学生文理兼备，做既有理科知识，又有人文修养的通才学生。

斯坦福大学商学院和哈佛大学商学院一样，被认为是美国最好的商学院。所不同的是，哈佛商学院代表比较传统的经营管理培训模式，培养的是"西装革履"式的大企业管理人才，而斯坦福则更强调开创科技新企业的中小企业精神，培养的是"穿 T 恤衫"的新一代小企业家。

说起斯坦福大学，许多人都知道他与美国"硅谷"的关系，公认的"硅谷之父"佛瑞德·特尔曼在担任斯坦福大学电子工程系主任期间，为他的学生出谋划策建立了著名的惠普公司。1951 年，特尔曼和当时的校长华莱士决定将 655 英亩的校园土地出租给从事高科技产业的公司，创建了斯坦福研究园，也就是后来的硅谷雏形。

斯坦福大学与中国有较深的渊源，迄今为止，斯坦福为中国培养了不少著名学者和科技英才，如我国著名植物学家裴鉴，著名医学家张孝骞，国际知名数学家李骏，中国科学院院士谢家麟等。在新一代中国留学生中，有一位神童邹求真非常出类拔萃，他是 CDMA 这项世界通信顶尖技术的主要研制者。邹求真原是南京东南大学少年班的学生，15 岁初中毕业后直接考入大学。1992 年，18 岁的邹求真被推荐到斯坦福大学深造，获得了该校留学生的特殊待遇。入学后，邹求真仅用了 8 个半月，就获得了斯坦福大学电子工程硕士学位。

何谓大学

因时间匆匆，我们未能详细参观斯坦福大学的全貌，但它给我们留下了深刻而美好的印象。除了斯坦福，美国还有哈佛、耶鲁、麻省理工、普林斯顿、哥伦比亚、宾夕法尼亚等一批世界顶尖的大学，在这些大学里，聚集着一大批思想大师、经济学家、科学巨匠和科技精英等一流人才。它们不但为美国也为世界输送了数以万计的青年才俊（目前美国授予的博士学位 30% 被外国学生获得），而且还发明创造了大量的科研成果。可以说，美国的大学对美国经济社会发展、科学技术创新、思想文化进步、对外文化交流所产生的影响是巨大而深远的。正如现任耶鲁大学校长理查德·莱文所说："在漫长的历史中，大学从未像现在这样成为国家竞争的工具和缔造和平的途径。它们是推动经济发展的中心，是取得和保持竞争优势所需的人才教育的中心。"
因此说，大学不仅是培养人才的高地，而且是国家战略的智囊库，思想创新
的蓄水池，科技进步的助推器，民族精神的涵养园。

纵观美国著名大学，它们无不因产生了像诺贝尔奖得主这样的世界级大
师，培养了众多的名人政要、企业精英等一流人物而闻名于世。尽管美国大
学多数都不像斯坦福大学那样拥有规模宏大的校园，但盛产大师、成果卓著、
富有活力却是它们的共同特征，正如清华大学老校长梅贻琦先生所说："所
谓大学者，非谓有大楼之谓也，有大师之谓也。"

路在何方

改革开放 30 年来，我国高等教育发生了翻天覆地的变化，高等院校总体
规模和综合水准有了显著提升。到 2005 年底，中国高校在校学生超过 230 万人，
毛入学率达到了 21%。

但不容回避的是，近年来，社会上浮躁逐利的风气也刮进了大学校园，
严重毒害了大学风气。国内许多大学盲目追求教育产业化、院校规模化、校园
现代化，从而导致贷款猛增，学费攀升，教学质量下降，毕业生就业困难。我
国大学教育质量的滑坡，大学人文精神的旁落已成为中外媒体评论的热点，并
为社会公众所垢病。实实在在地讲，今日中国之大学，不论是地方普通院校，
还是国家名牌学府，不但与欧美大学的办学水准差距较大，而且与我国传统教
育所推崇的人文精神相去甚远。特别是上世纪 90 年代末至今十来年间，尽管
国内大学规模迅速膨胀，校园设施大大改善，大学经费成倍增长，教师收入大
幅度提高，但大学毕业生的总体质量竟赶不上上世纪 80 年代毕业生的水平。

最近，从《半月选读》杂志看到一篇《中外大学校长反思中国高等教育》
的综述报道，这些大学掌门人在"第三届中外大学校长论坛"上，对现行中
国高等教育弊端的质疑、批评和反思，对大学体制、教学模式变革创新的呼
声和意见，无不触及中国教育的软肋。

哈尔滨工业大学校长王树国幽默地说："我是研究机器人的，希望机器
越来越像人，但作为校长，我担心把人培养得像机器。"

大连海事大学校长王祖温感慨地讲，"西南联大在那么艰苦的条件下培

Chinese-Foreign University Presidents Forum

养出了大思想家和诺贝尔奖获得者，而中国 50 多年的高等教育培养了这么多学生，为什么一个也没有？"

东北林业大学校长李坚直抒心中的困惑："中国学者的智商绝对不差，待遇也越来越好，优秀教授的年薪能超过 20 万元，究竟是什么原因导致中国在世界上少有顶尖的人才出现？"

华东理工大学校长钱旭红戏称被应试教育"摧残"的学生，是"被格式化的一代"：没有时间玩耍，甚至没有时间梦想，他们被一纸试卷扼杀了创意。

校长们异口同声地讨伐目前大学培养人才的方法：过于强调知识的灌输，不断重复考查学生对课本知识的掌握，扼杀了学生对知识的兴趣和好奇心。"这也许是我们与国外在人才培养方面最大的差别。"

复旦大学党委书记秦绍德一针见血地指出，高考指挥棒不改变，"唯分数论"的培养人才模式不改变，中国的素质教育将成为一句空话，"一张再好的试卷也无法考查考生的综合素质"。

针对这些年高校层出不穷的剽窃、抄袭等学术造假现象，中国科技大学校长朱清时认为，"现在的学术风气，在各个学校已经降到了最低点"。

　　对此，西安外语大学的王天定教授得出一个悲观的结论：今天的大学，已经不利于真正有志于学术追求的人生活，包括年轻教师在内的大学老师正处于一种比较萎靡的状态。"大家在一起常常议论的不是房子孩子，就是如何找关系发论文，学问连提都不提。"

　　"大学要办好，就是八个字'大学自治、学术自由。'"湖南师范大学校长刘湘荣掷地有声地说，"在这方面，我们与国外的差别可能是更本质的"。

　　侃侃而谈，肺腑之言，忧教忧国，真知灼见。看来，中国大学教育质量滑坡并不是校长无能，也不是学生不行，而是教育体制、社会环境、历史枷锁、官办方式使然。

　　面对社会各界的批评，面对大学校长们的呼声，面对国家强盛、民族复兴对高等教育的期待，我们必须将变革大学体制、改革高考制度、创新办学方式等实际举措提到议事日程。果真如此，1977 年中国恢复高考制度之后高等教育的第二个春天也就快要到了，中国名牌大学赶上世界一流大学的日子也就为期不远了。

What to Buy in the United States?

What shall we buy in the United States? Mainly three things: products of name brand, the local specialty and the cheap stuff. In fact, the things that cost you a dollar in the United States can also be bought with one Yuan in China. According to the actual purchasing power of RMB, the GNP and living standards in China are much higher than those in the United States. Whether you are an official or a civilian in China, as long as you drive your own private car, you have to cut down on expenses.

It is common to buy something for relatives, friends and colleagues, and sometimes for ourselves, when we Chinese visit the developed countries as it is not that easy to go abroad.

Brands and Specialty

Then what to buy? A plane? Technologically advanced, but can seldom be afforded. A car? They are really cheaper when bought here but cannot be driven back. Electronic products? They are fashionable and easy to carry, but they are already very common in domestic markets. Although it was hard to find things before the reform and opening up, China now has an abundance of goods for everyday consumption with much cheaper prices, and many products in the United States market now are found to be made in China. Without a long list of items to buy, we did not spend a huge amount of money in America. We did decide to buy three types of things: first, the name-brand products, mainly clothes and shoes, which cost much less there than in China, second, local specialties such as dietary supplements that are newly produced and have not yet been exported to China, and third, the cheap stuff. The average Chinese prefer to buy something for less than a hundred dollars or even less than a dollar, since they cannot afford many expensive goods.

Nike Factory Store

On the afternoon of May 19, on our way to Washington, alongside the Maryland highway, we stopped at a Nike store, which sold all sports shoes and sportswear. A pair of Nike sports shoes, which priced ¥ 600 to ¥ 700 in China, could be bought with 49.99 dollars. With the 5% sales tax added, the total cost would only be 52.5 dollars, that is, a bit more than ¥ 400. Although all marked "Made in China," the products were of very good quality. In fact, most of the items in this store were imported, while few were produced in the United States. The sports shoes I tried on were quite comfortable. What's more, the price was 30% cheaper than that in China, so I bought one pair happily and could not wait to wear them inWashington the next morning.

As said before, when we left Las Vegas for Los Angeles, we stopped at a little town named Bastogne to shop. In the suburb of the town there were many factory outlet stores, mainly selling clothes and shoes. One shop sold several types of Nautical jackets, which would be priced about ¥ 1000 in China, and around $100 in the shopping mall in the United States. However, the price here was only between 39.9 to 59.9 dollars, that is, 300 to 500 Yuan. The men in our group thought the price was right and the products were fine, so they bought one or two for themselves or their family.

In the United States, the price would always be set below a round number, normally less than 5 or 10, which meant 50 to 100 dollars, so that the customers felt the price was cheaper. This way of promotion has already been learnt by Chinese businessmen. But their American counterparts keep creating some new means, for example, if one wants to buy two pairs of shoes, for the first pair you will be charged full price, but for the second pair, you will get a 50% discount. If there is the third pair, it will be free. Because of the relatively cheaper price and the attractive discounts, the Chinese would inevitabley buy more than two pairs of shoes. The sales tax varies in different states, for example, the tax in Maryland is 5%, while in California it is 8.5%.

Chinese visitors like buying dietary supplement as is sold in many Chinese stores in New York, Washington, Los Angeles, San Francisco, etc, which, many tourists patronize. In the stores, Deep-sea Fish Oil, Lecithin Phosphate, Brain Age and Multi-Vitamin are normally are sold. Some stores sell Viagra but without doctor's prescription.

The biopharmaceutical industry in California is highly developed and thriving. There are hundreds of enterprises producing health care products, and almost all the dietary supplements mentioned above are made there. Due to the blind faith in American medicines and health care products, and also the illness of affluence caused by over-nutrition, Chinese tourists like to buy a lot of such products, some for themselves and most for their friends.

We have also visited two $1 Markets in

Wal-Mart CEO Lee Scott

Washington and Los Angeles. The size of the $1 Markets in the United States is not as small as we thought; there are many items being offered for one dollar. You can buy a lot of useful things there. Mr. Wu from China National Publications Import & Export Corporation bought some petroleum jelly for his colleague, introduced that it was just like the moisturizer people used in winter in the north of China, popular and good in quality.

"Purchasing Power Parity"

Most Chinese would think about the rate of exchange before they determine to buy anything abroad. But it is not wise to do so. It is much wiser to calculate only the cost of the currency in corresponding countries. The prices of American products are decided by the income level of the Americans. Except for luxuries, taking price ratio out of consideration, the general price of food, clothes and other commodities are not higher but about the same in China. For example, a tankard of Coke costs 2.4 dollars, and in China it is about two or three Yuan. That is to say, the things that need one dollar in the United States will also cost one Yuan in China. As a result, when measured on a purchasing power parity (PPP) basis, the exchange rate between the renminbi and the U. S. dollar is not as high as 8:1, although the income standard is much lower in China. In fact, Yuan always rises to higher ratio against the dollar.

In this way we can see that the basic living standards of Chinese is about the same as the Americans, while the weaker part is in the purchase of car, house, yacht, real estate and travelling abroad, that is the so called Purchasing Power Parity named by some economists, who think that when measured on the PPP basis, the GNP and living standard of Chinese are much higher than that of the Americans.

"Made in China"

The United States is a country with a developed economy, prosperous business and strong consumer demand. Wherever there are residents, there are different types of stores, which can be divided into the following: boutique, supermarket, shopping mall, factory outlet store, monopoly store, $1 Market, flea market, junk shop and garage sales. In recent years on-line shopping, teleshopping and mail-order have also become very popular.

Among all these types, the supermarket stands out as a great innovation by the Americans, who have the biggest chain supermarket in the world—Wal-Mart. Its founder Sam Walton started with a grocery store in Arkansas and achieved great success later by managing chain discount shops. After 40 years' hard work, he became the biggest retailer in the world. In 2001, Wal-Mart ranked first in the Fortune Global 500 with the highest operation revenue of 220 billion dollars, and has stayed at No.1 for four successive years. It was surpassed by Exxon Corporation in 2005, but it returned to be No.1 only one year later. Our tour guide told us that 90% of the merchandise in Wal-Mart is made in China, which had taken up 10% of the total exported goods from China to the United States.

While shopping in the United States, Chinese-made products can be seen

Washington Mall

everywhere. About ten years ago the "Made in China" products could be found only on the cheap goods, Now they can be found in the high-and medium-end stores, and even in boutiques. The large number of American imports of Chinese-made products has certainly promoted the development of the Chinese manufacturing industry, but the United States has also benefited from it. The price of these products would be much higher, maybe even ten times higher. For example, a lighter is priced ¥1 in China, while in the United States it cost up to 1 dollar or 1.5 dollars. So, American consumers can still save money by buying Chinese-made products. According to the estimate of American economists, every American family would save 621 dollars per year through the Sino-US trade.

American people also budget their money. During our visit to the U.S. international oil prices were skyrocketing, which had greatly influenced the life of the Americans and their driving habits. At that time, a litre of 97# gasoline in China cost almost 5 Yuan. In the United States, a gallon (about 3.8 liters) of 87# gasoline was about 3 dollars, which meant 1 Yuan higher per liter than that in China, when converted to RMB (the 87# in America is equal to 97# in China according to the gas standard). Not only did the price vary from place to place in the U.S., but it might be different at two gas stations on either side of the same road. The difference ranged from a few cents to several cents.

Our tour guide Peter Cai drove a Ford Wagon with an air displacement of 5.8 L. On our way from New York to Washington, as soon as there was a gas station with a cheaper price, he would get gas there. Afterwards, he would apologize, saying, "I'm so sorry, but the oil price is high, I have to save as much as possible." The local Chinese newspapers also reported that Bird Man, the minister of the U. S. Department of Energy, said that his wife always drove from one place to another to find cheap gas too. Thus, it can be seen that everyone, officials or common people, would like to find a cheaper way, when it comes to their car.

到美国买什么

一是买名牌，二是买特色，三是买便宜。在美国花一美元能买到商品，在中国也是一块钱左右，按人民币的实际购买力计算，中国的国民生产总值和国民生活水平还要高一大截。不管是高官还是平民，开的只要是私家车，自己掏腰包就得算经济账。

去趟美国不容易，总得给亲戚、朋友、同事和家人买点东西回来，碰上有自己合适的也买上一件，这是我们中国人出国尤其是去发达国家的通常心理。

名牌与特色

到美国买什么呢？飞机先进买不起，汽车便宜开不回，电子产品国内又不缺。现在的中国已不同于改革开放初期，一般日用消费品国内很丰富，而且比美国的价格低得多，就连美国市场上的消费品很多都是中国制造的。因为可买的东西不多，所以，到美国走了一圈，并没有拼血大购物。最后盘点，觉得有三类东西可以买：一是买名牌，如服装、皮鞋之类，价格比国内同类品牌合算。二是买特色，如营养保健品，有些是美国的最新产品，国内尚缺。三是买便宜。到了美国，普通中国人的口袋捉襟见肘，一般都买些几十、几块甚至一美元的商品。

5月19日下午，我们团队在赶往华盛顿的途中，在马里兰州公路边的耐克工厂直销店停留参观。店内全部是运动鞋和运动装，一双在国内售价600到700元人民币的耐克牌运动鞋，标价49.99美元，加上5%的消费税，不过52.5美元，折合人民币400元多一点。虽然标明中国制造(Made in China)，但质量很好，实际是中国企业为耐克公司加工的产品。美国商店出售的很多日用商品部是美国公司委托外国工厂加工的，本土生产的很少。运动鞋试穿后感觉轻松舒适，价格又比国内便宜三分之一，于是我就买了一双，第二天就穿上它走在华盛顿大街上了。

在拉斯维加斯通往洛杉矶的途中，有个小城镇叫巴斯通，往来两地的游客多在此地停留用餐和购物。城郊有一排建筑全是工厂直销店，基本都是销售服装和鞋类商品的。在一家店里有几种款式的 Nautica 牌夹克衫，这些夹克衫在中国品牌店一般卖 1000 多元人民币一件，在美国大商场也要卖 100 多美元，该店的标价在 39.9 到 59.9 美元之间，折合人民币 300 到 500 元。几位同行感觉物美价廉，赶紧掏腰包给自己或家人买了一两件。

美国商店的商品定价通常不超过一个整数，如定在 5 或 10 数值之下，50 元或 100 元以内，让消费者觉得价格便宜，现在国内商家早就学会了这些促销招数。美国店家还有些新的优惠促销手段，如卖鞋，第一双收全价，买两双第二双减半，买三双第三双赠送。本来价格不贵加上优惠促销，诱使许多中国游客纷纷购买两双以上的鞋子。美国的消费税各州不同，如马里兰州是 5%，而在加利福尼亚州则是 8.5%。

营养保健品是中国游客的最爱，在纽约、华盛顿、洛杉矶、旧金山等地都有华人经营的此类商店，而且是导游带团必去的地方。这些华人商店卖的大体都是深海鱼油、卵磷酸酯、脑白金、综合维生素之类的保健品，也有的商店出售"伟哥"，属于未经医生处方的交易行为。美国加利福尼亚州生物制药业发达，仅生产保健品的企业就有几百家，上述品种基本都是该地所产。对于美国药品和保健品的迷信，加上生活水平提高后营养过剩带来的富贵病，使许多中国游客大包小包地购买上述保健品，有的自己用，多数是送朋友。

这次在华盛顿和洛杉矶也转了两家一元店 (1 $ Market)。美国一元店的规模并不小，里面的商品琳琅满目，都是新品，而且都卖一美元，在这里你可选购到许多可心的东西。中图公司的老吴受同事所托，在一元店买到了几盒美国产的凡士林油，就像前些年北方人冬天擦手用的蛤蜊油，说是质量很好，颇受欢迎。

"购买力平价"

普通中国游客在美国购物，看上的东西先算算比价合不合适，然后再决定买不买。这样算虽然心理平衡但并不科学，在哪个国家购物就应按那个国家的货币收入来算账。美国的商品价格是按美国人的收人水平来确定的，如果不是奢侈品，不算比价，美国普通吃、穿、用的商品并不贵，与中国同类商品人民币的价格不相上下。如在美国快餐店，买一大杯可乐 2.4 美元，在国内也就是 2 至 3 元人民币，也就是说，就基本生活资料而言，在美国花一美元能买到的商品在中国也是一块钱人民币左右。如此算来，中国人挣钱虽少，但同样数额人民币与美元的收入，按实际购买力来算账并不是 8∶1 的概念，人民币的实际比价还会高一些。因此，中国城镇居民的基本生活水平比美国人差不了太多，所差的也就是汽车、住房、游艇等高档品、不动产和出国旅游等方面，这也就是国际上一些经济学家所谓的"购买力平价"说。他们认为，若按人民币的实际购买力计算，中国的国民生产总值和国民生活水平还要高一大截。

中国制造

美国是一个经济发达、商业繁荣、消费旺盛的国家，凡是有人群居住的地方，都开有各种各样的商店。美国的商店可大致分为：精品店、超级市场、大型购物中心 (Mall)，工厂直销店、专业商场、一元店、跳蚤市场、旧货商店和家庭车库售货等。此外，近些年还兴起了网上购物、电话购物和邮购等各种新型购物方式。

在所有商店类型中，超级市场是美国人的一大发明，美国有全球最大的连锁超级市场——沃尔·玛特（Wall Mart，即沃尔玛）。它的创始人山姆·沃顿早年从阿肯色州一个小镇上干杂货店起家，后来开设折扣连锁店取得巨大成功，经过 40 年的奋斗，一跃成为全球最大的零售企业。2001 年，沃尔玛以 2200 亿美元的历史最高营业收入跃居世界 500 强榜首，并且连续 4 年蝉联 500 强冠军，虽 2005 年被埃克森石油公司超过，屈居第二，但 2006 年又重新夺回第一。据导游介绍，目前沃尔玛经营的商品 90% 是中国制造的，它采购的中国商品已占到中国出口美国商品总额的 10%。

在美国逛商场，随处可见中国制造的商品，也许 10 年前，"中国制造"只能在廉价货位上才能看到，现在高、中、低档商品都有了，即使在精品店里，"中国制造"也随处可见。美国进口了那么多"中国制造"，当然拉动了中国制造业的发展，但美国商家也因经营"中国制造"赚了不少钱。我们看到，中国制造的商品，在美国商店一般都加价几倍到十倍出售，如国内售价仅一块钱的一次性打火机，美国人则卖到 1 至 1.5 美元。美国消费者因购买"中国制造"也节省了很多钱。据美国经济学家测算，美国每个家庭每年从中美贸易中受益 621 美元。

美国人虽然有钱，但也很注意节省，处处精打细算。这次在美国访问期间，正赶上国际石油价格一路飙升，油价上涨对于"汽车上的民族"美国人的生活影响很大。当时中国一公升 97 号汽油已接近 5 块钱，美国一加仑（合 3.8 升）87 号汽油约 3 美元，折合成每升价格比中国贵一块多钱（美国 87 号汽油标准相当于中国 93 号）。美国油价不但各地不同，就是同一路口两边的加油站价格也不相同，差价从几美分到几十美分不等。

导游蔡彼德开着他的排气量 5.8 的福特牌中巴旅行车，拉着我们从纽约至华盛顿，途中见了有便宜油的加油站就进去加上一点儿，他客气地对我们说："不好意思，油价太贵，能省一点儿是一点儿"。当地华人报纸报道，美国能源部部长伯德曼说，他的夫人也开着车到处找便宜油。看来，不管是高官还是平民，开的只要是私家车，自己掏腰包就得算经济账。

Chinese and Americans in My Eyes

There are many examples that prove that individual Chinese is generally intelligent and diligent. But the Chinese community, as a whole, lacks cohesion and team spirit. The gap between the Chinese and the Americans lies not merely in the difference in appearance, but mostly in temperament and spirit. Maybe it is just the Americans insistence and perseverance, never being fickle and opportunistic, the so-called "stupidity" in the eyes of most Chinese that has made them more successful.

During our visit to the United States, our Chinese compatriots took charge of the whole reception process. The twelve-day journey could be summarized in six sentences: "lived in American hotels, traveled by American car, enjoyed American Scenery; but ate Chinese food, visited Chinese shops, and purchased Chinese products." Although we were abroad, we felt not far away from China.

Always among the Chinese

We never felt the culture shock during our visit to the United States, even at the first moment we arrived. When we just landed in New York's Kennedy Airport, our tour guide Peter Cai, who I introduced in the chapter "First Step on the United States", was already there to pick us up. A Hong Konger with the U.S. green card, Mr. Cai has been a tour guide for more than ten years since he migrated to the United States in the 1980s. During the four days from New York to Washington, he proved to be a perfect guide and driver who introduced us to everything and had a well-planned out agenda.

In Las Vegas and Los Angeles, our tour guide was Mr. Ge, who had been in America for almost three years. Before that, he worked at a foreign trade company in China where he was well paid, but he did not like the restrictive atmosphere of the state-owned company. Since his sister and brother-in-law all lived in Los Angeles, he came to the United States as a visiting

Tour Guide Peter Cai (right) with Shi Li

relative several years ago, and later became a tour guide. Mr. Ge, who came from Shandong Providence, was very outgoing and talkative. He brought us to many places and introduced us to a lot of sites in Las Vegas, the Great Canyon and Los Angeles.

In San Francisco, the one waiting for us was a 26-year-old Chinese youngster. The young fellow came from Shanghai. After getting his B.A. degree in China, he chose to further his study of computers at the University of California in San Francisco. Unfortunately, he graduated when there was waning enthusiasm in the IT industry, so he could not find an appropriate job and had to take a makeshift job as a tour guide. Compared with Peter Cai, the tour guides from mainland were not as qualified and professional, with haphazard schedules and not as informative, indicating the need for the American travel agency to improve its service.

With language barriers and cultural differences, Chinese tourists surely feel it more convenient to be received by their fellow countrymen in the United States. In that case, just as an old Chinese proverb says, rich water should be kept in one's own fields; at least the one who pays and the other who earns are from the same "field," China. We asked our tour guide if Chinese travelling groups are always received by the Chinese. He said they mostly are, and he told us that the Japanese and Koreans also have their own reception groups, which aren't usually available to foreigners. Although it is quite helpful for us to enjoy the exotic landscapes of the United States, I felt regretful to have missed more chances to interact with the Americans, as it was a perfect opportunity to do so. Visiting abroad is different than being in our country, since we spend more money, time as well as energy. We did widen our horizons a little bit through traveling, but it seemed that we have wasted more, sources and opportunities, to obtain some substantial achievement.

The "Bad Habits" of Chinese Tourists

During our ten days' visit to the United States, except for the Americans, we had seen more Chinese than any other people. In recent years, with the development of our national strength, and many people in the country becoming wealthier, the number of outbound Chinese tourists, government-sponsored and self-supported, rocketed to 31.02 million in 2005, in 117 countries and areas. Surely it is good for us to broaden our horizon and spread Chinese culture. But as the material wealth of our countrymen has increased, the spiritual wealth seems not to have changed accordingly. Some disgraceful acts of the Chinese fellow travelers have severely damaged China's international image as an ancient civilized country, a "nation of etiquette" and a newly rising giant. In recent years, together with the praises for Chinese development, complaints and criticisms about Chinese tourists have constantly been in the news at home and abroad. Last year, China's Central Government's Office of the Spiritual Civilization Development Steering Commission cooperated with the National Tourism Administration to collect "The Frequent Bad Behaviors of Chinese Citizens Who Travel Abroad," and listed ten categories:

1. Littering, spitting, and not flushing the toilet;
2. Smoking in non-smoking areas;
3. Snatching seats in any means of transportation; queue-jumping;
4. Talking loudly in public;
5. Lack of respect for religion and local customs;
6. Taking off shoes and socks; sloppily dressed in public; cross-legged; blatantly picking teeth in public;
7. Talking dirty; behaving rudely; losing temper easily and cursing when annoyed;

8. Bargaining in places offering no bargains; pressing foreigners for group photo;
9. Being involved in gambling and visiting red-light districts;
10. Deliberately wasting food in buffets; taking away the non-gifts from hotels; refusing to give tips after service.

The above points of uncivilized behaviors have really made us Chinese upset and shameful. We were once looked down upon when we were poor, but we cannot take it for granted that when we get rich, we'll definitely win respect from others. It takes just a generation's striving to make a millionaire in a person, but several generations' polish to form a gentleman in mind. The gap between us and the westerners lies not only in appearance, but in temperament and spirit. The bad habits of Chinese people have grown over the years, the lack of modern civilized qualities like credibility, observance of law, courtesy, helpfulness, hygiene and orderly behavior might be the reasons why we are despised by the westerners. I am not a worshiper of foreign things. I just want to be honest and hope my countrymen can face directly their "ugliness", and get rid of the bad habits. Only when we take stock of ourselves and our behavior, how can we get the respect from the world and be truly "a nation of etiquette".

All those who have been abroad have the same feeling. In western countries, there are many successful Chinese individuals, intelligent and industrious, like the famous scientist Yang Zhenning , Li Zhengdao and the famous politicians in the United States, such as Elaine Chao, and Gary Faye Locke. According to *Wall Street Telegraph*, nearly 50 mayors in the United States were Chinese in 2005, which proved that more and more Chinese have stood out from the others and had been gradually accepted by the American mainstream society. It also indicated that Chinese could not only achieve splendid successes in the fields of economy, science and technology, arts, medicine and sports, but also in American politics.

However, as a whole, the Chinese community appears to lack cohesion and team spirit compared with the Japanese, Vietnamese and other Asians. The Chinese seem to be fond of getting together for fun, but actually always

Elaine Chao

for internecine struggles. This might be a reason for the overseas Chinese's status and impact to be not proportional to their population and wealth. For example, nowadays more and more Chinese have taken part in American politics, but in the huge melting pot of the American society, they remain only a very small minority. We have a long way before we are fully embrace on the international political stage.

The "Stupidity" of the Americans

Although we did not often interact with the Americans during our journey, I still got some intuitive impressions of them, since I did encounter them in hotels, restaurants, scenic spots or just on the streets. All the Americans seemed optimistic, generous and relaxed. Whether they were waiting for a bus, shopping or traveling, they would always line up patiently and would wait their turn. Moreover, they'd always nod first and say hello to me when we saw each other and they would always be ready to help or apologize when necessary.

Once during our visit to the natural museum in Washington, when we were about to cross the street, we saw a car coming on our right side. We stopped to wait for it to pass, but the driver stopped and beckoned us to go first. Another day when we were at the Grand Canyon, while I was walking along a path on the edge of the canyon, a middle-aged couple holding a child came from the opposite direction. The wife said "Hello" kindly, which made me feel very welcome in this foreign country.

The Americans dress casually. You seldom see people in suits in the street, nor do you see two people wearing the same clothes. Many Americans are plump or stout, maybe resulting from their bad eating habits. People of more than 100 kilograms are commonplace while those over 200 kilograms are not surprising. In the Aerospace museum, we

Casual Americans

An American Mom with Two Kids

saw a tall and stout middle-aged man, who seemed to weigh more than 250 kilograms. According to research, the United States has the largest number of overweight people in all the developed countries. One out of three Americans in average is considered obese. Obesity has become a kind of sickness and burden to the Americans, and every year they spend more than 90 billion dollars in the treatment of it and its related diseases. Meanwhile, Americans also exercise a lot. On a Sunday while we were visiting Washington, along the street, there were always people of different ages running past us with mineral water in tow.

During our visit, we found a common phenomenon on many different occasions. That is, we often saw a young mother taking two children with her, holding one at the age of two or three by the hand, while wheeling the other, normally an infant. Later we learned that in the United States, it is really an example of eugenics to bear two children in succession, as it can both save the raising cost and benefit the children's growth. At the same time, the young mother can recover from the trauma of birth earlier to regain her youth and vitality. Thus both bearing and rearing children take a lot of learning. What the Americans have done might accord with the natural law the more.

Americans are mostly white, but they are a nation of immigrants. In the metropolises in the United States, bustling crowds of different nations, different ethnic groups and different skin colors shuttle back and forth. The United States is really a melting pot, with diversifications in race, culture, religion, lifestyle, state law and geographical landscape.

As a nation of immigrants, the nature of the Americans is adventurous and creative. In agriculture, the Americans have created a highly developed planting industry and animal husbandry, in order to grow huge amounts of soybean, rice, wheat, cotton, fodder and have become the major exporter of agricultural products. In industry, the Americans have the biggest automobile manufacturing and plane manufacturing industry, the most advanced chemical military, as well as biopharmaceutical industry. Ford Motor, Boeing aircraft, Coca Cola and IBM have been the representatives of American industrial civilization in different periods. In commerce, the Americans have created many globally famous commercial wonders, such as the chain-store kingdom, Wal-Mart and the fast-food magnate, McDonalds. In education, the Americans have set up Harvard, Yale and other world top-class universities and cultivated numerous talents and masters. In art and culture, the Americans have created Hollywood and Disneyland, favorites of the whole world. In sports, they have NBA and Punch-Out, now the known and followed throughout the world. In promoting military power, they own the strongest armed forces and keep updating their army with modern combat technologies, and take the lead in the researches of atomic bomb, neutron bomb and other destructive nuclear weapons as well as other sophisticated conventional weapons. In science and technology, from Edison's electric light, Bell's telephone to Bill Gates' Microsoft and internet, all these inventions were made by Americans. In aerospace industry, from Apollo, which landed on the moon to the aerospace plane, the Martian probe, Americans have reached great heights of space technology.

Here we are not discussing the hegemonic United States, but the creative one. Facing their brilliant achievements, we have to think about a question: Since we are the same as human beings, but why is the creativity of the Americans more prosperous and everlasting? Is it their economic and social systems that provide them a stage to exert their individual creativity or is it the gifted spirit of the Americans to be scientific and pragmatic?

Some say that the Americans are of one-track mind, which means they are not flexible enough. But actually it is perhaps just this "stupidity," with perseverance and concentration behind that has made them more successful than others.

同胞形象与美国人印象

华人作为个体聪明勤奋，成功者很多，但是，作为一个族群，华人社团则往往缺乏凝聚力和团队精神。我们中国人的差距不仅是块头形体上的，主要还是精神气质上的。或许正因为美国人"傻"，做事认真执著，不朝三暮四，不投机取巧，才能够把事情做成功。

访美期间，全程都是由华人同胞负责接待，12天的行程可用六句话来概括：住美国店，坐美国车，看美国景；吃中国饭，逛华人店，买中国制造。人虽到了外国，但事仍没离开中国。

走不出的华人圈

从我们踏上美国国土的那一刻起，就有同胞负责接机，在纽约肯尼迪机场迎接我们的导游叫蔡彼德，在《初踏美利坚》一文中已经介绍，蔡彼德是一位持美国绿卡的香港人，上世纪80年代移居美国，做了十多年的导游接待。从纽约到华盛顿4天行程，蔡彼德一人既做导游又兼司机，日程安排得井井有条，参观讲解满有素质。

到拉斯维加斯和洛杉矶两站，陪同我们的是移居美国不到三年的导游小葛，他来美国前在国内一家外贸公司工作，待遇虽然不错，但他不愿受国有单位的约束，姐姐、姐夫又在洛杉矶，几年前就以探亲名义来到美国，后来做起了导游。小葛是山东人，既豪爽也健谈，在拉斯维加斯、大峡谷和洛杉矶带着我们看了很多地方，也介绍了不少情况。

到了旧金山，负责接站和陪同我们的是一位26岁的年轻人。小伙子是上海人，在国内大学毕业后来到美国求学，在旧金山加州分校攻读计算机专业研究生，毕业一年多，因美国IT产业热浪消退，暂时找不到合适的工作，也做起了导游接待。比起蔡彼德，大陆去的导游属半路出家，在专业素质上有明显差距，日程活动安排随意性强，讲解缺乏知识性和系统性，说明负责接待中国团队的美国旅行社亟需提高业务水准。

受语言、文化和饮食习惯等限制，中国人去美国访问由华人接待自然有许多方便之处，起码中国人的钱由同胞赚，肥水不流外人田。我们问导游，来自中国的团队是不是都由华人接待？导游回答，基本是这样。并解释说，日本人和韩国人也都有自己一条龙的接待圈子，外国人很难挤进去。如此虽好，但好不容易去趟美国，除了看西洋景，没有接触几个美国人，难得与人家对话交流，岂不是憾事？出国访问不同国内出差，费了好多周折，花了不少银子，如果只是走马观花，旅游购物，虽说也长了点见识，但对人家的事情毕竟只了解了点皮毛，没有实质性的收获，既是资源的浪费，也是机会的损失。

难改的国人陋习

在美十多天，除了美国人，见到最多的就是中国人。近年来，随着我国国力的提升，国人腰包的鼓起，公派团队和私人出国（境）旅游的人数急剧增加，2005 年中国出国（境）人数达到 3102 万人次，出行目的地国家和地区达到 117 个。中国人开始有钱了，出国旅游观光的人越来越多了，对于国人开阔眼界，传播中华文明是件好事情。但是，在物质财富增加的同时，国人的精神财富却似乎没有相应增长，某些中国人在国（境）外的种种不雅表现给文明古国大丢脸面，使我们新兴大国的国际形象大打折扣。近年来，国际舆论在大力赞扬中国发展成就的同时，对中国游客的批评经常见诸报端。去年，中央文明办和国家旅游局公开征集我国公民出国（境）旅游常见的不文明行为，归纳起来有如下 10 种表现：

1. 随处抛丢垃圾、废弃物，随地吐痰、擤鼻涕、吐口香糖，上厕所不冲水，不讲卫生留脏迹；

2. 无视禁烟标志想吸就吸，污染公共空间，危害他人健康；

3. 乘坐公共交通工具时争抢拥挤，购物、参观时插队加塞，排队等候时跨越黄线；

4. 在车船、飞机、餐厅、宾馆、景点等公共场所高声接打电话、呼唤朋友、猜拳行令、扎堆吵闹；

5. 在教堂、寺庙等宗教场所嬉戏、玩笑，不尊重当地居民风俗；

6. 大庭广众之下脱去鞋袜、赤膊袒胸，把裤腿卷到膝盖以上、跷"二郎腿"，酒足饭饱后毫不掩饰地剔牙，卧室以外穿睡衣或衣冠不整，有碍观瞻；

7. 说话脏字连篇，举止粗鲁专横，遇到纠纷或不顺心的事大发脾气，恶语相向，缺乏基本社交修养；

8. 在不打折扣的店铺讨价还价，强行拉外国人拍照、合影；

9. 涉足色情场所，参加赌博活动；

10. 不消费却长时间占据消费区域，吃自助餐时多拿浪费，离开宾馆饭店时带走非赠品，享受服务后不付小费，贪占小便宜。

上述 10 种表现概括得既全面又准确，委实让人感到汗颜。殊不知，人穷了让人瞧不起，富了也未必能赢得尊重。要成为富豪，只需一代人的奋斗；而要成为绅士，则需要几代人的修养。与欧美人相比，我们中国人的差距不仅是块头形体上的，主要还是精神气质上的。长期以来，国人身上积累的陋习太多，诚信、守法、礼貌、助人、卫生、秩序等现代文明素养欠缺，这也许是某些西方人从骨子里瞧不起我们中国人的重要原因。本人决不是崇洋媚外、自贬家人，而是想说点实话，希望国人有勇气面对自己的丑陋，改掉自己的毛病。知耻而后勇，只有痛下决心、洗心革面，才能赢得世人的尊敬，成为真正的文明之邦。

去过欧美的国人都有这样的同感：在国外，华人作为个体聪明勤奋，成功者很多，特别是美籍华人，成就非凡。从前产生了像杨振宁、李政道等一批著名科学家，近些年又在美国政坛涌现出像赵小兰、骆家辉等一批担任联邦部长、州长和市长的政界人物。据《华尔街电讯》报道，2005 年有近 50 位华人在美国当市长。这说明，越来越多的华人脱颖而出，已经融入美国主流社会；说明华人不但在经济、科技、文艺、医学、体育等领域能够取得辉煌成就，还可以登上美国政治舞台一显身手。

但是，作为一个族群，与日本人、越南人等其他亚洲人相比，华人社团往往显得缺乏凝聚力和团队精神。中国人表面喜欢扎堆凑热闹，实际上常搞内耗，习惯"窝里斗"。因此，华人在海外居住国的地位和影响力，与其人数和财富不成正比。比如在美国，尽管华人参政的越来越多，但在偌大的美国，仍然是寥若晨星，华人在政坛上的真正崛起，进而成为不可忽视的力量，还有很长的路要走。

美国人的"傻"

虽然很少直接和美国人打交道，但在宾馆、餐厅、景点、大街上天天碰到美国人，逐渐地对美国人形成了一些直观的印象。普通美国人看上去大多单纯乐观、朴实大方、随意自然。他们在等车、购物、参观时自觉地排队等候，没有一点急不可耐的样子。在很多场合与美国人面对面碰上了，他们会主动地点头微笑、打招呼，帮忙、道歉也是美国人的日常功课。

我们在华盛顿参观自然史博物馆时，正要过路，右侧驶过来一辆大轿车，我们停下来示意让它先过，但司机停下车，连连摆手让我们先通过。参观大峡谷时，我沿着峡谷边缘的小路正往前游走，有对中年夫妇领着孩子也从对面走来，女主人 Hello 一声，主动打招呼，让人在异国他乡感到亲切。

美国人衣着随便，在大街上很少看到有人西装革履的，更看不到穿同样衣服的人。可能是饮食结构的关系，人高马大的美国人胖子很多，100 多公斤的胖子随处可见，200 公斤的也非个别。在航空航天博物馆，我们见到一位高大肥胖的中年男子，看上去足有 250 多公斤。据统计，美国是发达国家中肥胖和超重人口最多的国家，平均每三个人中就有一名胖人。肥胖对美国人来说是一种病态和负担，美国人每年用于治疗肥胖症及相关疾病的费用高达 900 多亿美元。当然，美国人很注意锻炼，星期天我们在华盛顿街头参观，不时遇到跑步的男女老少，有的身上还背着瓶矿泉水。

一路走来，在很多场合发现一个同样的现象，美国年轻的妈妈同时携带两个孩子，一个两三岁，手里牵着；一个襁褓中，身上背着或小车推着。分析加询问，才明白美国年轻人结婚后连续生两个孩子确是优生之道，既节省家庭养育成本，也对孩子成长有利，也好让年轻的妈妈早点从生育负担中解脱出来，恢复青春和活力。看来怎样生孩子、带孩子、养孩子是一门很大的学问，美国人的做法可能更符合人类生育和孩子成长规律。

美国是个以白人为主的移民国家，在美国各大城市熙熙攘攘的人群当中，你会看到各个国家、各个民族、各种肤色的人，可以说，美国是世界人种的大杂汇。有人讲，多样化是美国的重要特征：种族的多样化、文化的多样化、宗教信仰的多样化、生活方式的多样化、各州法律的多样化、地理景观的多样化……

移民国家的美国人本性勇于冒险、富于创造。搞农业，美国人创造了高度发达的种植业和畜牧业，每年向世界市场提供大量的大豆、稻米、小麦、棉花、饲料粮等，成为世界上重要的农产品出口大国；搞工业，美国人拥有世界上最大的汽车、飞机制造业，最先进的化学工业、军事工业以及生物制药业，美国人发明的福特汽车、波音飞机、可口可乐、IBM 计算机等成为各个时期美国工业文明的象征；搞商业，美国人造就了连锁帝国沃尔玛、快餐大王麦当劳等影响世界的商业王国；办教育，美国人创办了哈佛、耶鲁等一大批世界顶尖大学，造就了为数众多的一流科学家和大师级人才；搞文化，美国人打造的好莱坞影城和出产的大片、创造的迪斯尼乐园风靡全球；搞体育，美国的 NBA 职业篮球赛、拳王争霸赛成为全世界关注的热点；搞军事，美国不但拥有世界上最强大的军队，而且不断更新军队体制，创新现代化作战方式，率先研制出原子弹、中子弹等毁灭性核武器和各种尖端常规武器；搞发明，从爱迪生发明电灯、贝尔发明电话，再到当今比尔·盖茨的微软帝国、互联网世界无一不是美国人的杰作；搞航天，从阿波罗登月到航天飞机，再到火星探测器，美国的科技水平登峰造极……

这里，我们谈论的不是美国人的霸道，而是美国人的创造，面对美国人创造的辉煌业绩，我们不能不思考这样一个问题：同为地球人，为什么美国人会有如此长盛不衰的创造力？是美国的经济社会体制能够充分发挥个人的创造才能，还是美国人天生就有一种科学务实的探索精神？

有人讲，美国人一根筋，意指美国人做事不够灵活，不善变通。其实，或许正因为美国人"傻"，做事认真执著，不朝三暮四，不投机取巧，才能够把事情做成功。

Bibliography

1. Shen Mingde, *A General Survey of the United States*, Beijing: China Maps Press, 2004.

2. Yu Lihua, *Travel Through the Whole World: the United States*, Beijing: China Tourism Press, 2003.

3. Shi Peijun, *Knowing a Country from Its Capital.*

4. Xue Shengxiong, Xue Jie, "Washington: The Capital of the United States," *Traveller*, 2001, 5.

5. Shi Cheng, "The Vietnam War," *Global Times*, April 30, 2004.

6. "Defeat in the Vietnam War," Sina.com.

7. "The Most Authoritative Detailed Data of the Injuries and Deaths in the Korean War," Tongxing Net.

8. Duan Yong, *Contemporary American Museums*, Beijing: Science Press, 2003.

9. "Some National Treasures Taken To Foreign Countries from 1860 to 1900," *Beijing Evening News*, August 14, 2000.

10. Li Zhengxin, "The One Hundred Year's Great Changes in Las Vegas of the United States: from a Desert to a Luxury Gambling Town," *Global Times*, May 18, 2005.

11. Tan Xuelai, "The Father of the Gambling Town Creating a New Landmark with 2.7 Billion Dollars," *National Business Daily*, April 29, 2005.

12. Liu Aicheng, "The Poisonous Weeds Turning into Fragrant Flowers: an Observation of the Gambling in the United States Seen from Las Vegas," *The People's Daily*, September 25, 2005.

13. "Grand Canyon Colorado," Sina. com.

14. Chen Shixu, "Miscellaneous Knowledge about the United States," *Petrel*, 2006. 7.

15. *Manual for Exploring the Yarlung Zangbo Grand Canyon*.

16. Zhi Xiaomin, *The National Government's Three Gorges Project.*

17. "The World's Number One Dam Fully Completed," *The Xinhua News Agency*, May 20, 2006.

18. Liu Geli, Gao Yijuan, "Cracking the Ecological Bewilderment in Constructing the Huge Dam."

19. Jiang Wandi, "A Look into the Chinese Scenery at the Book Trade Fair," *The People's Daily*, May 30, 2006.

20. "The Basic Information of the National News and Publishing in 2005," *China News and Publishing Journal*, August 18, 2006.

21. "The Country's National Reading and Buying Intention Sampling Survey Report 2006," China Publishing Science Institute.

22. "A Glimpse of the Global Reading," *China News and Publishing Paper*, August 30, 2006.

23. "Los Angeles, the City of Angels: The Pearl on the West Coast of the United States," Xinhuanet.com.

24. "Chinese Contestants First Seen at the 1932 Los Angeles Olympic Games," *Beijing Entertainment Economic Journal*, July 3, 2006.

25. San Francisco, "The Cultural and Financial Center of the Western United States," Xinhuanet.com.

26. Jiang Lexing, Zhou Guobao, A Journey to the World-Famous Universities, *China Waterpower Press*, 2006.

27. *Half-moon Selected Readings*, 2006, 16.

28. "Shopping in the United States," sina.com.

29. List of Top Global 500 in 2005 published by *Fortune* of the United States.

30. "The Number of Person-time of Chinese Citizens Leaving China Reached 3102 in 2005," Chinanews.com.

31. "The Black List of Bad Habits Seen in Tourism Home and Abroad," *Shenzhen Commercial News*, September 23, 2006.

32. He Qun, "Pattern-matching Production: the Text Production in Hollywood Movie Industry."

33. Hu Zhengrong, "The Core and Operating Strategy of the American Movie Industry," *Film Art*, 2005.1.

34. Zhang Jiangyi, "An Analysis of the International Competition

Development of China's Movie Industry."

35. Tian Yannan, "The American Blockbusters Are 'Political Commodities' ."

36. "How Disneyland Enjoyed 50 Years of Happiness," *Jingbao*, July 18, 2005.

37. "The Disneyland Landmark of Orlando in America," Google. Earth. Observation.

38. "The State of Operation of China's Theme Parks Is Not Satisfactory," people. cn.

39. "A Survey Report of the Construction of China's Theme Parks," 163.com.

40. "Los Angeles: Capital of the American Homeless People," quoted from the *European Times.*

41. Xu Xiaoping, "The Extremely Rich American Philanthropist," Sina.com.

参考文献

1. 沈明德，《美国一览》，北京：中国地图出版社，2004.

2. 虞丽华，《走遍全球：美国》，北京：中国旅游出版社，2003.

3. 史培军，《从首都认识一个国家》

4. 薛胜雄、薛洁，"美国首都华盛顿"，《旅行家》，2001(5).

5. 史诚，"越南战争"，《环球时报》，2004-04-30.

6. "溃败在越南战场"，新浪网.

7. "朝鲜战争伤亡最权威的翔实数据"，同行网.

8. 段勇，《当代美国博物馆》，北京：科学出版社，2003.

9. "1860-1900 年流失海外的部分国宝"，《北京晚报》，2000-08-14.

10. 李正信，"美国拉斯维加斯百年巨变：从荒芜沙漠到豪华赌城"，《 环球时报》，2005-05-18.

11. 谭学莱，"赌城之父 27 亿打造新地标"，《每日经济新闻》，2005-04-29.

12. 刘爱成，"草变香花——从拉斯维加斯看美国赌业"，《人民日报》，2005-09-25

13. "科罗拉多大峡谷"，新浪网

14. 陈世旭，"美国杂识"，《海燕》，2006(7).

15. 《雅鲁藏布大峡谷探险手册》

16. 智效敏，《国民政府的三峡工程》

17. "世界第一坝全线建成"，新华社电，2006-05-20.

18. 刘戈力、高弋绢，《破解大坝建设中的生态困惑》

19. 江宛棣，"书业盛会上看中国风景"，《人民日报》，2006-05-30.

20. "2005 年全国新闻出版业基本情况"，中国新闻出版报，2006-08-18.

21. 《全国国民阅读与购买倾向抽样调查报告（2006）》，中国出版科学研究所.

22 "环球阅情一瞥"，《中国新闻出版报》，2006-08-30.

23. "美国西海岸的明珠——天使之城洛杉矶"，新华网.

24. "1932 年洛杉矶奥运会首见中国选手"，《北京娱乐信报》，2006-07-03.

25. "美国西部的文化和金融中心——旧金山"，新华网.

26. 江乐兴、周国宝，《世界名校之旅》，中国水利水电出版社，2006.

27.《半月选读》，2006(16).

28. "在美国购物"，新浪网.

29. "美国《财富》杂志公布 2005 年度全球 500 强企业名单".

30. "2005 年中国公民出境人数达到 3102 万人次"，中国新闻网.

31. "境内外旅游陋习黑榜公布"，《深圳商报》，2006-09-23.

32. 何群，《配方式生产：好莱坞电影产业的文本制作》

33. 胡正荣，"美国电影产业的核心与经营策略"，《电影艺术》，2005(1).

34. 张江艺，"中国电影产业国际竞争力发展分析"

35. 田雁南，"美国大片是'政治商品'"

36. "迪斯尼如何快乐 50 年"，《竞报》，2005-07-18.

37. "美国奥兰多迪斯尼乐园地标"，Googl. Earth 观察.

38. "中国主题公园经营状况不理想"，人民网.

39. "中国主题公园建设调查报告"，网易.

40 "洛杉矶成美国无家可归者之都"，转自《欧洲时报》.

41. 徐小平，"富可敌国的美国慈善家"，新浪网.

Epilogue

It was a delightful experience to visit the United States last year. My long-cherished dream came true, and the journey left an unforgettable impression on me. I did not intend to write a book when I started my journey, but after I came back, I felt so excited and could not help but write my thoughts down when I read my travel journal and looked at my photos. I began with *Reading: An Indispensable Spiritual Cultivation of Chinese*, and *The Magnificent Grand Canyon* which were published respectively on *Hebei Daily* and *Tourism Overview*. Encouraged by my friends who read my journals, I concentrated on my writing and finished my entire travel journal about the United States.

To get a coherent narration and reading, the nineteen articles are basically arranged in accordance with my travel schedule. I have described American cities and geographical landscape, gave my impression of American culture and education, and made an observation of the American social and economic problems, with some reflection of the United States' national spirit. Although my topics are rambling and broad, the main idea is focused on the United States and its reflection on China. Through the description of American phenomenon especially the narration and interpretation of American culture, I appeal for more reflection about Chinese culture and national spirit.

Some people might think that I am unqualified to write something valuable as there are numerous books about America and I have only been there for ten days. Indeed, these concerns are reasonable, as the limitation of time and area, I couldn't get a comprehensive impression on every aspect of America. But I think whether one can write good travel notes or not does not totally depend on one's length of stay, but on the depth of the author's knowledge and his insights, the concentration of the author's emotion and the beauteousness of the author's language. I do not hint that I have reached such a high level, but I have spent a lot of time and effort to do a better job. Since the beginning of June of last year, I have read hundreds of thousands of words and related books and articles in my spare time and spent four months finishing my first draft, and then after a half-year's accumulation, through repeated editing I eventually finalized the draft. Fortunately, different from an academic or research report, I feel free to be creative and write whatever I like from my travel notes as it is my interpretation and an expression of my personal experience.

Through the writing and editing process, I have gotten earnest encouragement and help from my colleagues who had traveled with me, including Du Shuhua , Wu Guojing , Liu Zhengpei, Zhao Hengfeng, Shi Li, Man Xiangwei and Sun Luyin, and my special thanks goes to Liu Zhengpei from The Commercial Press, who have made careful modification to my book.

Some of my workmates and friends had also gave me sincere help, including Du Lihua , Pan Haibo, Wang Dianzhong, Rong Huiyong , Zhang Shengli, who have read my articles thoroughly and gave me a lot of suggestions. In a word, they have done a lot for me.

I am especially grateful to Hu Zhenmin, the party secretary and executive vice president of China Federation of Literary and Art, who read my articles with his busy schedule and wrote me a letter in person, gave me detailed advice in forms, opinions and expressions. I have learned a lot from him.

I should also show my thanks to my wife and son for their support both mentally and physically.

What's more, my thanks also go to Hao Jianguo, Xu Zhanbo from Hebei

Education Press's editorial office. They have done a lot on the editing part.

Most of the pictures in the book were shot by me, some were shot by my colleagues, and a few were from the Internet, as I do not know the photographer, I cannot list their names one after another, therefore I want to extend my special apologies.

Although this book was written by me, it coagulated the thoughts and efforts from my leader, colleagues, friends and family I have listed above, so I am grateful to all of them for suggestions and help.

Du Jinqing
March 31, 2007, written in Shijiazhuang

后记

去年访美是一次愉快的旅程，实现了多年的夙愿，留下了难忘的印象。出国时，本没有写书的打算。回国后，翻阅访美日记，浏览录像照片，一路行程回放脑海，诸多思绪激荡胸怀，心有所思，情有所动，于是便动起笔来。开始，只写了《阅读·国民不可或缺的精神涵养》和《壮丽的科罗拉多大峡谷》两篇，分别在《河北日报》和《旅游纵览》杂志上发表，受到了朋友们的鼓励。接下来便一鼓作气，把整个访美行程过滤筛选，把点滴心得归纳成篇，最终形成这本书稿。

为了叙事方便和阅读连贯，19篇文章基本是按照访美日程顺序来写的，有描写美国城市和地理景观的，有解读美国文化和教育现象的，有观察美国社会和经济问题的，有思考美利坚民族精神的。虽然题目拉杂，内容宽泛，但各篇文章的主旨都是围绕话说美国、思考中国这个大题目来写的。试图通过对美国现象特别是美国文化的叙述与评说、观察与解读，从而对中华文化复兴和民族精神熔铸作一点反省与思考、呐喊与呼唤。

有的朋友可能会说，目前国内外关于美国的著述如汗牛充栋，阁下只在美国呆了十多天，怎么能写出好看的东西来呢？的确，访美时间短暂，接触面有限，不可能充分体验美国的方方面面、深刻思考有关问题。但我以为，能否写出好的游记作品，并不完全取决于作者在一个地方逗留时间的长短，而主要在于作者本人知识的厚度、见识的深度、情感的浓度和文字的美度。作者绝不敢夸口自己的文章具备了这四个"度"，而是想说，为了写好这部书稿，自己是下了一番功夫、费了一番心血的。从去年6月初开始，我利用大部分周末和节假日，翻阅了几十万字的有关书籍和文章资料，先是用四个月写就初稿，然后又沉淀了半年时间，征求意见、补充提炼、反复修改才打磨成现在的模样。好在游记文章不同于学术专著或研究报告，作者可以信马由缰、纵横骋怀，不管生动与否、识见高低，总还是作者的一点志趣、一种追求吧。

在这部书稿写作和修改过程中，和我一同访美并结下友情的各位同行杜淑华、伍国京、刘正培、赵恒峰、石丽、满向伟和孙录印给了我热情的鼓励和帮助，特别是商务印书馆的刘正培老兄对文稿作了细心的文字修改，校正了多处谬误。

我的几位同事和朋友杜力华、潘海波、王殿忠、戎慧勇、张胜利等真诚相助，他们有的认真阅读了每篇文稿，提出中肯的修改意见，有的帮我查阅、整理资料，做了很多有益的工作。

尤其令我感动的是，中国文联党组书记、常务副主席胡振民同志在百忙中阅读了书稿，并亲自给我写信，从体裁写作、思想观点到具体表述，都给予了悉心指点，令我获益良多。

还有我的妻子悉心照料我的生活、支持我的写作，正在大学读书的儿子也帮我查找了许多重要的资料和数据。

河北教育出版社综合读物编辑室郝建国主任、徐占博编辑精心编校和设计，付出了很多辛苦。

需要说明的是，书中图片大部分为作者所摄，部分由一同赴美的各位同行所提供，少量选自网络媒体，因无法确认作者，故不能一一署名。

本书虽是我的创作，但也凝结着他们的热情、智慧和心血。在此，让我对上述各位领导、同事、朋友和家人一并表示由衷的感谢！

杜金卿

2007 年 3 月 31 日于石家庄

Note for Second Edition

It has been 8 years since the book *Taking a Bite of the "Big Apple"* was initially published in 2007. The first edition was printed 3,000 copies. Many of them were sent out, some of them were sold off. The book received a favorable response from colleagues and friends. It also enjoyed good reviews in the press. Most of the essays were reproduced by newspapers and websites, which might be good for the society.

I had neither considered publishing the second edition nor publishing the book overseas in both Chinese and English until the coincidence last spring. In February 2014, Mr. Wang Xin, the president of Sinomedia International Group Inc. which is one of overseas branches of China International Publishing Group, came to Hebei Publishing & Media Group to talk over with cooperation. Before his leaving, I sent him a copy of the book. He found it so interesting that he suggested publishing the English version by their company and put it into market sometime in America. But it took a long time to do translation and I was busy doing lots of other things later on, the plan had to be delayed for almost one year. At the end of last year, I got to know that China, being the Guest of Honor, would participate in the New York Book Fair in the upcoming May. Therefore, the old plan was put back onto the agenda. My colleagues suggested making the book quickly to catch up the New York Book Fair. It not only fulfilled the old agreement, but also added one more overseas project for our group company. That's why we did the bilingual *Taking a Bite of the "Big Apple"*.

Besides revising some words in several chapters, the photos were adjusted as well in the second edition. In order to meet the needs of readers abroad, the graphic design had been done in a new way, as the book is bilingual and published overseas.

Before ending, I would like to sincerely thank Li Zhengshuan and Nan Fang, the president and teacher from institution of foreign studies in Hebei Normal University, for their refined translations. Thank Liu Zheng and Sun Hailiang from Beijing Songyafeng Culture & Media Company, Xu Fan and Shao Hong from publishing department of Hebei Publishing & Media Group, for their passions and efforts. Hope the new "Big Apple" is more tasty.

Du Jinqing
May 2015

再版说明

    《品味"大苹果"》自 2007 年面世至今 8 年了，初版印了 3 千册，多数赠送，少量销售，同事朋友反响尚可，媒体评价也还不错，其中大部分文章被报刊或网络媒体转载，对社会也算有所裨益吧。

    本来没有再版的想法，更没有输出海外的奢望，这次之所以推出中英文双语版，是因为去年春天的一次机缘。2014 年 2 月，中国外文局海外分支机构华媒（美国）国际集团总裁王欣先生来集团公司洽谈合作，临别时我将此书赠送，王欣先生翻阅后认为该书写得挺有意思，便提出由他们公司出版英文版，择机在美国上市发行。因为翻译费时加上诸事耽搁，此事放了将近一年。去年年底，得知今年 5 月中国作为主宾国参加美国纽约书展，于是旧事重提，同事们建议抓紧成书并在纽约展会上亮相，既履行了事先的约定，也给集团公司赠加了一项走出去的成果，所以就有了今天这部中英文的《品味"大苹果"》。

    需要说明的是，这次再版，除了个别篇章在文字上作了些修订，配图照片也作了调整，因为是中英文双语版式又在海外发行，故在装帧设计上采取了新的样式，以适应海外读者的需求。

    该书再版之际，由衷地感谢河北师范大学外语学院李正栓院长、南方老师等为翻译此书所付出的心血，感谢北京颂雅风公司刘峥、孙海亮，集团公司出版部徐凡、邵红等诸位同仁的热心与付出，希望新版"大苹果"能给大家带来新的品读感受。

杜金卿于 2015 年 5 月